Betty Crocker

Why It Works

Betty Crocker
Why It Works

✎ Insider Secrets to Great Food

KEVIN RYAN, Ph.D.
Food Scientist, General Mills

WILEY
Wiley Publishing, Inc.

Library of Congress Cataloging-in-Publication Data:

Betty Crocker why it works : insider secrets to great food / by the editors of Betty Crocker.
    p. cm.
    Includes index.
    ISBN-13: 978-0-471-75305-6
    ISBN-10: 0-471-75305-X (cloth)
  1. Cookery. 2. Food. I. Crocker, Betty.
    TX651.B486 2006
    641.5—dc22
                       2005032316

Manufactured in the United States of America

10 9 8 7 6 5 4 3 2 1

Cover photo: Chicken with Chipotle-Peach Glaze (page 107)

General Mills

Director, Book and Online Publishing: Kim Walter

Manager, Cookbook Publishing: Lois Tlusty

Editor: Heidi Losleben, Sharon Secor

Recipe Development and Testing: Betty Crocker Kitchens

Photography and Food Styling: General Mills
    Photography Studios

Wiley Publishing, Inc.

Publisher: Natalie Chapman

Executive Editor: Anne Ficklen

Editor: Kristi Hart

Production Editor: Leslie Anglin

Cover Design: Suzanne Sunwoo

Interior Design: Fritz Metsch

Interior Layout: Northeastern Graphic, Inc.

Photography Art Direction: Paul DiNovo

Manufacturing Manager: Kevin Watt

The Betty Crocker Kitchens seal guarantees success in your kitchen. Every recipe has been tested in America's Most Trusted Kitchens™ to meet our high standards of reliability, easy preparation and great taste.

**Find more great ideas and
shop for name-brand housewares at**

Betty Crocker.com

Dear Friends,

Everyone has the potential to be a great cook. I sincerely believe that. Yes, even your sister who made that terrible tuna casserole last weekend, or your Uncle Bob with his infamous Chicken Surprise. Anyone can cook because cooking is first and foremost about love and second about technique and ingredients. Many people confuse that order, thinking that because they don't know a whisk from a spatula they are not good cooks. Cooking doesn't have to be difficult, gourmet or sophisticated to be good. I'd rather eat a ham sandwich prepared by someone who cared about me than a five-course meal assembled by a chef in a restaurant. For that reason, I think that you—yes, you!—have all the makings of a great cook. You care about someone so much (even if that person is yourself) that you are willing to create something just for them. That is the most important first step to cooking well.

"...this book is designed to help you understand food and recipes in a whole new way."

The second step is where this cookbook comes into play. Whether you are new to cooking or a seasoned pro, this book was designed to help you understand food and recipes in a whole new way. Recipes are like very short stories. They have a beginning (the ingredients), a middle (the method) and an end (the actual eating of the meal). If you tell the story right, you end up with great-tasting food. But who wants to hear the same story every day? What if you want to have baking soda play the part of baking powder? Will the recipe still end the same delicious way? In tips titled "Why It Works," this book gives you the "behind-the-scenes" information on the whole story, and allows you to see how recipes work from the inside out. Before you know it, you will be creating your own recipes and changing mine (go ahead, I don't mind).

As you glance through the book, you may notice that some of the recipes are longer than you're used to and take extra time to prepare. Don't let a lengthy ingredient list or prep time scare you off. None of the recipes are unnecessarily complex or fancy; it's just that some recipes can't be shortened without compromising flavor. Also keep in mind that once you learn and become familiar with the techniques involved, they can be applied to other foods you make.

Chances are, you're a great cook—you just don't know it yet!

Warmly,

Kevin Ryan

Contents

Ask the Food Doctor

Q&A with Kevin Ryan

So, who is this guy and why should you trust him with your dinner? Kevin Ryan is a foodie in all aspects of the word. He's been a caterer, a wedding cake creator and a cooking class instructor. Currently he works as a food scientist, developing everything from soup to vegetables. Kevin credits his lifelong fascination with food to a tomato he picked from his mother's garden when he was four. "The flesh of the tomato was still warm from the sun; the skin was paper thin, and the taste was extraordinary!" he says. "To this day, I compare all tomatoes to that tomato." Kevin says it was the first time he remembers really *tasting* food. "It made me realize that my senses could be engaged at a level I had never known before."

Q: **Why did you want to write** ***Why It Works?***

A: In the cooking classes I teach, I get a wide range of students with varying skill levels. All of them are looking to better understand cooking in general, not just make a particular dish. When they learn they can cook almost anything better with a few simple tips and techniques about how ingredients work together, it makes them very happy. I realized I could share that knowledge with many more people via a book.

Q: **What do you think people will like best about** ***Why It Works?***

A: I tried to make sure there was a good mix of simple and involved foods in the book. Along the way, I've shared secrets I've learned in my study of food science, history/anthropology or just observation. I hope these secrets not only give them assurance that they are getting a perfect recipe, but confidence to change the recipe to suit their taste as well. As the saying goes, "Give a man a fish and you feed him for a day, but teach a man to fish and you feed him for a lifetime." By showing people the internal workings of a recipe and its ingredients, I want to take the fear out of cooking.

Q: **Who does the cooking in your home?**

A: I do a large part of the cooking at home. My wife, who is also a food scientist, enjoys cooking occasionally, but lets me handle the task most weekdays.

Q: **What are ten ingredients you always have on hand?**

A: Along with the usual suspects (flour, sugar and salt) I try to keep the following in my fridge and pantry.

Refrigerator:
- Fresh lemons
- Good Parmesan cheese
- Flat leaf parsley
- Butter
- Eggs

Pantry:
- Balsamic vinegar
- Low-sodium chicken broth (in aseptic box, not canned)
- Extra-virgin olive oil
- Dry white wine
- 100% durum semolina pasta (spaghetti or linguini)

Q: What's your favorite dish to prepare?

A: I don't so much have a favorite dish as I do a favorite cuisine: Mexican. I love the processes involved and the time it takes. The anticipation of getting everything just right is fun. Rendering lard, chopping vegetables, grinding chiles and patting tortillas gets you so involved in the making of the meal. When you put so much effort into the process, you put so much of yourself into a food's overall success.

Q: When it comes to buying items like cheese and olive oil, there is such a wide range of prices. What ingredients are worth paying top-dollar for?

A: Some ingredients play such a dominant role in dishes, that replacing them with lower-quality versions really hurts your cooking. Here are the top five items I never substitute with cheaper alternatives:

- **Extra-virgin olive oil:** The good stuff is *not* always imported or expensive! It is also a myth that the greener an olive oil, the fresher the flavor. Tasting is the true test of quality. The best olive oil is the one you like the taste of the most, so try as many as you can. Choose one that is not too strong because you don't want it to overwhelm your dish. Conversely, you don't want it to be too mild; otherwise a cheaper vegetable oil could have been used instead. I don't put much stock in the word "cold press" on the label. Extra-virgin olive oil, by its very name and the regulations surrounding it, has to be pressed at cold or room temperature. Adding heat to the press gets a little more oil out, but then it can't be labeled "extra virgin."

- **Chocolate:** With everyone watching calories these days it's not worth wasting your time on bad chocolate. The best chocolate is smooth, slightly bitter and melts almost instantly on your tongue. Many of the best chocolates are imported, but some of my favorites are produced domestically, so don't discount American producers. As with olive oil, the best way to choose a chocolate is by tasting it. If it tastes good plain, it will be wonderful in your finished dish.

- **Parmesan cheese:** Good Parmesan cheese is so far removed from the dried, boxed variety we all grew up with that it is almost a different product altogether. The complex taste and wonderful aroma of quality Parmesan can make even the most overcooked bowl of pasta edible. You do not have to buy Parmigiano-Reggiano, the original Parmesan, but you should if you can afford it because it is the best. There are, however, some smaller producers that make top-quality cheese.

- **Wine:** Picking a wine is like picking out jewelry; it is a very personal experience and sometimes you just like what you like. I have two rules: Never cook with a wine you would not drink, and never cook with "cooking wine" (it is mostly salt and other additives).

- **Steak:** I try to limit my intake of steak to times of celebration. When I do eat it, I will only settle for the best. Look for meat labeled "prime" and expect to pay for this rare treat.

Q: What was your biggest cooking mistake or kitchen disaster?

A: Early in my catering career, I agreed to make a classical French dinner for a group of about twenty-five people. The guest of honor made a point of requesting chocolate soufflé for dessert. As the evening progressed, all the courses went spectacularly well and my ego was significantly pumped up. I whipped up the soufflés and placed them in the oven. As the time for dessert approached, I peeked in the convection oven to see how the custards were doing (not a wise thing to do with soufflés). Instead of tall crowns, I found hollowed out dishes and a thick, smoldering smear of chocolate on the oven door! In my haste, I had forgotten to turn off the convection fan on the stove after removing the chateaubriand! The fan blew the soufflés off as they rose in their dishes. I quickly whipped up another batch, delayed dessert and turned off the fan. Never again will I be that cocky.

Q: Do you have any "secret" ingredients to enhance flavor?

A: No one should ever be able to identify secret ingredients in your cooking, except when they are missing. They intensify the natural flavors of food and brighten aromas. Here are my favorites:

- **Splash of lemon juice:** Added at the last minute to soups, sauces and meats, lemon juice makes everything just a little more fresh tasting.

- **Anchovies:** You may turn up your nose at the mention of these tiny fish, but you would be amazed at how many top chefs use good-quality anchovies in some of their most popular dishes. I add anchovies to tomato sauces, stews and sauces for an unidentifiable oomph.

- **Alcohol endings:** Sometimes cooking takes away the "up-front" flavors in soups and sauces. I add character back by finishing these dishes with a little wine, brandy or vermouth.

- **Soy sauce:** Although we tend to think of it as an Asian condiment, soy sauce can add a great amount of flavor to soups and sauces. Just a splash makes your beef taste more beefy and gravy good enough to eat on its own.

- **Frozen concentrate orange/lemon juice:** Not just for drinking, these juices are—as the name implies—concentrated. They can conveniently add a lot of complex taste in cooking.

Q: How have your cooking tastes changed over the years?

A: I started off as a complete snob! As a teenager, I began studying the "classic" cuisine of France. I considered anything boxed, canned or processed to be nearly inedible. If it didn't take five hours to make, I wasn't interested. As I got older, I realized that food has more to do with people than with a certain technique or kind of equipment used. Food connects us to families and friends; it often holds our culture together—via family barbecues, Thanksgiving and everything in between. I realized that connection can be made just as well with a box of mac and cheese as with a cheese soufflé, as long as the food is served with love. Food tastes best, not when it stimulates your taste buds, but when it excites your memory! No stew ever tastes as good as the one your mom made, no matter if your mom lived in New York, Paris, Addis Ababa or Quito! Now I am a food snob of a different sort. I insist all the food I make be "genuine." By that I mean it can't merely be fuel to feed the body, it has to be food to feed the soul.

Q: Are there convenience foods that don't sacrifice quality or flavor?

A: Convenience foods are great because they allow us to prepare the foods we love on a busy schedule. Although some leave much to be desired as far as taste is concerned, some are just as good as their regular versions.

- **No-boil lasagna noodles:** All of the taste and texture of regular noodles, but without the fuss of having to boil water (and no burnt fingers either!).

- **Canned broth:** In a perfect world, we would all make our own stocks from scratch, but who has time for that? Canned broths are a great alternative, with all of the taste of good-quality stock. For best results, use a lower-sodium broth.

- **Frozen vegetables:** We've been using them for years as an additive to stews and soups, but the real surprise is that frozen vegetables are often just as good as fresh, even on their own.

- **Canned tomatoes:** This is one product that is often even better than its fresh counterpart. For most of the year, I rarely use fresh tomatoes, and use good-quality canned for all of my cooking.

- **Bagged salad:** Chopped, mixed and ready to go. Bagged salad makes eating healthy so much easier.

Q: What small appliances do you consider "must-haves"?

A: I find I am most efficient owning the least number of kitchen "gadgets." Most gadgets get in my way and are hard to store. Instead, I like to have a few multi-purpose tools I can use everyday. Here are the appliances I think every good kitchen must have:

- **Food processor:** From chopping vegetables to kneading bread dough, there is no end to the number of uses I find for this contraption. The medium-size processor (seven to nine cups) is my favorite. Plan on spending at least $100 for a good model.

- **Stick, or immersion, blender:** Perfect for soup, sauces and even drinks. These days I save my regular blender for the bar.

- **Coffee grinder:** Although I'm not much of a coffee drinker, I can't imagine cooking without this appliance. Spices and herbs are at their best when left whole until ready to use. A coffee grinder is a modern-day mortar and pestle, grinding to release great flavor in your cooking.

- **Ice-cream maker:** There was a time when making ice cream was a strenuous, all-day process. Today, ice-cream makers have changed all that. Just place the canister in the freezer and fresh churned ice cream is only about forty minutes away.

- **Standing mixer:** A good standing mixer, if treated right, can be used for generations. From kneading bread to whipping egg whites and even stuffing sausages, a standing mixer is like having an extra set of hands in the kitchen.

Q: What was the first holiday you cooked for?

A: When I was about eight I remember begging my mom to let me help make part of the Thanksgiving meal. Turkey Day was a big deal in the Ryan household. We had a full house with my parents, two brothers, two sisters, grandma, two cousins, two aunts and assorted nephews. To feed so many people, my mom had to buy a twenty-five-pound turkey and get up at 5:00 am to prepare it. One of the stipulations for me helping was that I had to get up that early as well. To this day I can remember the anticipation I had the night before—it was like Christmas! The next morning, mom put me to work, boiling water for the deviled eggs, stirring the onions in the bottom of the pot for her famous wild rice casserole and chopping up the sweet potatoes. The windows in the kitchen got steamy as the heat rose in the kitchen. I remember the pride I felt as we served that Thanksgiving meal. As the years wore on I made more and more of the dishes, but none were as satisfying as that first one I had a hand in.

Q: What is your most cherished cooking memory?

A: I had just started dating the woman who would later become my wife. At the time, I owned and operated a catering/wedding cake business and went to college full time, so time was tight. One late Saturday afternoon, I mentioned that I would love to make her a meal. I had never cooked for her and I really wanted it to be special. I sat her down at the kitchen table and went to work. Having a pantry and refrigerator full of produce, I whipped up a nice spring salad. Being a bread fanatic, I always had dough starter somewhere in the kitchen. I quickly kneaded a small loaf and set it aside. I threw together some flour, eggs, salt and oil and created a rich egg pasta. As I let that sit, I combined some tomatoes and spices for a sauce. I rolled out the pasta, threw the bread on the hot quarry tiles lining my oven and within forty minutes we had a romantic dinner for two! Years later my wife confessed—to paraphrase a now-famous line—"You had me at the pasta."

Good Morning!

BREAKFAST THE WAY

YOU REMEMBER

Yogurt-Granola Parfaits with Berries

2 containers (6 oz each) strawberry, raspberry, key lime or banana-cream pie fat-free yogurt

3/4 cup blueberries, raspberries or sliced strawberries

6 tablespoons granola

2 mint leaves, if desired

In each of 2 clear 8-ounce dishes (or use 2 martini glasses or wine goblets for a more elegant touch), spoon one-third of the yogurt from 1 container, 2 tablespoons of the berries and 1 tablespoon of the granola; repeat layers 2 more times. Garnish each serving with a mint leaf if desired. Serve immediately.

1 Serving: Calories 280 (Calories from Fat 35); Total Fat 4g (Saturated Fat 1.5g; Trans Fat 0g); Cholesterol 0mg; Sodium 110mg; Total Carbohydrate 52g (Dietary Fiber 3g; Sugars 40g); Protein 10g • **% Daily Value:** Vitamin A 0%; Vitamin C 15%; Calcium 30%; Iron 4% • **Exchanges:** 1/2 Fruit, 2 Other Carbohydrate, 1 Skim Milk, 1/2 Fat • **Carbohydrate Choices:** 3 1/2

WHY IT WORKS:

GOOD BACTERIA Over 3,000 years ago, yogurt was probably invented as a way to preserve fresh milk. Today, even with refrigerators, we enjoy the creamy, acidic taste of yogurt, and the process of making it hasn't changed much. Ingredients used are milk (fat-free [skim], 2% or whole) and bacteria. In the beginning, the bacteria might have been added by simply letting warm milk sit uncovered in hopes that the correct bacteria would come along. Today, the process is more controlled (and safer): Pure bacteria are added directly to milk. As the bacteria "eat" the sugar in the milk, it produces acid. And it's this acid that causes the milk to thicken into yogurt.

Yogurt-Granola Parfaits with Berries

Strawberry Freezer Jam

PREP TIME: 15 MINUTES • **START TO FINISH:** 24 HOURS 20 MINUTES   ABOUT 5 HALF-PINTS JAM

1 quart (4 cups) strawberries,
    cut in half
4 cups sugar
3/4 cup water
1 package (1 3/4 oz) powdered
    fruit pectin

1. In large bowl, mash strawberries with potato masher (or process in food processor) until slightly chunky (not pureed) to make 2 cups crushed strawberries. Stir sugar into strawberries in large bowl. Let stand at room temperature 10 minutes, stirring occasionally. (This not only sweetens the strawberry mixture, but also helps to relieve the strawberries of their juices.)

2. In 1-quart saucepan, mix water and pectin. Heat to boiling, stirring constantly. Boil and stir 1 minute. Pour hot pectin mixture over strawberry mixture; stir constantly 3 minutes.

3. Immediately spoon mixture into freezer containers, leaving 1/2-inch headspace. Wipe rims of containers; seal. Let stand at room temperature about 24 hours or until set.

4. Store in freezer up to 6 months or in refrigerator up to 3 weeks. Thaw frozen jam in the refrigerator and stir before serving.

1 Tablespoon: Calories 45 (Calories from Fat 0); Total Fat 0g (Saturated Fat 0g; Trans Fat 0g); Cholesterol 0mg; Sodium 0mg; Total Carbohydrate 11g (Dietary Fiber 0g; Sugars 11g); Protein 0g • **% Daily Value:** Vitamin A 0%; Vitamin C 8%; Calcium 0%; Iron 0% • **Exchanges:** 1/2 Other Carbohydrate • **Carbohydrate Choices:** 1

WHY IT WORKS:

JELLING THE JELLY If you enjoy the consistency of jams, jellies and preserves, you owe a debt of gratitude to a carbohydrate called pectin. Found mostly in the seeds and skins of fruits (especially apples), pectin traps and holds water so that your jelly is wobbly, not runny or clumpy. In order for this to happen, pectin needs the help of sugar and acid (usually lemon juice)—which "pull" the individual pieces of pectin as far away from one another as possible, allowing room for more water. This process requires a lot of sugar, so don't be tempted to cut back on the sugar in a recipe unless you want strawberry sauce instead of jam!

Blueberry Turnovers

PREP TIME: 30 MINUTES • START TO FINISH: 50 MINUTES   12 TURNOVERS

2 cups fresh or frozen blueberries

1/4 cup packed brown sugar

1 tablespoon cornstarch

1 tablespoon grated orange peel

1/4 teaspoon ground cinnamon

Dash of ground allspice

2 sheets frozen puff pastry (from 17.3-oz package), thawed

6 tablespoons firm butter, each tablespoon cut into 4 pieces

2 egg yolks

2 tablespoons milk

1/4 cup granulated sugar

1. Adjust oven rack to lower third of oven. Heat oven to 400°F. Cover 2 large cookie sheets with cooking parchment paper; set aside.

2. In medium bowl, mix blueberries, brown sugar, cornstarch, orange peel, cinnamon and allspice. Let stand 20 to 30 minutes to allow the juices to exude.

3. Place 1 sheet puff pastry on work surface lightly dusted with flour. (Keep other sheet covered in refrigerator.) Use rolling pin to roll pastry sheet into 12 × 9-inch rectangle. Use pizza cutter to cut dough into 6 squares (don't worry if squares are uneven).

4. Stir blueberry mixture well; spoon about 2 rounded tablespoons filling onto center of each pastry square, leaving about 1 inch around edges. (Don't add more filling; it will ooze out during baking and burn onto cookie sheet.) Place 2 pieces butter on each mound of filling.

5. In small bowl, mix egg yolks and milk with fork. Use pastry brush or your fingertip to paint edges of each square with egg mixture. Fold each square over, corner to corner, to form a triangle. Use your fingertip to lightly press edges shut. Use fork to crimp edges. Move turnovers to a cookie sheet.

6. Paint tops of turnovers with additional egg mixture and sprinkle each with 1 teaspoon granulated sugar. Cut one or two 1-inch steam vents on top of each turnover using tip of sharp knife. While the first 6 turnovers bake, repeat with remaining pastry sheet and filling.

7. Bake turnovers 15 minutes or until flaky and golden. (Check after 10 minutes because they brown quickly. If they look like they may burn, cover with foil and continue baking.) Remove from oven and cool 5 minutes. Remove turnovers from parchment and place on wire rack. Serve warm or at room temperature.

1 Turnover: Calories 310 (Calories from Fat 180); Total Fat 20g (Saturated Fat 8g; Trans Fat 1.5g); Cholesterol 90mg; Sodium 130mg; Total Carbohydrate 29g (Dietary Fiber 1g; Sugars 11g); Protein 3g • **% Daily Value:** Vitamin A 6%; Vitamin C 4%; Calcium 2%; Iron 10% • **Exchanges:** 1 Starch, 1/2 Fruit, 1/2 Other Carbohydrate, 4 Fat • **Carbohydrate Choices:** 2

WHY IT WORKS:

PUFF PASTRY Question: How is puff pastry like a sandwich? Answer: Both are made from layers. Puff pastry has two separate parts: dough and fat (usually butter). The pastry is made by first rolling the dough into a thin sheet. Next, a sheet of cold butter about half the size of the dough is placed on top and the dough is folded over to create a sandwich. This sandwich is then re-rolled and re-folded numerous times, each time gaining layers of dough and butter. During baking, the butter melts and its water (butter is 20% water) turns to steam, pushing up each layer of dough as it rises. The result is a dramatic, flaky pastry.

Baked Apple Oatmeal

2 2/3 cups old-fashioned oats

1/2 cup raisins

4 cups milk

1/3 cup packed brown sugar

2 tablespoons butter, melted

1 teaspoon ground cinnamon

1/4 teaspoon salt

2 medium apples, chopped (2 cups)

1/2 cup chopped walnuts or almonds,
   if desired

Additional milk, if desired

1. Heat oven to 350°F. In 2-quart casserole, mix oats, raisins, 4 cups milk, the brown sugar, butter, cinnamon, salt and apples.

2. Bake uncovered 40 to 45 minutes or until most of the liquid is absorbed. Top with walnuts if desired. Serve with additional milk if desired. (Leftover oatmeal can be covered and refrigerated. To reheat: Place 1 cup oatmeal in microwavable bowl. Cover and microwave on high about 1 minute or until hot. Top with additional milk.)

1 **Serving:** Calories 280 (Calories from Fat 60); Total Fat 7g (Saturated Fat 3g; Trans Fat 0g); Cholesterol 15mg; Sodium 160mg; Total Carbohydrate 45g (Dietary Fiber 4g; Sugars 24g); Protein 9g • **% Daily Value:** Vitamin A 8%; Vitamin C 0%; Calcium 15%; Iron 10% • **Exchanges:** 2 Starch, 1/2 Other Carbohydrate, 1/2 Low-Fat Milk, 1 Fat • **Carbohydrate Choices:** 3

WHY IT WORKS:

FEELING YOUR OATS Oats are available in many forms, each requiring a slightly different preparation. Whole oats, or "groats," take the longest time to prepare—up to 2 hours. When cut into two or three pieces, the groats are called "Scotch oats" or "steel-cut oats" and need slightly less cooking (about an hour). Rolled oats—also called old-fashioned oats—are groats that have been steamed and pressed between heavy rollers. This process speeds up the cooking time 15 minutes. Instant oats are groats that have been pre-cooked and then dried, resulting in oats that can be cooked in minutes.

Baked Apple Oatmeal

Banana-Chocolate Bread

PREP TIME: 15 MINUTES • START TO FINISH: 3 HOURS 25 MINUTES   1 LOAF (16 SLICES)

1/2 cup butter, softened

1 cup sugar

2 eggs

2 tablespoons buttermilk

1 cup ripe bananas (3 to 4 medium), mashed

2 cups all-purpose flour

1/2 cup unsweetened baking cocoa

1/2 cup miniature semisweet chocolate chips

1 1/2 teaspoons baking powder

1/2 teaspoon baking soda

1/2 teaspoon salt

1/4 cup miniature semisweet chocolate chips

1 teaspoon vegetable oil

1. Heat oven to 350°F. Grease bottom only of 9 × 5-inch loaf pan with shortening or spray bottom with cooking spray; lightly flour.

2. In large bowl, beat butter and sugar with electric mixer on medium speed until creamy. Beat in eggs. Beat in buttermilk and bananas. Stir in remaining ingredients except 1/4 cup chocolate chips and 1 teaspoon oil until dry ingredients are moistened. (Batter should be lumpy. Overmixing will make the bread tough and cause tunnels.) Spread in pan.

3. Bake 50 to 60 minutes or until toothpick inserted in center of bread (not chocolate chips) comes out clean. Cool in pan 10 minutes; remove from pan to wire rack. Cool completely, about 2 hours.

4. In small microwavable bowl, mix 1/4 cup chocolate chips and 1 teaspoon oil. Microwave uncovered on High 1 minute; stir until melted. Drizzle chocolate over loaf. (Bread can be tightly wrapped in plastic wrap and stored at room temperature up to 4 days, or refrigerated up to 10 days.)

WHY IT WORKS:

TOP BANANA In addition to providing flavor and moistness to banana bread, bananas actually have an effect on the bread rising. Like many fruits, bananas are acidic, and that means they react with baking soda to produce gas bubbles, which causes rising. But check your bananas. As bananas ripen they become sweeter and more flavorful, but they also lose their acidity. Banana bread recipes that contain only baking soda rely on the acid in the bananas to make the bread rise. The solution? Keep using ripened bananas, but use recipes that use both baking soda *and* baking powder to ensure a tall loaf.

RECIPE R$_x$: BAD BREAD RISING So you used baking powder and baking soda but your bread still didn't rise? Before you throw the loaf away, let's figure out what happened. The most likely culprit is your baking soda or baking powder. Both of these leaveners go bad

(one year is about their maximum life) and should be replaced often (don't use the baking soda deodorizing your fridge; it already has a job). To test baking soda for freshness: Add 1 1/2 teaspoons baking soda to a small bowl along with 1 tablespoon white vinegar. If the mixture fizzes, the baking soda is still good. If it doesn't, it's time to get a new box. For baking powder, place 1/2 teaspoon in a small bowl and add 1/4 cup hot water. The mixture should bubble dramatically. Discard the box if it doesn't. (By the way, don't throw away that loaf. Cut up the sunken creation and make it into dainty finger sandwiches with some cream cheese.)

1 Slice: Calories 240 (Calories from Fat 90); Total Fat 10g (Saturated Fat 5g; Trans Fat 0g); Cholesterol 40mg; Sodium 210mg; Total Carbohydrate 34g (Dietary Fiber 2g; Sugars 19g); Protein 4g • **% Daily Value:** Vitamin A 6%; Vitamin C 0%; Calcium 4%; Iron 8% • **Exchanges:** 1 Starch, 1 Other Carbohydrate, 2 Fat • **Carbohydrate Choices:** 2

Banana-Blueberry Muffins

PREP TIME: 10 MINUTES • **START TO FINISH**: 30 MINUTES   12 MUFFINS

. . . .

2/3 cup milk

1/4 cup vegetable oil

1/2 cup mashed very ripe banana
   (1 medium)

1 egg

2 cups all-purpose flour

2/3 cup sugar

2 1/2 teaspoons baking powder

1/4 teaspoon ground nutmeg

1 cup fresh or frozen (thawed and
   well drained) blueberries

1. Heat oven to 400°F. Place paper baking cup in each of 12 regular-size muffin cups, or grease bottoms only.

2. In large bowl, mix milk, oil, banana and egg with fork. Stir in remaining ingredients except blueberries just until flour is moistened. (Muffin batter should be lumpy. If you overmix the batter, muffins will be tough and have pointed, rather than rounded, tops.) Gently stir in blueberries. Divide batter evenly among muffin cups (cups will be almost full). Sprinkle with sugar if desired.

3. Bake 18 to 20 minutes or until golden brown. Immediately remove from pan.

1 Muffin: Calories 190 (Calories from Fat 50); Total Fat 6g (Saturated Fat 1g; Trans Fat 0g); Cholesterol 20mg; Sodium 115mg; Total Carbohydrate 32g (Dietary Fiber 1g; Sugars 14g); Protein 3g • **% Daily Value:** Vitamin A 0%; Vitamin C 2%; Calcium 8%; Iron 6% • **Exchanges:** 1 Starch, 1 Other Carbohydrate, 1 Fat • **Carbohydrate Choices:** 2

WHY IT WORKS:

KEEP YOUR COLOR Have you ever opened a delicious looking blueberry muffin only to be greeted with streaks of green? What you've witnessed is a reaction between the blueberries and the baking soda. Blueberries get their color from a group of pigments called anthocyanins (literally "blue plant"). These are the same pigments that color apples, cherries and red cabbage. When exposed to a base, such as baking soda, the blueberries turn green. To avoid this colorful surprise, use only baking powder in your blueberry muffins. Because the amount of banana called for is so slight in this recipe, you do not need to use baking soda to ensure the muffins rise (see Banana-Chocolate Bread, page 20).

Dried Cherry–Lemon Scones

2 cups all-purpose flour

1/4 cup sugar

2 teaspoons grated lemon peel

1 1/2 teaspoons cream of tartar

3/4 teaspoon baking soda

1/4 teaspoon salt

1/2 cup firm butter, cut into 8 pieces

1/3 to 1/2 cup buttermilk

1/2 cup dried cherries

Milk

Additional sugar, if desired

1. Heat oven to 425°F. In medium bowl, mix flour, sugar, lemon peel, cream of tartar, baking soda and salt. Cut in butter, using pastry blender (or pulling 2 table knives through ingredients in opposite directions), until mixture looks like fine crumbs. (Butter must be firm so it can be easily cut into the flour mixture.) Stir in enough buttermilk so dough leaves sides of bowl and forms a ball. Stir in cherries.

2. Onto ungreased cookie sheet, drop about 1/3 cupfuls of dough about 1 inch apart. Brush with milk. Sprinkle with additional sugar if desired.

3. Bake 10 to 15 minutes or until light brown. Immediately remove from cookie sheet. Serve warm, or cool on wire rack.

1 Scone: Calories 220 (Calories from Fat 90); Total Fat 10g (Saturated Fat 5g; Trans Fat 0.5g); Cholesterol 25mg; Sodium 230mg; Total Carbohydrate 30g (Dietary Fiber 1g; Sugars 9g); Protein 3g • **% Daily Value:** Vitamin A 10%; Vitamin C 0%; Calcium 2%; Iron 8% • **Exchanges:** 1 1/2 Starch, 1/2 Other Carbohydrate, 1 1/2 Fat • **Carbohydrate Choices:** 2

WHY IT WORKS: **BUTTERED UP** Despite its name, buttermilk is not full of butter. In fact, it is similar to 2% or skim milk in fat content. Traditional buttermilk is a fermented beverage made from the liquid that remained after butter was churned from fresh cream. Today, buttermilk is made by exposing milk to good bacteria (just like making yogurt), causing it to become acidic. Buttermilk's acid makes it a great baking ingredient. This acid tenderizes cakes and muffins by preventing the proteins in flour from binding and becoming stretchy like they do in bread. It also enhances flavor, just like a squirt of lemon brightens a soup.

Dried Cherry-Lemon Scones

Banana Pancakes

WITH MAPLE-PECAN SYRUP

PREP TIME: 10 MINUTES • **START TO FINISH:** 40 MINUTES ⋯⋯⋯⋯⋯⋯⋯⋯⋯⋯⋯⋯⋯⋯⋯⋯⋯ TWENTY-SEVEN 4-INCH PANCAKES

Syrup

1 cup pure maple syrup
1 tablespoon butter
1/4 cup chopped pecans

Pancakes

2 eggs
2 cups all-purpose flour
2 cups buttermilk
2 cups mashed ripe bananas
   (4 medium)
1/4 cup granulated or packed
   brown sugar
1/4 cup vegetable oil
2 teaspoons baking powder
1 teaspoon baking soda
1/2 teaspoon salt

1. In 1-quart saucepan, heat syrup and butter over medium heat, stirring occasionally, until butter is melted; remove from heat. Stir in pecans.

2. In medium bowl, beat eggs with wire whisk or egg beater until foamy. Beat in remaining ingredients just until smooth. For thinner pancakes, stir in additional 1 to 2 tablespoons buttermilk.

3. Heat griddle to 375°F or heat skillet over medium heat. Grease griddle with butter if necessary. (To test griddle, sprinkle with a few drops of water. If bubbles jump around, heat is just right.)

4. For each pancake, pour slightly less than 1/4 cup batter from cup or pitcher onto hot griddle. Cook pancakes until small holes appear on top and pancakes are puffed and dry around edges. Turn and cook other sides until golden brown. (It's a good idea to make a test pancake to ensure your batter is the right consistency. If the outside edge of the pancake is golden brown but the middle is uncooked, thin the batter with a tablespoon or two of milk.)

1 **Pancake:** Calories 140 (Calories from Fat 35); Total Fat 4g (Saturated Fat 1g; Trans Fat 0g); Cholesterol 20mg; Sodium 170mg; Total Carbohydrate 23g (Dietary Fiber 0g; Sugars 9g); Protein 2g • **% Daily Value:** Vitamin A 0%; Vitamin C 0%; Calcium 4%; Iron 4% • **Exchanges:** 1 Starch, 1/2 Other Carbohydrate, 1/2 Fat • **Carbohydrate Choices:** 1 1/2

WHY IT WORKS:

KITCHEN CHEMISTRY Combining an acid and a base (alkaline) forms a gas. When you watch little holes form on top of your pancake as it cooks on the griddle, you're witnessing this reaction. One of the most important aspects of baking is achieving the right balance of acid and base in your recipe. Too much of either can ruin the taste and texture. When baking soda (the most common base in your pantry) is used with an acid (lemon juice, molasses, vinegar, etc.), gas is produced immediately. This works in recipes that contain an acidic ingredient, but what about those that don't, or that just have a tiny bit of acidity? Use some baking powder, which contains both acid and base.

Banana Pancakes with Maple-Pecan Syrup

Spiced Crepes
WITH STRAWBERRY FILLING

PREP TIME: 55 MINUTES • START TO FINISH: 55 MINUTES   6 SERVINGS (2 CREPES EACH)

Crepes

3/4 cup instant flour

1 tablespoon granulated sugar

1/4 teaspoon ground nutmeg

1/8 teaspoon salt

1 cup milk

3 eggs

3 tablespoons butter, melted
   and cooled

1/2 teaspoon almond extract

1 teaspoon vegetable oil

Filling

2 tablespoons butter

2 1/2 cups strawberry halves

2 tablespoons packed brown sugar

2 tablespoons orange juice

1 tablespoon balsamic vinegar or
   red wine vinegar

1 teaspoon vanilla

Dash of salt

Topping

2 tablespoons powdered sugar

1. In medium bowl, mix flour, granulated sugar, nutmeg and 1/8 teaspoon salt; set aside. In another medium bowl, beat milk, eggs, 3 tablespoons butter and the almond extract with wire whisk. Make a well in center of dry ingredients and pour in wet ingredients. Gradually beat together until no dry flour mixture is visible. The batter should have the consistency and look of beige house paint. If it's too thick, add more milk, 1 tablespoon at a time.

2. In 8-inch nonstick skillet or crepe pan, pour about 1 teaspoon oil. Use a folded paper towel to wipe oil around entire interior of skillet. Heat skillet over medium heat until hot (a drop of water should skitter across the bottom). Add about 3 tablespoons batter to skillet and immediately tilt skillet to swirl batter so it covers bottom of skillet. Cook until tiny bubbles form around the edge and crepe is lightly browned on bottom. Use a spatula to loosen and flip crepe. Cook other side just a few seconds. Turn finished crepe out onto plate. (Your first crepe may not turn out perfect—that's okay. The second one will.)

3. Repeat with remaining batter. If crepes stick, re-oil bottom of skillet using the same paper towel. Stack crepes, placing a piece of cooking parchment paper or waxed paper between each so they don't stick together. Cover crepes with a kitchen towel so they don't dry out before making the filling. (Stacked crepes, wrapped in plastic wrap, can be stored in the refrigerator 1 day. Bring to room temperature before filling.)

4. In 10-inch skillet, melt 2 tablespoons butter over medium heat. Add strawberries and brown sugar. Cook, stirring occasionally, until strawberries become slightly soft and exude some juice. Add orange juice, vinegar, vanilla and dash of salt. (Mixture will bubble up and you may want to avert your head; the fumes from the vinegar can take your breath away.) Cook uncovered 2 minutes, stirring occasionally, until liquid becomes slightly syrupy. Remove from heat.

5. Remove a crepe from the stack and place it on clean work surface. (Be sure to fill crepes so the more attractive side will be on the outside.) Place about 2 tablespoons warm strawberry filling (try not to include too much of the juice) down middle of crepe. Fold sides of crepe, one at a time, over filling until they meet in the middle and overlap slightly. Repeat with remaining crepes and filling. Dust with powdered sugar.

WHY IT WORKS: **ADD INSTANT FLOUR** Some crepe recipes call for all-purpose flour and tell you to mix your batter and let it rest for hours to allow the flour to absorb the liquid. An easier and faster way is to use instant flour. In a process similar to the manufacture of instant milk, instant flour is made by combining low-protein flour with water before being dried. This pre-wetting process allows instant flour to absorb liquid very quickly without clumping. This guarantees thin delicious crepes every time!

1 Serving: Calories 270 (Calories from Fat 130); Total Fat 14g (Saturated Fat 6g; Trans Fat 0.5g); Cholesterol 135mg; Sodium 220mg; Total Carbohydrate 29g (Dietary Fiber 2g; Sugars 16g); Protein 7g • **% Daily Value:** Vitamin A 10%; Vitamin C 30%; Calcium 8%; Iron 8% • **Exchanges:** 1 Starch, 1/2 Fruit, 1/2 Other Carbohydrate, 3 Fat • **Carbohydrate Choices:** 2

Whole Wheat Waffles

WITH MAPLE-APPLE SYRUP

PREP TIME: 10 MINUTES • START TO FINISH: 40 MINUTES   SIX 7-INCH ROUND WAFFLES

Syrup

1/2 cup pure maple syrup
1/4 cup frozen apple juice
    concentrate

Waffles

2 eggs
2 cups whole wheat flour
1 3/4 cups milk
1/2 cup vegetable oil
1/4 cup frozen apple juice
    concentrate
1 tablespoon granulated or packed
    brown sugar
4 teaspoons baking powder
1/4 teaspoon salt

1. In 1-quart saucepan, heat syrup ingredients over medium heat, stirring occasionally, until juice concentrate is melted and mixture is warm.

2. Heat waffle iron. (Waffle irons without a nonstick coating may need to be brushed with vegetable oil or sprayed with cooking spray before batter for each waffle is added.)

3. In large bowl, beat eggs with wire whisk or egg beater until fluffy. Beat in remaining ingredients just until smooth.

4. For each waffle, pour slightly less than 3/4 cup batter from cup or pitcher onto center of hot waffle iron. (Check manufacturer's directions for recommended amount of batter.) Close lid of waffle iron.

5. Bake about 5 minutes or until steaming stops. Carefully remove waffle and serve immediately. Top with syrup.

1 Waffle: Calories 500 (Calories from Fat 200); Total Fat 22g (Saturated Fat 4g; Trans Fat 0g); Cholesterol 75mg; Sodium 520mg; Total Carbohydrate 65g (Dietary Fiber 5g; Sugars 24g); Protein 10g • **% Daily Value:** Vitamin A 6%; Vitamin C 0%; Calcium 30%; Iron 15% • **Exchanges:** 3 Starch, 1 1/2 Other Carbohydrate, 4 Fat • **Carbohydrate Choices:** 4

WHY IT WORKS:

THE "WHOLE" TRUTH Wheat kernels are much like eggs. The "shell" is the bran, the "white" is the endosperm and the "yolk" is the germ. All-purpose flour is made by removing the bran and germ and grinding the endosperm. Flour labeled as "whole wheat" is made from the entire wheat kernel. Although nutritious, the bran and germ can wreak havoc on your baked goods. Just like a shell, the bran is hard and sharp. When ground into flour it can "cut" into the structure of your bread or muffin, ruining the tender crumb and making it dense and soggy. If you want to use whole wheat flour in recipes that call for all-purpose flour, it's best to substitute no more than half whole wheat flour for all-purpose flour in baking.

Better-than-the-Mall Cinnamon Rolls

PREP TIME: 25 MINUTES • START TO FINISH: 2 HOURS 30 MINUTES   12 LARGE CINNAMON ROLLS

Rolls

1 teaspoon salt
4 1/2 cups all-purpose flour
1/2 cup granulated sugar
2 packages fast-acting dry yeast
1 cup warm milk (105°F to 115°F)
1/3 cup butter, melted
2 eggs

Filling

1 cup packed brown sugar
2 tablespoons ground cinnamon
1/3 cup butter, softened

Frosting

1 package (3 oz) cream cheese,
    softened
1/4 cup butter, softened
1 1/2 cups powdered sugar
1/2 teaspoon vanilla

1. Measuring carefully, place all roll ingredients in bread machine pan in the order recommended by the manufacturer.

2. Select Dough/Manual cycle. Do not use Delay cycle.

3. Remove dough from pan, using lightly floured hands; place on lightly floured surface. Cover dough and let rest 10 minutes.

4. Meanwhile, in small bowl, mix brown sugar and cinnamon; set aside.

5. Grease bottom and sides of 13 × 9-inch pan with shortening or spray with cooking spray. Roll dough into 20 × 16-inch rectangle. Spread 1/3 cup butter over dough; sprinkle evenly with brown sugar-cinnamon mixture. Roll up dough, beginning at 20-inch side; pinch edge of dough into roll to seal. Cut into 12 slices. (Use dental floss to cut clean slices that hold their shape. Place a piece of floss under the roll, bring ends of floss together and crisscross at top. Pull ends in opposite directions.) Place slices in pan. Cover and let rise in warm place 35 to 45 minutes or until dough has almost doubled in size.

6. Heat oven to 375°F. Bake 20 to 25 minutes or until golden brown. Meanwhile, in medium bowl, beat all frosting ingredients with electric mixer on medium speed until smooth and spreadable. Let rolls stand 5 minutes before frosting. Spread frosting on warm rolls. (Leftover rolls should be stored in refrigerator, due to cream cheese frosting.)

1 Roll: Calories 510 (Calories from Fat 160); Total Fat 18g (Saturated Fat 9g; Trans Fat 1g); Cholesterol 80mg; Sodium 340mg; Total Carbohydrate 80g (Dietary Fiber 2g; Sugars 42g); Protein 8g • **% Daily Value:** Vitamin A 15%; Vitamin C 0%; Calcium 8%; Iron 20% • **Exchanges:** 2 1/2 Starch, 3 Other Carbohydrate, 3 Fat • **Carbohydrate Choices:** 5

WHY IT WORKS:

BABY YOUR BREAD Yeast is alive and it is eating your dough! The yeast used to make your cinnamon rolls is actually a fungus related to the common button mushroom. When added to dough, yeast goes to work eating as much sugar as it can. In return, the yeast produces gas that makes your rolls rise. The more comfortable you make the yeast, the faster it will eat. Ideally yeast likes it warm, but not too warm (about 80°F). Too much sugar or spice (such as cinnamon) can slow down or even kill yeast. A good rule of thumb is to use no more than 1/4 teaspoon cinnamon per cup flour in the dough. Overly rich doughs, like those used for coffee cake, may need extra time to rise or extra yeast in the dough.

Better-than-the-Mall Cinnamon Rolls

Apple Cinnamon–Raisin Bread Pudding

PREP TIME: 25 MINUTES • **START TO FINISH:** 1 HOUR 45 MINUTES 12 SERVINGS

Bread Pudding

6 cups cubed day-old cinnamon-
    raisin bread (8 slices)
2 cups thinly sliced peeled apples
    (2 medium)
4 eggs
3/4 cup granulated sugar
1/4 teaspoon salt
3 cups milk
1 teaspoon vanilla

Streusel Topping

3/4 cup all-purpose flour
1/2 cup old-fashioned oats
1/2 cup packed brown sugar
1 teaspoon ground cinnamon
1/4 cup butter, melted

1. Heat oven to 350°F. In ungreased 13×9-inch glass baking dish, toss bread and apples.

2. In large bowl, beat eggs, granulated sugar and salt with wire whisk until well blended. Beat in milk and vanilla. Pour milk mixture over bread and apples. Let stand 5 minutes.

3. Meanwhile, in small bowl, mix all streusel topping ingredients; sprinkle evenly over unbaked pudding.

4. Bake 40 to 50 minutes or until center is puffed and golden. Cool at least 30 minutes.

1 Serving: Calories 280 (Calories from Fat 70); Total Fat 8g (Saturated Fat 3.5g; Trans Fat 0g); Cholesterol 85mg; Sodium 200mg; Total Carbohydrate 45g (Dietary Fiber 2g; Sugars 30g); Protein 7g • **% Daily Value:** Vitamin A 8%; Vitamin C 0%; Calcium 10%; Iron 8% • **Exchanges:** 1 Starch, 2 Other Carbohydrate, 1/2 High-Fat Meat, 1 Fat • **Carbohydrate Choices:** 3

WHY IT WORKS: CAREFUL WITH THE CUSTARD

Successful custard, such as the one in this pudding, should be creamy and smooth, with no pooling of water on the top or holes inside. The secret to this success rests firmly with the way you treat your eggs. As eggs cook in custard, their proteins unwind and spread out, trapping all of the milk and thickening the mixture. If this heating happens quickly, the egg proteins may recombine, and the trapped liquid will squeeze out, leaving you with a watery mess. To make sure this doesn't happen, cook custard at a low temperature and remove it from the oven when it is almost done (it will continue to cook on the counter). For extra insurance, you can add sugar to the custard to slow the cooking of the eggs.

Apple Cinnamon–Raisin Bread Pudding

Apricot-Stuffed French Toast

PREP TIME: 55 MINUTES • **START TO FINISH:** 1 HOUR 10 MINUTES　　　　　6 SERVINGS (2 SLICES EACH)

1 loaf (8 oz) or 1/2 loaf (1-lb size)
　　day-old French bread
1 package (3 oz) cream cheese,
　　softened
3 tablespoons apricot preserves
1/4 teaspoon grated lemon peel
3 eggs
3/4 cup half-and-half or milk
2 tablespoons granulated sugar
1 teaspoon vanilla
1/8 teaspoon salt
1/8 teaspoon ground nutmeg,
　　if desired
2 tablespoons butter, melted
Powdered sugar, if desired

1. Spray 13 × 9-inch pan with cooking spray.

2. Cut bread crosswise into 12 1-inch slices. Cut a horizontal slit in the side of each bread slice, cutting to—but not through—the other edge.

3. In medium bowl, beat cream cheese, preserves and lemon peel with electric mixer on medium speed about 1 minute or until well mixed. Spread about 2 teaspoons of the cream cheese mixture inside the slit in each bread slice. Place stuffed bread slices in pan.

4. In medium bowl, beat eggs, half-and-half, granulated sugar, vanilla, salt and nutmeg if desired, with fork or wire whisk until well mixed. Pour egg mixture over bread slices in pan, and turn slices carefully to coat. Cover and refrigerate at least 30 minutes but no longer than 24 hours.

5. Heat oven to 425°F. Uncover French toast and drizzle with melted butter. Bake 20 to 25 minutes or until golden brown. Sprinkle with powdered sugar if desired.

1 Serving: Calories 310 (Calories from Fat 150); Total Fat 16g (Saturated Fat 8g; Trans Fat 1g); Cholesterol 145mg; Sodium 380mg; Total Carbohydrate 32g (Dietary Fiber 1g; Sugars 11g); Protein 9g • **% Daily Value:** Vitamin A 10%; Vitamin C 0%; Calcium 8%; Iron 10% • **Exchanges:** 1 Starch, 1 Other Carbohydrate, 1 High-Fat Meat, 1 1/2 Fat • **Carbohydrate Choices:** 2

WHY IT WORKS: **A ZEST FOR FLAVOR** You might be surprised to learn that the most flavorful part of a lemon is the part you normally throw away: the peel. The yellow part of the lemon peel (called the rind or the zest) contains lemon oil, a powerful concentrate of citrus. Including the zest of the lemon in your cooking adds a refreshing flavor without the acidity of lemon juice. Care must be taken when removing the zest so you don't remove the bitter white pith that lies just underneath. Although you can use a box grater, the best tool is called a microplane grater (similar to an old-fashioned wood rasp). It grates the zest evenly but avoids scraping the underlying pith.

Cheesy Apple-Bacon Strata

PREP TIME: 25 MINUTES • START TO FINISH: 3 HOURS 20 MINUTES   12 SERVINGS

3 tablespoons butter

3 medium Granny Smith apples, peeled and coarsely chopped (3 cups)

3 tablespoons packed brown sugar

4 cups cubed day-old firm bread (such as Italian or French bread)

1 lb bacon, crisply cooked and coarsely chopped

2 cups shredded sharp Cheddar cheese (8 oz)

2 1/2 cups milk

2 teaspoons Worcestershire sauce

1 teaspoon ground mustard

1/4 teaspoon salt

1/8 teaspoon pepper

5 eggs

1. Spray a shallow 2-quart casserole or 11 × 17-inch glass baking dish with cooking spray.

2. In 10-inch skillet, melt butter over medium heat. Cook apples in butter 2 to 3 minutes, stirring occasionally, until crisp-tender. Stir in brown sugar; reduce heat to low. Cook 5 to 6 minutes, stirring occasionally, until apples are tender.

3. Layer half each of the bread, bacon, apples and cheese in casserole. Repeat with remaining bread, bacon, apples and cheese.

4. In bowl, mix remaining ingredients; pour over cheese. Cover tightly and refrigerate at least 2 hours but no longer than 24 hours.

5. Heat oven to 350°F. Bake uncovered 40 to 45 minutes or until knife inserted in center comes out clean. Let stand 10 minutes before serving (strata will be easier to cut or spoon into serving pieces).

1 Serving: Calories 270 (Calories from Fat 160); Total Fat 18g (Saturated Fat 9g; Trans Fat 0g); Cholesterol 130mg; Sodium 450mg; Total Carbohydrate 15g (Dietary Fiber 0g; Sugars 10g); Protein 13g • **% Daily Value:** Vitamin A 10%; Vitamin C 0%; Calcium 20%; Iron 6% • **Exchanges:** 1 Other Carbohydrate, 2 High-Fat Meat • **Carbohydrate Choices:** 1

WHY IT WORKS:

STALE BREAD When bread dough begins to bake, water is evenly mixed within the dough. However, as the dough's starch cooks, the starch pulls the water to itself. This combination of water and starch forms the texture of bread. After baking, the water in the loaf moves again, this time away from the starch towards the crust. This process is called staling, and you can see it happen as the interior of the bread gets dry and the crust gets leathery. The good news is that stale (or day-old) bread is perfectly willing to absorb a new liquid, such as the custard in this casserole.

Apple, Cheddar and Sausage Sandwiches

PREP TIME: 25 MINUTES • **START TO FINISH:** 25 MINUTES

8 oz bulk pork sausage

1 tablespoon vegetable oil

2 eggs

Salt and pepper, if desired

1/4 cup apple butter

4 slices (1/2 inch thick) Italian bread

1/2 cup shredded sharp Cheddar cheese (2 oz)

2 tablespoons butter, softened

1. Heat 12-inch nonstick skillet over medium heat. Divide sausage in half and shape into flat patties slightly bigger than the diameter of each bread slice. Place patties in hot skillet and cook about 8 minutes, turning once, until pork is no longer pink in center. Drain on paper towel–lined plate. Drain fat from skillet and wipe out with a wadded paper towel.

2. In same skillet, heat oil over medium heat until hot. Break each egg into skillet and sprinkle with salt and pepper if desired. Cook until whites of eggs are set. Flip eggs so yolks face down (flip eggs away from you to avoid being splashed with hot oil). Use tip of spatula to pierce each yolk. Cook eggs 1 minute or until yolks are set. Remove eggs from skillet and place directly on top of sausage patties on paper towels.

3. Spread 2 tablespoons apple butter on one side of 2 bread slices. Top each slice with sausage and egg. Sprinkle each with 1/4 cup cheese. Cover with remaining bread slices. Spread half of the butter over the top slices of bread.

4. In same skillet, place sandwiches butter sides down. Spread remaining butter over top slices of bread. Cook uncovered over medium heat about 5 minutes or until bottoms are golden brown. With spatula, carefully turn sandwiches over. Cook 2 to 3 minutes longer or until bottoms are golden brown and cheese is melted. Serve hot.

1 Sandwich: Calories 730 (Calories from Fat 460); Total Fat 51g (Saturated Fat 21g; Trans Fat 1g); Cholesterol 315mg; Sodium 1240mg; Total Carbohydrate 40g (Dietary Fiber 2g; Sugars 18g); Protein 28g • **% Daily Value:** Vitamin A 20%; Vitamin C 2%; Calcium 25%; Iron 15% • **Exchanges:** 1 1/2 Starch, 1 Other Carbohydrate, 3 1/2 High-Fat Meat, 4 1/2 Fat • **Carbohydrate Choices:** 2 1/2

WHY IT WORKS:

THE MELT FACTOR Considering the wide variety of cheese available, it's amazing that they all start as milk. Although some cheeses are made from milk other than cow's, the main flavor differences between cheese varieties are due to the type of bacteria used and the way it is fermented or aged. Aging also affects how cheese cooks. In general, the drier a cheese, the better its melting characteristics. Fresh cheeses, like creamy fresh mozzarella, usually resist melting. The very best melting cheeses are hard cheeses (like Cheddar) and very hard cheeses (like Parmesan, if grated finely). To ensure a good melting texture and prevent separation, keep cooking temperatures low and cooking times brief.

Apple, Cheddar and Sausage Sandwiches

Classic Eggs Benedict

PREP TIME: 30 MINUTES • START TO FINISH: 30 MINUTES 6 SERVINGS

. . . .

Hollandaise Sauce

3 egg yolks
1 tablespoon lemon juice
1/2 cup firm butter

Eggs Benedict

3 English muffins
3 tablespoons butter, softened
1 teaspoon butter
6 thin slices Canadian-style bacon
    or fully cooked ham
4 teaspoons distilled white vinegar
6 eggs
Paprika, if desired

1. In 1-quart saucepan, vigorously stir egg yolks and lemon juice with wire whisk. Add 1/4 cup of the butter. Heat over very low heat, stirring constantly with wire whisk, until butter is melted.

2. Add remaining 1/4 cup butter. Continue stirring vigorously until butter is melted and sauce is thickened. (Be sure butter melts slowly so eggs have time to cook and thicken sauce without curdling.) If the sauce curdles (mixture begins to separate and melted butter starts to appear around the edge of the pan and on top of the sauce), add about 1 tablespoon boiling water and beat vigorously with wire whisk or egg beater until smooth. Keep warm.

3. Split English muffins; toast. Spread each muffin half with some of the 3 tablespoons butter; keep warm.

4. In 10-inch skillet, melt 1 teaspoon butter over medium heat. Cook bacon in butter until light brown on both sides; keep warm.

5. Wipe out skillet; fill with 2 to 3 inches water. Add vinegar to water. Heat to boiling; reduce to simmering. Break cold eggs, one at a time, into custard cup or saucer. Holding dish close to water's surface, carefully slip eggs into water. Cook 3 to 5 minutes or until whites and yolks are firm, not runny (water should be gently simmering and not boiling). Remove with slotted spoon.

6. Place 1 slice bacon on each muffin half. Top with egg. Spoon warm sauce over eggs. Sprinkle with paprika if desired.

1 **Serving:** Calories 410 (Calories from Fat 290); Total Fat 32g (Saturated Fat 14g; Trans Fat 1.5g); Cholesterol 390mg; Sodium 670mg; Total Carbohydrate 14g (Dietary Fiber 0g; Sugars 5g); Protein 15g • **% Daily Value:** Vitamin A 25%; Vitamin C 0%; Calcium 10%; Iron 10% • **Exchanges:** 1 Starch, 2 Medium-Fat Meat, 4 Fat • **Carbohydrate Choices:** 1

WHY IT WORKS: PERFECT POACHING

Everyone knows that heat cooks an egg, but did you know vinegar does as well? Vinegar, as well as other acids like lemon juice, has the same effect on egg protein as does boiling water: It sets the white. This can be used to your advantage when poaching eggs. A small amount of vinegar (no more than a teaspoon per quart of water) stops the egg white from spreading before the heat of the poaching water has a chance to cook the egg.

RECIPE Rx: BROKEN SAUCE If you returned to your hollandaise sauce after poaching your eggs only to find a pool of grainy butter floating on top, don't panic. What probably happened was that there was too much heat or butter for the emulsifier in the egg yolks

to do their job right. The solution is to add another yolk to the mix and start again. In another 1-quart saucepan or a double boiler over low heat, combine 1 large egg yolk and 1 tablespoon of cold water and whisk well. Very slowly drizzle in the broken sauce, whisking constantly. The sauce should return to its unseparated self. Serve right away, or keep covered over low heat, whisking occasionally.

Cheddar and Green Onion Biscuits
WITH SAUSAGE GRAVY

Biscuits

1 1/3 cups all-purpose flour

1 1/2 teaspoons baking powder

1/2 teaspoon salt

1/4 teaspoon baking soda

1/4 teaspoon ground mustard

4 medium green onions, sliced
(1/4 cup)

1/3 cup shredded Cheddar cheese

3/4 cup buttermilk

3 tablespoons vegetable oil

Gravy

12 oz bulk pork sausage

1/3 cup all-purpose flour

1/2 teaspoon salt

1/4 teaspoon coarse ground pepper

3 cups milk

1. Heat oven to 450°F. Spray cookie sheet with cooking spray.

2. In medium bowl, mix 1 1/3 cups flour, the baking powder, 1/2 teaspoon salt, the baking soda and mustard. Stir in green onions and cheese. In small bowl, mix buttermilk and oil; stir into flour mixture until soft dough forms and leaves side of bowl. (Dough will be soft and slightly sticky.)

3. Drop dough by 8 spoonfuls onto cookie sheet. Bake 9 to 11 minutes or until golden brown.

4. Meanwhile, crumble sausage into 10-inch skillet. Cook over medium-high heat, stirring frequently, until browned and no longer pink. (Don't drain the fat from the sausage; you'll need it later for the gravy.)

5. With wire whisk, stir in 1/3 cup flour, 1/2 teaspoon salt and the pepper. Gradually stir in milk. Cook until mixture thickens, stirring constantly.

6. Split warm biscuits; place on serving plates. Serve sausage mixture over warm split biscuits.

1 Biscuit: Calories 290 (Calories from Fat 140); Total Fat 15g (Saturated Fat 5g; Trans Fat 0g); Cholesterol 30mg; Sodium 780mg; Total Carbohydrate 26g (Dietary Fiber 1g; Sugars 6g); Protein 12g • **% Daily Value:** Vitamin A 6%; Vitamin C 0%; Calcium 20%; Iron 10% • **Exchanges:** 1 Starch, 1/2 Other Carbohydrate, 1 High-Fat Meat, 1 1/2 Fat • **Carbohydrate Choices:** 2

WHY IT WORKS: **GETTING TO KNOW ROUX** Flour and water do not mix well. You can see this every time your gravy gets lumpy. This happens because flour would rather stick to itself than combine with water. To fix this situation, each grain of flour is surrounded with a nonstick coating, often a fat such as butter or oil. This mixture of flour and fat, called a roux, allows you to add liquid to flour without fear of lumps. Care must be taken when making and using a roux. The flour must be cooked either before or after adding the liquid to rid the flour of its raw taste. Although it adds a pleasant toasted flavor, browning a roux lessens the flour's thickening ability.

Extra-Moist Scrambled Eggs with Chives

PREP TIME: 10 MINUTES • **START TO FINISH:** 15 MINUTES   4 SERVINGS

6 eggs
1 tablespoon chopped fresh chives
1/4 teaspoon salt
1/8 teaspoon pepper, if desired
1/2 cup milk or half-and-half
3 tablespoons butter

1. In medium bowl, beat eggs, chives, salt and pepper if desired, with fork or wire whisk until well mixed.

2. In 10-inch skillet, heat milk and butter over medium heat just until butter melts and liquid is steaming. Pour egg mixture into skillet.

3. As mixture heats, portions of eggs will begin to set. Gently push cooked portions with metal spatula to the outside edge of skillet. Avoid stirring constantly. As more egg sets, push it to the edge as well and stack it on top of the set egg mixture already there. Cook 5 to 6 minutes or until eggs are thickened throughout but still *moist*.

1 Serving: Calories 210 (Calories from Fat 150); Total Fat 17g (Saturated Fat 7g; Trans Fat 0.5g); Cholesterol 345mg; Sodium 310mg; Total Carbohydrate 2g (Dietary Fiber 0g; Sugars 2g); Protein 11g • **% Daily Value:** Vitamin A 15%; Vitamin C 0%; Calcium 8%; Iron 6% • **Exchanges:** 1 1/2 Medium-Fat Meat, 2 Fat • **Carbohydrate Choices:** 0

WHY IT WORKS: **HANDLE WITH CARE** Eggs, like meat, are made mostly of protein. Like towels, proteins can hold a lot of water. The more you heat eggs—or other high-protein foods—the more these proteins are wrung dry. With just a little heat, eggs turn out moist; with too much heat, the egg proteins are squeezed so tightly that they leave a puddle of liquid on your plate. The secret to moist scrambled eggs lies in gentle heat. By starting eggs cooking in liquid, you slowly raise their temperature without overheating. Pushing them off to the side of the pan when they are completed stops the cooking and saves your breakfast!

Extra-Moist Scrambled Eggs with Chives

Cheesy Cheddar Hash Browns

5 cups frozen shredded hash brown
   potatoes, thawed
3 medium green onions, thinly sliced
   (3 tablespoons)
1/2 teaspoon salt
1/4 teaspoon pepper
2 tablespoons olive oil
1 1/2 cups shredded Cheddar
   cheese (6 oz)

1. In large bowl, mix potatoes, onions, salt and pepper. Coat 10-inch non-stick skillet with slanted side with 1 tablespoon of the oil and heat over medium heat. Spread 2 1/2 cups of the potato mixture evenly over bottom of skillet, pressing down with back of broad spatula. Top with cheese to within 1 inch of edge. Spread remaining potatoes over cheese, pressing down again with back of broad spatula.

2. Cook over medium heat about 15 minutes or until potatoes are well browned and crisp. Loosen edge of potatoes with spatula. Place a heatproof plate upside down over skillet, then carefully turn skillet upside down over plate to remove potatoes.

3. In skillet, heat remaining 1 tablespoon oil over medium heat. Slide potatoes from plate into skillet so uncooked side is down. Cook about 10 minutes or until potatoes are well browned and tender. Slide onto serving plate and cut into wedges.

1 Serving: Calories 310 (Calories from Fat 130); Total Fat 14g (Saturated Fat 7g; Trans Fat 0g); Cholesterol 30mg; Sodium 420mg; Total Carbohydrate 35g (Dietary Fiber 4g; Sugars 2g); Protein 10g • **% Daily Value:** Vitamin A 8%; Vitamin C 10%; Calcium 15%; Iron 4% • **Exchanges:** 2 1/2 Starch, 1/2 High-Fat Meat, 1 1/2 Fat • **Carbohydrate Choices:** 2

WHY IT WORKS:

PRE-COOKED POTATOES The ideal hash brown is crispy on the outside and tender on the inside. When cooked over high heat, shredded raw potatoes brown nicely. But unless you spread them thinly in the pan, the outside will burn before the inside ever becomes soft. Because potatoes are mostly starch, high heat breaks the starch on the outside of the hash brown down into sugar, making for the golden color. The starch on the inside of the hash browns needs steam and time to cook through. The answer to the perfect hash brown is simple: Start with cooked potatoes.

Maple-Glazed Peppered Bacon

PREP TIME: 10 MINUTES • START TO FINISH: 55 MINUTES   6 SERVINGS (2 SLICES EACH)

1 lb thick-cut bacon (about 12 slices)
1/2 cup real maple syrup
2 tablespoons apple jelly
Freshly ground pepper

1. Adjust oven rack to middle position. Heat oven to 375°F. Line cookie sheet with sides with foil.

2. Place bacon on cookie sheet in single layer. Bake 10 minutes. Drain off fat.

3. Meanwhile, in 1-quart saucepan, heat syrup and jelly, stirring occasionally, until jelly melts and syrup is warm. Remove from heat.

4. Use pastry brush to brush about half the syrup mixture on bacon (you don't have to use it all, just enough to moisten bacon), then sprinkle with pepper. Bake 15 minutes.

5. Flip bacon, brush with remaining syrup mixture and sprinkle with pepper. Bake 20 minutes longer or until bacon is glazed and done. Serve warm.

1 Serving: Calories 210 (Calories from Fat 90); Total Fat 10g (Saturated Fat 3.5g; Trans Fat 0g); Cholesterol 20mg; Sodium 340mg; Total Carbohydrate 22g (Dietary Fiber 0g; Sugars 19g); Protein 6g • **% Daily Value:** Vitamin A 0%; Vitamin C 0%; Calcium 2%; Iron 4% • **Exchanges:** 1 1/2 Other Carbohydrate, 1 High-Fat Meat • **Carbohydrate Choices:** 1 1/2

WHY IT WORKS:

KEEP IT CLEAN There are two ways to make American bacon. The current way is to quickly brine the belly of the pig in a salt/sugar solution. The second way, commonly used years ago, is to rub the belly with salt and spices, a slower but more flavorful process. Unfortunately, the former process leaves a large amount of liquid in the bacon. When this liquid escapes from the bacon as it cooks, it encounters the hot melted fat. The result is a lot of popping and a big mess. The solution? Bake your bacon in the oven instead of frying it on the stovetop. Because the heat is more evenly distributed in the oven, there's less mess.

Snacks and Starters

BIG FLAVORS

FOR SMALL PLATES

Cheddar-Apple Soup

3 tablespoons butter

1 large apple (preferably Golden
    Delicious), peeled, cored and
    finely chopped (1 cup)

1 medium onion, finely chopped
    (1/2 cup)

1 medium carrot, finely chopped
    (1/2 cup)

2 tablespoons all-purpose flour

1 1/2 cups chicken broth

1 cup apple juice

2 cups half-and-half

1/2 cup whipping (heavy) cream

1 dried bay leaf

1 tablespoon apple brandy,
    dry vermouth or frozen apple
    juice concentrate

Dash of ground cinnamon

Dash of ground red pepper (cayenne)

3 cups shredded sharp Cheddar
    cheese (12 oz)

1 teaspoon salt

White pepper

Chopped fresh parsley, if desired

1. In 4-quart Dutch oven, melt butter over medium-low heat. Add apple and onion. Cook 12 to 15 minutes, stirring frequently, until soft but not brown. Add carrot and cook 5 minutes longer or until carrot just begins to soften. Increase heat to medium. Add flour and cook 1 minute, stirring constantly as mixture thickens. Add 1/2 cup of the broth, stirring constantly with wire whisk to prevent lumps. As soon as broth is incorporated (about 20 seconds), add another 1/2 cup broth and stir again until incorporated. Add remaining broth and the apple juice.

2. Increase heat to high. Heat soup to boiling, stirring occasionally. Stir well and add half-and-half, whipping cream and bay leaf. Reduce heat to medium-low and simmer gently 15 minutes. (Do not let mixture boil or soup may curdle.)

3. Remove bay leaf. Add brandy, cinnamon and red pepper. Gradually stir in cheese until completely melted and smooth, about 8 minutes. Season with salt and white pepper. Garnish with parsley if desired.

1 Serving: Calories 390 (Calories from Fat 270); Total Fat 30g (Saturated Fat 18g; Trans Fat 1g); Cholesterol 95mg; Sodium 810mg; Total Carbohydrate 15g (Dietary Fiber 1g; Sugars 11g); Protein 14g • **% Daily Value:** Vitamin A 50%; Vitamin C 2%; Calcium 30%; Iron 4% • **Exchanges:** 1 Other Carbohydrate, 2 High-Fat Meat, 3 Fat • **Carbohydrate Choices:** 1

WHY IT WORKS: CHEESE AND FRUIT COMBO

Cheese begins its life as milk, but after being heated, salted and mixed with bacteria, the end results are quite different. Dramatic flavor changes are due in part to the breakdown of chemicals that made up the original milk. Some of the new chemicals formed as cheese ages are similar to chemicals naturally found in fruit. Successful flavor combinations are often the result of pairing similar flavors. For instance, a mild Cheddar cheese that hints of an apple's tart sweetness is complemented when served with a Granny Smith apple. A sharp Cheddar would better complement a sweet Golden Delicious apple, as in the recipe above.

Cheddar-Apple Soup

French Onion Soup

PREP TIME: 20 MINUTES • **START TO FINISH:** 1 HOUR 30 MINUTES   4 SERVINGS

2 tablespoons butter

4 medium onions, sliced

2 cans (10 1/2 oz each) condensed
   beef broth

1 1/2 cups water

1/8 teaspoon pepper

1/8 teaspoon dried thyme leaves

1 dried bay leaf

4 slices French bread, 3/4 to
   1 inch thick, toasted

1 cup shredded Gruyère, Swiss or
   mozzarella cheese (4 oz)

1/4 cup grated Parmesan cheese

1. In 4-quart nonstick Dutch oven, melt butter over medium-high heat. Stir in onions to coat with butter. Cook uncovered 10 minutes, stirring every 3 to 4 minutes.

2. Reduce heat to medium-low. Cook onions 35 to 40 minutes longer, stirring well every 5 minutes, until onions are light golden brown (onions will shrink during cooking).

3. Stir in broth, water, pepper, thyme and bay leaf. Heat to boiling; reduce heat. Cover and simmer 15 minutes. Remove bay leaf.

4. Set oven control to broil. Place toasted bread in 4 ovenproof bowls or individual ceramic casseroles (do not use glass). Place bowls on cookie sheet or in pan with shallow sides. Pour onion soup over bread. Top each with 1/4 cup Gruyère cheese and 1 tablespoon Parmesan cheese.

5. Broil with cheese about 5 inches from heat 1 to 2 minutes or just until cheese is melted and golden brown. Watch carefully so cheese does not burn. Serve with additional French bread if desired.

1 Serving: Calories 450 (Calories from Fat 170); Total Fat 19g (Saturated Fat 10g; Trans Fat 1g); Cholesterol 50mg; Sodium 1400mg; Total Carbohydrate 44g (Dietary Fiber 4g; Sugars 7g); Protein 25g • **% Daily Value:** Vitamin A 15%; Vitamin C 6%; Calcium 45%; Iron 15% • **Exchanges:** 3 Starch, 2 1/2 Lean Meat, 2 Fat • **Carbohydrate Choices:** 3

WHY IT WORKS:

NO MORE TEARS Cutting onions for French Onion Soup can cause a lot of tears. When cut, sulfur-containing chemicals in the onion combine, irritating your eyes and making you cry. Fresh, juicy onions contain the most potent of these chemicals. In nature, this reaction stops predators from nibbling away at the onion, but in the kitchen it can be annoying. Although not completely preventable, there are ways to lessen the problem. Chilling the onion about 30 minutes slows the reaction, and washing large chopped pieces rinses away the chemicals. Some people swear contact lenses are the answer.

RECIPE Rₓ: CARAMELIZING ONIONS Browned onions are browned onions, right? Not necessarily. The onions in this recipe start to brown within about 15 minutes of cooking. However, the true flavor of this soup is developed when the onions are cooked down and really brown (see photo). French onion soup served in Paris is a rich and much sought-after meal. In many American restaurants, French onion soup is often looked down upon as too salty and lacking in flavor. The secret to getting the best flavor of this simple but elegant soup is browning, but not burning, the onions. So take your time and don't rush this step.

French Onion Soup

Creamy Corn Chowder

PREP TIME: 1 HOUR 10 MINUTES • START TO FINISH: 1 HOUR 10 MINUTES   5 SERVINGS (1 1/2 CUPS EACH)

4 slices thick-cut bacon

1/4 cup butter

1 large onion, finely chopped (1 cup)

1 small carrot, finely chopped
(1/3 cup)

1 medium stalk celery, finely
chopped (1/2 cup)

2 cloves garlic, finely chopped

3 tablespoons all-purpose flour

2 1/2 cups chicken broth

1/2 cup dry white wine or
chicken broth

3 cups frozen extra-sweet whole
kernel corn (from 1-lb bag)

2 medium potatoes (Yukon Gold or
other medium-starch potato),
each cut into 8 chunks

3 cups half-and-half

1 teaspoon chopped fresh thyme
leaves or 1/2 teaspoon dried
thyme leaves

1 teaspoon salt or to taste

Freshly ground pepper, if desired

1 dried bay leaf

Dash of ground nutmeg

Chopped fresh parsley, if desired

1. In 4-quart Dutch oven, cook bacon over medium heat 7 to 10 minutes, turning once, until crisp. Drain on paper towels; leave bacon drippings in pan. When cool, crumble bacon and set aside.

2. In same pan, cook butter, onion, carrot, celery and garlic over medium heat 10 to 12 minutes, stirring constantly, until vegetables soften but do not brown.

3. Sprinkle flour over vegetables and stir well with wire whisk to incorporate. Cook about 2 minutes. Stirring constantly, slowly add broth and wine (make sure to scrape bottom of pan as flour tends to stick). Stir in corn, potatoes, half-and-half, thyme, salt, pepper if desired, bay leaf and nutmeg. Heat soup to a gentle simmer. Cook 15 minutes, stirring occasionally, until potatoes are tender. (Corn can be naturally salty depending on the season, so make sure to taste before adding extra salt.) Remove bay leaf.

4. Garnish with parsley if desired, and crumbled bacon.

1 Serving: Calories 490 (Calories from Fat 260); Total Fat 29g (Saturated Fat 16g; Trans Fat 1g); Cholesterol 85mg; Sodium 1230mg; Total Carbohydrate 43g (Dietary Fiber 5g; Sugars 11g); Protein 13g • **% Daily Value:** Vitamin A 60%; Vitamin C 10%; Calcium 20%; Iron 8% • **Exchanges:** 2 Starch, 1/2 Other Carbohydrate, 1 Vegetable, 1 High-Fat Meat, 4 Fat • **Carbohydrate Choices:** 3

WHY IT WORKS:

ALCOHOL ENHANCES FLAVOR Food is made up of thousands of chemicals. (Chocolate alone contains over 2,000!) Some of these chemicals dissolve in water while others dissolve only in fat. When you chew a food, you taste only those substances that are dissolved. But many soups get most of their flavor from chemicals that need to be dissolved in fat. How to bring out a soup's flavors without adding extra fat to a recipe? Adding alcohol can help. Alcohol is unique in that it can act like water and fat. That's why a splash of wine or liquor at the end of cooking will heighten the flavor of dull soups or stews.

Tomato and Cannellini Bean Soup
WITH GARLIC AND BASIL

PREP TIME: 1 HOUR • **START TO FINISH:** 1 HOUR 35 MINUTES 10 SERVINGS (1 1/2 CUPS EACH)

4 cloves garlic, unpeeled
3 tablespoons olive oil
3 slices pancetta or bacon, finely
   chopped
1 medium onion, finely chopped
   (1/2 cup)
1 medium carrot, finely chopped
   (1/2 cup)
1 medium stalk celery, finely
   chopped (1/2 cup)
3 large cloves garlic, finely chopped
2 quarts chicken broth
1 1/2 cups water
2 cans (15 oz each) cannellini beans,
   drained
1 can (28 oz) crushed tomatoes,
   undrained
1 tablespoon tomato paste
4 good-quality anchovy fillets
   (packed in oil or salt, bone
   removed if necessary), finely
   chopped
1 piece (2 inches) Parmesan
   cheese rind
2 dried bay leaves
1 large sprig fresh rosemary
1 tablespoon butter, softened
1 teaspoon salt
1/4 teaspoon crushed red pepper
Dash of freshly ground pepper
1/2 cup fresh basil leaves, torn
   into pieces

1. In 8-inch skillet, heat unpeeled garlic over low heat (you are dry-roasting the garlic, so there is no need for oil) 25 to 30 minutes, turning occasionally, until peel is light brown and clove feels soft inside when you touch it. (Don't rush the process by turning up the heat; garlic may burn and become bitter.) Remove garlic from skillet; set garlic aside.

2. In 3-quart saucepan, heat oil over medium heat. Add pancetta and cook about 3 minutes, stirring occasionally, until slightly crisp around edges. Add onion, carrot and celery. Cook about 5 minutes, stirring occasionally, until vegetables soften but do not brown. Add finely chopped garlic and cook 30 seconds, stirring constantly. Add broth, water, beans, tomatoes, tomato paste, anchovies, the cheese rind, bay leaves and rosemary; heat to boiling. (When you've used a piece of Parmesan cheese, save the rind in the freezer. If you don't have a rind, you may want to sprinkle each serving with grated Parmesan cheese.) Reduce heat and simmer 30 minutes, stirring occasionally.

3. Peel cooled, roasted garlic cloves and place in small bowl. Add butter, salt, red pepper and pepper. Use a fork to mash garlic to a smooth paste. Spoon garlic paste into hot soup and stir well to incorporate. Sprinkle with basil and stir well. Remove bay leaves and rosemary sprig.

1 Serving: Calories 230 (Calories from Fat 70); Total Fat 8g (Saturated Fat 2g; Trans Fat 0g); Cholesterol 5mg; Sodium 1310mg; Total Carbohydrate 26g (Dietary Fiber 6g; Sugars 3g); Protein 14g • **% Daily Value:** Vitamin A 35%; Vitamin C 10%; Calcium 15%; Iron 20% • **Exchanges:** 1 Starch, 2 Vegetable, 1 High-Fat Meat • **Carbohydrate Choices:** 2

WHY IT WORKS:
FLAVORFUL FISH The culinary world is full of references to using fish in small amounts as a flavor enhancer. In Asia, as well as in ancient Greece and Rome, small fish are steeped in salt water to make a sauce (*nam pla* in Thailand, *nuoc mam* in Vietnam and *garum* in ancient Rome) used in hundreds of dishes. In the Mediterranean, anchovies are the fish of choice. To most Americans, anchovies are the overly fishy and salty pieces sometimes found on a pizza. However, these do not adequately represent the flavor of true anchovies. High-quality anchovies should smell like the sea, not like rotten fish. To experience the best, buy anchovies packed in salt. Rinse them well under water and, if you like, insert your thumb through the center to remove their small bone. Chopped finely, they add a great depth of flavor to many dishes.

Pork Pot Stickers
WITH CHIPOTLE HONEY SAUCE

Sauce

1 cup honey

4 chipotle chiles in adobo sauce
   (from 7-oz can), finely chopped

2 tablespoons adobo sauce
   (from can of chiles)

Pot Stickers

4 medium dried shitake mushrooms

1 lb lean ground pork

1/3 cup finely chopped canned
   bamboo shoots

4 medium green onions, finely
   chopped (1/4 cup)

1 tablespoon dry white wine or
   nonalcoholic wine

1 tablespoon water

1 teaspoon cornstarch

1 teaspoon salt

1 teaspoon sesame oil

Dash of white pepper

2 cups all-purpose flour

1 cup boiling water

1/2 cup vegetable oil

2 cups water

1. In small bowl, mix all sauce ingredients; set aside.

2. In another small bowl, soak mushrooms in enough hot water to cover 20 minutes or until soft, drain. Rinse in warm water; drain. Squeeze out excess moisture. Remove and discard stems; chop caps finely.

3. In large bowl, mix mushrooms, pork, bamboo shoots, green onions, wine, 1 tablespoon water, the cornstarch, salt, sesame oil and white pepper.

4. In medium bowl, mix flour and 1 cup boiling water until a soft dough forms. Knead dough on lightly floured surface about 5 minutes or until smooth. Divide dough in half. Shape each half into a 12-inch-long roll; cut each roll into 24 slices, each about 1/2 inch thick.

5. Roll 1 slice of dough into a 3-inch circle on lightly floured surface. (If the circle springs back, cover the slices with a towel and let rest about 10 minutes or until slice is easy to roll and stays in a circle.) Place 1 tablespoon pork mixture on center of circle. Pinch 5 pleats on edge of one-half of circle. Fold circle in half, pressing pleated edge to unpleated edge. (Or instead of pleating the edge, you can fold the circle in half and press edges together with a fork.) Place the dumpling, pleated edge up, on cookie sheet. Gently press dumpling to flatten the bottom. Repeat with remaining slices of dough.

6. Heat wok or skillet until hot. Add 2 tablespoons of the vegetable oil; tilt wok to coat side. Place about 12 dumplings in single layer in wok; fry 2 minutes or until bottoms are golden brown. Add 1/2 cup of the water. Cover and cook 6 to 7 minutes or until water is absorbed. Repeat with remaining dumplings. (Add vegetable oil as necessary.) Serve with sauce.

1 Serving: Calories 90 (Calories from Fat 35); Total Fat 4g (Saturated Fat 1g; Trans Fat 0g); Cholesterol 5mg; Sodium 70mg; Total Carbohydrate 10g (Dietary Fiber 0g; Sugars 6g); Protein 2g • **% Daily Value:** Vitamin A 0%; Vitamin C 0%; Calcium 0%; Iron 2% • **Exchanges:** 1/2 Other Carbohydrate, 1 Fat • **Carbohydrate Choices:** 1/2

WHY IT WORKS: **DUMPLING DOUGH** When mixed with water, flour is naturally sticky and elastic—a texture caused by a protein in wheat called gluten. All batters and doughs made from wheat flour benefit and suffer from the properties of gluten. In dumpling dough, the gluten helps hold the dough together when rolling and when submerged in the boiling water. The downside is that gluten sometimes makes the dough difficult to roll out. Because it is elastic, the gluten tends to snap the dough back after it is stretched. The secret is to allow the gluten to relax after mixing the dough and before rolling. After a short rest, the dough will roll out without fighting back.

Pork Pot Stickers with Chipotle Honey Sauce

Chicken Satay
WITH PEANUT SAUCE

PREP TIME: 15 MINUTES • START TO FINISH: 2 HOURS 25 MINUTES

4 SERVINGS

Satay

3 tablespoons lime juice
1 teaspoon curry powder
2 teaspoons honey
1/2 teaspoon ground coriander
1/2 teaspoon ground cumin
1/8 teaspoon salt
2 cloves garlic, finely chopped
1 lb boneless skinless chicken
   breasts, cut into 1-inch cubes

Sauce

2/3 cup vanilla yogurt
1/4 cup coconut milk (not cream of
   coconut)
1/4 cup creamy peanut butter
1 tablespoon soy sauce
1/4 to 1/2 teaspoon red pepper sauce

1. In small bowl, mix all satay ingredients except chicken. Place chicken in resealable plastic food-storage bag or shallow glass or plastic dish. Pour lime juice mixture over chicken; stir chicken to coat with lime juice mixture. To marinate, seal bag or cover dish and refrigerate 2 hours, stirring occasionally.
2. Meanwhile, in medium bowl, mix all sauce ingredients with wire whisk; refrigerate.
3. Set oven control to broil. Spray rack in broiler pan with cooking spray.
4. Remove chicken from marinade; set marinade aside. Thread chicken on eight 8-inch skewers, leaving space between each piece. (If using bamboo skewers, soak in water at least 30 minutes before using to prevent burning.) Place skewers on rack in broiler pan.
5. Broil with tops about 3 inches from heat for 4 minutes. Turn skewers; brush with marinade. Broil 4 to 5 minutes longer or until chicken is no longer pink in center. Discard any remaining marinade. Serve chicken with sauce.

1 Serving: Calories 330 (Calories from Fat 140); Total Fat 15g (Saturated Fat 5g; Trans Fat 0g); Cholesterol 70mg; Sodium 470mg; Total Carbohydrate 17g (Dietary Fiber 2g; Sugars 12g); Protein 32g • **% Daily Value:** Vitamin A 0%; Vitamin C 8%; Calcium 10%; Iron 10% • **Exchanges:** 1/2 Starch, 1/2 Other Carbohydrate, 4 Lean Meat, 1/2 Fat • **Carbohydrate Choices:** 1

WHY IT WORKS: **PAIRING PEANUTS** Believe it or not, peanuts are not really nuts at all! They're legumes (like beans). The peanut plant grows its nutlike seed underground encased in a papery brown skin. Only after the green leafy top withers and dies is the peanut ready to harvest. Rich in oil and vitamins, peanuts can be used in both sweet and savory cooking. Their flavor, without the sugar usually added in Western cooking, readily complements meat and poultry. In Africa, peanuts are known as groundnuts or nguba (where we get the synonym for peanuts—goobers) and are often included in stews. In Asian cooking the flavor of peanuts helps balance the heat of chiles.

52   *Betty Crocker*   WHY IT WORKS

Almond-Crusted Shrimp

PREP TIME: 20 MINUTES • **START TO FINISH:** 55 MINUTES   16 SHRIMP

1/2 cup all-purpose flour

1 1/4 teaspoons salt

1 egg

2 tablespoons water

1 cup panko or unseasoned dry bread crumbs

1/2 cup sliced almonds

16 uncooked peeled deveined extra-large shrimp (about 1 lb), thawed if frozen and peel left on tails

1/4 cup butter, melted

1. Heat oven to 375°F. Generously spray 15×10×1-inch pan with cooking spray.

2. In shallow dish, mix flour and salt. In another shallow dish, beat egg and water with fork or wire whisk until well mixed. In third shallow dish, mix bread crumbs and almonds.

3. Dip each shrimp into flour, turning to coat; then dip into egg, coating well, letting excess egg drip off. Finally, cover with bread crumb mixture, spooning mixture over shrimp and pressing to coat. Place coated shrimp in pan. Drizzle with butter.

4. Bake 30 to 35 minutes or until golden brown and shrimp are pink and firm.

1 Shrimp: Calories 100 (Calories from Fat 45); Total Fat 5g (Saturated Fat 2g; Trans Fat 0g); Cholesterol 40mg; Sodium 280mg; Total Carbohydrate 8g (Dietary Fiber 0g; Sugars 0g); Protein 4g • **% Daily Value:** Vitamin A 4%; Vitamin C 0%; Calcium 2%; Iron 6% • **Exchanges:** 1/2 Starch, 1/2 Very Lean Meat, 1 Fat • **Carbohydrate Choices:** 1/2

WHY IT WORKS: **PANKO** The secret to extra crispy coating comes from Portugal via Japan. Panko (from the Portuguese root *pan* for bread and the Japanese *ko* for "son of" or "made from") is traditionally used in Japanese dishes. The starting place for panko and American bread crumbs is the same: a loaf of bread. However, American bread crumbs are baked, and panko is heated with microwaves or in a special oven. The result is a coarser crumb that produces a lighter and crunchier coating or topping.

Margarita Shrimp Cocktail

PREP TIME: 25 MINUTES • **START TO FINISH:** 2 HOURS 30 MINUTES   ABOUT 26 SHRIMP

Shrimp

1 1/2 lb uncooked medium shrimp
   with shells (26 to 30 shrimp)
4 cups water
2 teaspoons salt
1 1/2 cups dry white wine or
   nonalcoholic wine
2 tablespoons lime juice
5 black peppercorns
Handful of fresh cilantro

Sauce

1/2 cup orange juice
1/2 cup ketchup
1/4 cup chopped fresh cilantro
1/4 cup lime juice
1/4 cup lemon juice
2 tablespoons tequila, if desired
2 tablespoons vegetable oil
1/2 teaspoon salt
1/8 teaspoon freshly ground pepper
Dash of red pepper sauce

1. Remove shells from shrimp, leaving tails intact. Set shells aside for the stock. Using a small, pointed knife or shrimp deveiner, make a shallow cut lengthwise down the back of each shrimp, then wash out the vein.

2. In 4-quart Dutch oven, heat shrimp shells, 4 cups water and 2 teaspoons salt to boiling over high heat. Add wine, 2 tablespoons lime juice, the peppercorns and handful of cilantro. Reduce heat to medium. Cover and cook 30 minutes.

3. Strain stock through strainer into large bowl and discard shells, peppercorns and cilantro. Return stock to same pan and heat to boiling over high heat. Add shrimp; remove pan from heat. Cover and let stand 8 to 10 minutes until shrimp are pink and firm.

4. Meanwhile, fill large bowl half full with ice and water. Strain stock through strainer and plunge shrimp into ice bath. (Strain stock over large bowl if you want to keep for another purpose.) Shrimp can be refrigerated in ice water for several hours.

5. In medium bowl, mix all sauce ingredients. (Don't use aluminum bowl because the acid in the sauce may react.) Stir in cooked shrimp to coat. Cover and refrigerate at least 30 minutes but no longer than 3 hours. (After 3 hours the acid in the sauce causes the shrimp to become chewy.) Serve cold.

1 Shrimp: Calories 30 (Calories from Fat 10); Total Fat 1g (Saturated Fat 0g; Trans Fat 0g); Cholesterol 25mg; Sodium 170mg; Total Carbohydrate 2g (Dietary Fiber 0g; Sugars 2g); Protein 3g • **% Daily Value:** Vitamin A 2%; Vitamin C 6%; Calcium 0%; Iron 2% • **Exchanges:** 1/2 Very Lean Meat • **Carbohydrate Choices:** 0

WHY IT WORKS:

SKIP THE MARINADE Marinades, whether for shrimp, poultry or meat, are used more often for flavor than for tenderizing. Tough cuts of meat, such as flank steak, can become more tender if soaked in an acidic marinade, but too long of a dip will make the outside of the meat mushy. Shrimp are naturally tender, so an overly acidic marinade can actually start the shrimp "cooking" before you even put them in the pan! If you want to marinate shrimp prior to cooking, don't use an acid—save it for your serving sauce.

Margarita Shrimp Cocktail

Three-Cheese Fondue

PREP TIME: 10 MINUTES • START TO FINISH: 25 MINUTES   2 SERVINGS

1/2 cup shredded Swiss cheese (2 oz)

1/2 cup shredded Colby cheese (2 oz)

1/2 cup shredded Monterey Jack cheese (2 oz)

2 teaspoons cornstarch

1 clove garlic, cut in half

1/2 cup dry white wine or nonalcoholic white wine

2 tablespoons dry sherry, kirsch or nonalcoholic white wine

1/4 teaspoon ground ginger

Several dashes of red pepper sauce

1/2 loaf (1-lb size) French bread, cut into 1-inch pieces, or vegetable dippers

1. In medium bowl, toss cheeses and cornstarch until cheese is coated.

2. Rub garlic on bottom and side of fondue pot, heavy 1-quart saucepan or skillet; discard garlic. Add wine. Heat over simmer setting or low heat just until bubbles rise to surface (do not boil).

3. Gradually add cheese mixture, about 1/4 cup at a time, stirring constantly with wooden spoon over low heat, until melted. (Stir gently. Vigorous stirring may cause the Swiss cheese to become stringy.) Stir in sherry, ginger and pepper sauce.

4. Keep warm over simmer setting. If prepared in saucepan or skillet, pour into a fondue pot or heatproof serving bowl and keep warm over low heat.

5. Spear bread with fondue forks; dip and swirl in fondue with stirring motion. If fondue becomes too thick, stir in small amount of heated wine.

NOTE: Nutrition information is only for fondue—does not include any dippers or bread.

1 Serving: Calories 650 (Calories from Fat 270); Total Fat 30g (Saturated Fat 17g; Trans Fat 1.5g); Cholesterol 80mg; Sodium 1070mg; Total Carbohydrate 63g (Dietary Fiber 3g; Sugars 3g); Protein 32g • **% Daily Value:** Vitamin A 15%; Vitamin C 0%; Calcium 80%; Iron 25% • **Exchanges:** 4 Starch, 3 High-Fat Meat, 1 Fat • **Carbohydrate Choices:** 4

WHY IT WORKS:

SMOOTH SAILING Cheese is a complex mixture of fat and protein. When correctly melted, cheese stays smooth and creamy. When overcooked or overheated, the fat separates from the cheese and the protein clumps. Fortunately, there are several steps you can take to avoid these pitfalls when making fondue. First, bringing the cheese to room temperature before melting means you don't have to use high heat. Second, cutting the cheese into small pieces speeds up the melting process. Third, adding a little starch to the fondue is a good idea too—it helps keep the fat from separating. Finally, adding some wine, with its acidity and minerals, lessens the stringiness of the cheese and helps keep the mixture smooth.

Roasted-Garlic Hummus

PREP TIME: 10 MINUTES • START TO FINISH: 1 HOUR 10 MINUTES

16 SERVINGS (2 TABLESPOONS
HUMMUS AND 2 PITA WEDGES EACH)

1 bulb garlic, unpeeled

2 teaspoons olive oil

1 can (15 to 16 oz) great northern
  beans, drained and 2 tablespoons
  liquid reserved

3 tablespoons lemon juice

1/2 teaspoon salt

Chopped fresh parsley

4 pita breads, each cut into 8 wedges

1. Heat oven to 350°F. Carefully peel paperlike skin from bulb of garlic, leaving just enough to hold garlic cloves together. Cut 1/2-inch slice off top of garlic bulb to expose the cloves. Place cut side up on piece of foil and drizzle with oil. Wrap garlic in foil. Bake 50 to 60 minutes or until garlic is soft when pierced with a knife; cool slightly.

2. Squeeze garlic into food processor. Add beans, reserved bean liquid, lemon juice and salt. Cover and process until uniform consistency.

3. Spoon dip into serving dish. Sprinkle with parsley. Serve with pita bread wedges.

1 **Serving:** Calories 80 (Calories from Fat 5); Total Fat 1g (Saturated Fat 0g; Trans Fat 0g); Cholesterol 0mg; Sodium 135mg; Total Carbohydrate 13g (Dietary Fiber 2g; Sugars 0g); Protein 4g • **% Daily Value:** Vitamin A 0%; Vitamin C 4%; Calcium 4%; Iron 8% • **Exchanges:** 1/2 Starch, 1 Vegetable • **Carbohydrate Choices:** 1

WHY IT WORKS: **GREAT GARLIC** Just as with its cousin the onion, garlic is notorious for its strong odor and flavor when raw. The smell that we associate with garlic is caused by a chemical reaction between two sulfur compounds in the garlic bulb. When cooked, these chemicals break down and the natural sugars in the flesh caramelize. The resulting garlic is smooth, buttery and quite sweet. Overcooked garlic is bitter and will ruin a dish. For the best flavor, cook garlic over low heat.

Caramelized Apple–Blue Cheese Spread

20 SERVINGS (3 TABLESPOONS SPREAD AND 2 SLICES BREAD OR 2 CRACKERS EACH)

1 tablespoon butter

1 teaspoon sugar

2 large firm apples (preferably Fuji or Braeburn), finely chopped (about 2 cups)

1 shallot, finely chopped

1 package (8 oz) cream cheese, softened

4 oz (1 cup) crumbled blue cheese (preferably Maytag or Roquefort)

3/4 cup mayonnaise

3/4 cup sour cream

1/2 teaspoon salt

1/2 cup chopped pecans

40 slices French bread or crackers

1. In 1-quart saucepan, melt butter over low heat. Stir in sugar until it dissolves, about 20 seconds. Add apples and shallot. Cook 20 to 30 minutes, stirring occasionally, until mixture turns golden brown and aroma is reminiscent of apple cider. (Do not rush process; color takes a while to form, but the flavor is worth it.) Set aside to cool completely.

2. Meanwhile, in small bowl, mix cream cheese, cheese, mayonnaise, sour cream and salt until well blended. Gently stir in cooled caramelized apple mixture and the pecans. Refrigerate 30 minutes before serving. Garnish with additional chopped pecans if desired. Serve with bread or crackers.

1 Serving: Calories 350 (Calories from Fat 170); Total Fat 19g (Saturated Fat 7g; Trans Fat 0.5g); Cholesterol 30mg; Sodium 600mg; Total Carbohydrate 37g (Dietary Fiber 2g; Sugars 4g); Protein 8g • **% Daily Value:** Vitamin A 6%; Vitamin C 0%; Calcium 10%; Iron 10% • **Exchanges:** 2 Starch, 1/2 Other Carbohydrate, 3 1/2 Fat • **Carbohydrate Choices:** 2 1/2

WHY IT WORKS:

BLUE CHEESE Blue cheese owes its color to a familiar mold: penicillin. The three most common blues are Roquefort (from France), Gorgonzola (from Italy) and Stilton (from England). Until quite recently, the process of introducing mold to these cheeses was left to Mother Nature. (Blocks of Roquefort were actually held in ancient caves where the mold lived!) Today the mold spores are usually mixed with the milk or the curd during cheesemaking (the mold is not injected as sometimes thought). Enzymes in the mold that eat and digest milk fat are responsible for the unique flavor of blue cheese. Over time, the mold penetrates the cheese causing "veins" to form and the cheese to become crumbly.

Caramelized Apple–Blue Cheese Spread

Parmesan-Tomato Rounds

PREP TIME: 45 MINUTES • START TO FINISH: 2 HOURS 50 MINUTES   ABOUT 7 1/2 DOZEN ROUNDS

3 cups shredded Parmesan
   cheese (12 oz)
1/2 cup butter, softened
1/4 cup tomato paste
1 1/2 cups all-purpose flour
1 teaspoon dried basil leaves
1/4 teaspoon salt
1/8 teaspoon ground red pepper
   (cayenne)

1. In food processor bowl, pulse cheese, butter and tomato paste 2 to 3 minutes or until well mixed. Add flour, basil, salt and red pepper and pulse until well combined. Dough should be firm but not dry. If dry, add water, 1 tablespoon at a time and pulsing 30 seconds after each addition, until mixture holds together and a soft, claylike dough is formed.

2. Wet a paper towel and rub it over work surface. Place 12-inch piece of plastic wrap on dampened surface (the dampness helps plastic wrap stick to work surface). Scoop half of dough onto plastic wrap and form into a rough log shape. Roll log in plastic wrap and seal ends (log should be about 12 inches long and 1 1/4 inches in diameter). Repeat with remaining half of dough. Refrigerate logs at least 2 hours or until firm. (Dough can be refrigerated 3 days or wrapped in foil and frozen 3 months. Thaw in refrigerator 2 hours before cutting.)

3. Heat oven to 400°F. Line 2 cookie sheets with cooking parchment paper.

4. Remove 1 log from refrigerator and remove plastic wrap. Use serrated knife to cut 1/4-inch slices from log. Place rounds about 1/2 inch apart on cookie sheets.

5. Bake 10 to 12 minutes or until lightly browned around edges. Remove cookie sheets from oven and cool 2 minutes. Remove rounds from cookie sheet to wire rack. Repeat with remaining dough. Serve warm or at room temperature. Store in airtight container.

1 Round: Calories 35 (Calories from Fat 20); Total Fat 2g (Saturated Fat 1g; Trans Fat 0g); Cholesterol 5mg; Sodium 90mg; Total Carbohydrate 2g (Dietary Fiber 0g; Sugars 0g); Protein 2g • **% Daily Value:** Vitamin A 0%; Vitamin C 0%; Calcium 6%; Iron 0% • **Exchanges:** 1/2 Fat • **Carbohydrate Choices:** 0

WHY IT WORKS: **IT'S IN THE WATER** In its simplest form, all dough is made up of flour suspended in water. The amount of water determines if the mixture will be a dough or a batter. Water also determines the final texture of the baked good. The more water that remains after baking, the less crisp the baked product will be. By altering the water level, you can make the dough shatteringly crisp, flaky or anywhere in between. Crispness occurs when the water in the dough/batter leaves rapidly. You can speed this process up by slicing or rolling a dough paper-thin and baking at a high temperature (driving off the water). This recipe calls for an intermediate texture, so a moderate oven temperature is used and the dough is not cut too thin.

Parmesan-Tomato Rounds

Yankee Corn Bread

PREP TIME: 10 MINUTES • START TO FINISH: 35 MINUTES   12 SERVINGS

1 cup milk
1/4 cup butter, melted
1 egg
1 1/4 cups yellow, white or blue
    cornmeal
1 cup all-purpose flour
1/2 cup sugar
1 tablespoon baking powder
1/2 teaspoon salt

1. Heat oven to 400°F. Generously grease bottom and side of 10-inch cast-iron skillet with shortening or spray with cooking spray. Heat greased skillet in oven about 5 minutes or until hot.

2. Meanwhile, in large bowl, beat milk, butter and egg with egg beater or wire whisk. Stir in remaining ingredients all at once just until flour is moistened (batter will be lumpy). Carefully remove skillet from oven. Pour batter into skillet.

3. Bake 20 to 25 minutes or until golden brown and toothpick inserted in center comes out clean. Serve warm if desired.

1 Serving: Calories 170 (Calories from Fat 45); Total Fat 5g (Saturated Fat 2.5g; Trans Fat 0g); Cholesterol 30mg; Sodium 260mg; Total Carbohydrate 29g (Dietary Fiber 0g; Sugars 10g); Protein 4g • **% Daily Value:** Vitamin A 4%; Vitamin C 0%; Calcium 10%; Iron 8% • **Exchanges:** 1 Starch, 1 Other Carbohydrate, 1 Fat • **Carbohydrate Choices:** 2

WHY IT WORKS: **CAST IRON** Cooking involves the transfer of heat. Yet some things transfer heat better than others. You can put your unprotected hand in a 350°F oven without fear of getting burned, but you can't touch the metal rack in that oven. Why? Metal holds and transfers heat better than air. But metals differ in their heat-efficiency. Iron—an excellent heat conductor—is ideal for cooking. But before you invest in cast iron, know that food will stick to a cast-iron pan unless you season it. A new cast-iron pan's surface is made of microscopic pits and bumps. By seasoning the pan (rubbing it with oil and baking it 1 hour at 300°F) you smooth out the surface, making it nonstick and rust proof.

Deviled Eggs with a Kick

PREP TIME: 10 MINUTES • START TO FINISH: 50 MINUTES   12 SERVINGS

6 eggs

3 tablespoons mayonnaise, salad dressing or half-and-half

1 tablespoon chopped fresh parsley

1 teaspoon prepared horseradish

1/2 teaspoon ground mustard

1/8 teaspoon salt

1/8 teaspoon pepper

1. In 2-quart saucepan, place eggs in single layer. Add cold water to at least 1 inch above eggs. Cover and heat to boiling; turn off heat. If necessary, remove pan from heat to prevent further boiling. Cover and let stand 20 minutes. Immediately run cold water over eggs or place them in ice water until completely cooled.

2. To remove egg shells, crackle shells by tapping gently all over; roll between hands to loosen. Peel, starting at large end. Cut lengthwise in half. (For a different twist, eggs can be cut crosswise in half. Cut a thin slice off the bottom of each egg so it will stand up without falling over.) Transfer yolks to small bowl; mash with fork. Set egg whites aside.

3. Stir mayonnaise, parsley, horseradish, mustard, salt and pepper into yolks. Fill whites with egg yolk mixture, heaping it lightly. (Use a teaspoon to fill the egg whites and to spread the yolk mixture easily and neatly into the whites.) Cover and refrigerate up to 24 hours.

WHY IT WORKS: **NO GREEN EGGS HERE** Hard-cooked eggs become tough and tinged with green when exposed to heat for too long. The more egg proteins are heated, the more water they lose. After too much heat (usually anything more than 20 minutes), the eggs turn rubbery, and a sulfur compound and the iron in the yolk react to make an unsightly green ring. You can avoid these problems by cooking the eggs only as long as necessary and stopping the cooking by plunging the cooked eggs into ice water. To avoid the green color, use recently purchased eggs; they do not react as easily.

RECIPE R_x: OFF-CENTERED YOLK You followed all the steps to cook a perfect egg only to discover, after peeling, that your yolk is positioned right on the edge or bottom of the white. Because deviled eggs are all about presentation (the special plate, garnish, etc.),

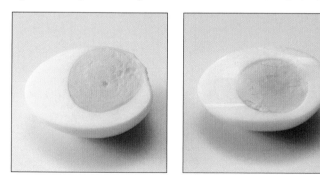

this can really mess up your plans. To prevent the yolk from moving off-center, simply store your raw eggs in the carton, on their side (overnight should do). The little strings that secure the yolk in the middle of the white will move it back to the center, and after boiling you will have perfect eggs to fill.

1 Serving: Calories 60 (Calories from Fat 50); Total Fat 5g (Saturated Fat 1g; Trans Fat 0g); Cholesterol 110mg; Sodium 75mg; Total Carbohydrate 0g (Dietary Fiber 0g; Sugars 0g); Protein 3g • **% Daily Value:** Vitamin A 4%; Vitamin C 0%; Calcium 0%; Iron 0% • **Exchanges:** 1/2 Medium-Fat Meat, 1/2 Fat • **Carbohydrate Choices:** 0

Corn Fritters
WITH PINEAPPLE-JALAPEÑO SAUCE

PREP TIME: 2 HOURS • **START TO FINISH:** 2 HOURS   ABOUT 32 SERVINGS (1 FRITTER AND 1 TABLESPOON SAUCE EACH)

Sauce

1 tablespoon vegetable oil

1 medium onion, finely chopped
    (1/2 cup)

2 teaspoons grated gingerroot

1 clove garlic, finely chopped

1 jalapeño chile, seeded and diced

1/2 teaspoon ground cumin

Dash of ground cinnamon

1/4 cup dark rum mixed with 1/4 cup
    pineapple juice, or 1/2 cup
    pineapple juice

1 can (20 oz) pineapple chunks,
    drained (about 2 3/4 cups)

1/2 cup packed light brown sugar

1/2 cup lime juice

1/4 teaspoon salt

3 tablespoons chopped fresh cilantro

Fritters

1 bag (1 lb) frozen whole kernel corn,
    thawed in refrigerator

1/4 red bell pepper

1/4 medium onion, cut into fourths

1 clove garlic, smashed

1/2 cup milk

3 tablespoons chopped fresh cilantro

1 tablespoon butter, melted

2 eggs

1 3/4 cups all-purpose flour

1/2 cup cornmeal (preferably
    stone-ground)

1 tablespoon granulated sugar

2 teaspoons baking powder

3/4 teaspoon salt

Vegetable oil

1. In 3-quart saucepan, heat 1 tablespoon oil over medium-low heat until hot. Add finely chopped onion and cook about 5 minutes, stirring occasionally, until softened. Add gingerroot, finely chopped garlic, chile, cumin and cinnamon. Heat about 1 minute or until fragrant.

2. Increase heat to medium. Add rum and pineapple juice mixture. Cook 3 to 5 minutes, stirring constantly, until there is no excess liquid in pan. Add pineapple chunks, brown sugar, lime juice and 1/4 teaspoon salt. Heat mixture to a simmer and cook 15 minutes, stirring occasionally, until pineapple is soft.

3. Remove mixture from heat and puree in food processor or blender. Stir in 3 tablespoons cilantro. Place in serving bowl and refrigerate. Bring to room temperature to serve.

4. In food processor, pulse corn, bell pepper, 1/4 onion and the smashed garlic about 10 seconds; remove cover and scrape sides of bowl with rubber spatula. Make sure bell pepper and onion are getting chopped. Replace cover and pulse 10 seconds longer or until bell pepper and onion pieces are about 1/4 inch in size. Add milk, 3 tablespoons cilantro, the butter and eggs. Pulse until mixture is blended; set aside.

5. In medium bowl, mix flour, cornmeal, granulated sugar, baking powder and 3/4 teaspoon salt with wire whisk. Make a well in center of dry ingredients and dump corn mixture on top. Use rubber spatula to mix wet and dry ingredients just until no dry flour mixture is visible. (Overmixing will toughen the fritters.) Set batter aside.

6. In 4-quart Dutch oven or deep fryer, heat 2 inches oil to 350°F. Drop tablespoonfuls of batter into hot oil (use 2 spoons, one to scoop up batter and another to push batter into hot oil). Fry 4 or 5 fritters at a time—more than that and you will crowd the fryer. Fry 3 minutes or until golden brown. Flip fritters (if you are adept at using them, long chopsticks work well for this) and fry other side about 2 minutes or until golden. Drain on wire rack (paper towels are not good for draining fried food because they don't wick away enough oil). Serve immediately with sauce.

1 Serving: Calories 150 (Calories from Fat 70); Total Fat 8g (Saturated Fat 1.5g; Trans Fat 0g); Cholesterol 15mg; Sodium 115mg; Total Carbohydrate 17g (Dietary Fiber 0g; Sugars 7g); Protein 2g • **% Daily Value:** Vitamin A 4%; Vitamin C 4%; Calcium 4%; Iron 4% • **Exchanges:** 1 Starch, 1 1/2 Fat • **Carbohydrate Choices:** 1

Corn Fritters with Pineapple-Jalapeño Sauce

Gather 'Round the Table

MAIN DISH MEALS

FOR THE FAMILY

Pulled Chicken Sandwiches

WITH ROOT BEER BARBECUE SAUCE

PREP TIME: 15 MINUTES • **START TO FINISH:** 40 MINUTES   4 SANDWICHES

Sauce

1/2 cup root beer
1/2 cup ketchup
3 tablespoons cider vinegar
2 tablespoons yellow mustard
1 tablespoon packed brown sugar
2 teaspoons Worcestershire sauce
1/4 teaspoon salt
1/4 teaspoon freshly ground pepper
1/8 teaspoon ground ginger
1 clove garlic, smashed
Dash of red pepper sauce

Sandwiches

1 deli rotisserie chicken (unflavored),
   skin and bones removed,
   shredded (about 3 cups)
4 kaiser rolls, split
2 cups purchased coleslaw

1. In 2-quart saucepan, heat all sauce ingredients to boiling over medium heat, stirring frequently. Reduce heat to medium-low and simmer 20 minutes, stirring occasionally to prevent scorching. Remove garlic clove.

2. Add shredded chicken to sauce and stir until chicken is evenly coated. Heat over low heat, stirring constantly, until chicken is hot.

3. Place about 1 cup chicken mixture on bottom of each roll and top with about 1/2 cup coleslaw and bun top.

1 Sandwich: Calories 560 (Calories from Fat 210); Total Fat 23g (Saturated Fat 4.5g; Trans Fat 1g); Cholesterol 100mg; Sodium 1160mg; Total Carbohydrate 53g (Dietary Fiber 3g; Sugars 22g); Protein 36g • **% Daily Value:** Vitamin A 60%; Vitamin C 20%; Calcium 10%; Iron 25% • **Exchanges:** 2 Starch, 1 1/2 Other Carbohydrate, 4 Lean Meat, 2 Fat • **Carbohydrate Choices:** 3 1/2

WHY IT WORKS: **THE DARK SIDE OF CHICKEN** Every Thanksgiving you hear the debate: Some people like dark meat and others white. Other than their location (white meat on the breast; dark meat the thigh and leg) what makes one different from the other? The answer lies in how the bird uses the muscles in these locations. Muscles used for endurance exercise (running and walking, for example) need plenty of blood flow and fat, qualities that make the meat in these areas darker. Conversely, those muscles that see little work (like the breast) have less blood flow and fat, making them light in color. This also explains why dark and white meats cook differently. Dark meat, dense with extra bits of fat, takes longer to cook compared to white.

Pulled Chicken Sandwiches with Root Beer Barbecue Sauce

Grilled Citrus Chicken

PREP TIME: 10 MINUTES • START TO FINISH: 2 HOURS 30 MINUTES   6 SERVINGS

Marinade

1/2 cup frozen orange juice
    concentrate, thawed
1/4 cup vegetable oil
1/4 cup lemon juice
2 tablespoons grated orange peel
1/2 teaspoon salt
1 clove garlic, finely chopped

Chicken

6 boneless skinless chicken breasts
    (about 1 3/4 lb)

1. In small bowl, mix all marinade ingredients.

2. Place chicken in resealable plastic food-storage bag or shallow glass or plastic dish. Pour marinade over chicken; turn chicken to coat with marinade. To marinate, seal bag or cover dish and refrigerate at least 2 hours but no longer than 24 hours, turning chicken pieces over occasionally.

3. Heat coals or gas grill for medium heat. (Check the temperature of the coals by placing your hand, palm side down, near but not touching the cooking grill rack. If you can keep your hand there for 2 seconds [one-thousand one, one-thousand two], the temperature is high; 3 seconds is medium-high; 4 seconds is medium; 5 seconds is low.)

4. Remove chicken from marinade; set marinade aside. Grill chicken covered 15 to 20 minutes, turning and brushing with marinade occasionally, until juice of chicken is no longer pink when center of thickest part is cut (170°F).

5. In 1-quart saucepan, heat remaining marinade to boiling; boil and stir 1 minute. Serve with chicken.

1 Serving: Calories 280 (Calories from Fat 120); Total Fat 13g (Saturated Fat 2.5g; Trans Fat 0g); Cholesterol 80mg; Sodium 270mg; Total Carbohydrate 10g (Dietary Fiber 0g; Sugars 9g); Protein 30g • **% Daily Value:** Vitamin A 2%; Vitamin C 30%; Calcium 2%; Iron 6% • **Exchanges:** 1 Other Carbohydrate, 4 Lean Meat • **Carbohydrate Choices:** 1/2

WHY IT WORKS:

FROZEN OJ TO THE RESCUE More than 80% of the Florida orange crop goes into making frozen orange juice—about 30 pounds of juice per person per year! The cooking possibilities of frozen orange juice are often overlooked. Which is a shame as the benefits of this freezer staple are immense. For one, frozen orange juice is concentrated, which means intense flavor. Also, it always has the same sweetness and acidity, unlike fresh oranges, where you gamble with flavor throughout the year. This is not to say that oranges are not useful in cooking—they are. Nothing can take the place of fresh orange juice in vinaigrettes and for finishing sauces. But when you need a reliable orange flavor for marinades, salad dressings and cooked sauces, look to the freezer.

Coffee Chicken
WITH QUICK MOLE SAUCE

PREP TIME: 35 MINUTES • **START TO FINISH:** 2 HOURS 35 MINUTES   6 SERVINGS

Chicken

4 cups water

1/3 cup salt

1/3 cup packed dark brown sugar

1 tablespoon cumin seed

1 tablespoon chili powder

1 lime, thinly sliced

1 cup strong-brewed coffee, at room
   temperature

6 boneless skinless chicken breasts
   (about 1 3/4 lb)

2 tablespoons vegetable oil

Sauce

1 medium onion, thinly sliced

2 cloves garlic, finely chopped

1 can (28 oz) crushed tomatoes,
   undrained

1 1/4 cups chicken broth

1 tablespoon creamy peanut butter

1 teaspoon granulated sugar

1/2 teaspoon ground cumin

Dash of ground cinnamon

1 oz unsweetened baking chocolate

2 chipotle chiles in adobo sauce
   (from 7-oz can), chopped

Salt and pepper, if desired

1. In 2-quart saucepan, heat water, salt, brown sugar, cumin seed, chili powder and lime slices over medium heat, stirring occasionally, until salt and brown sugar are dissolved. Remove from heat and stir in coffee. Cool mixture to room temperature.

2. Place chicken in 1-gallon resealable plastic food-storage bag or large bowl, and pour cooled coffee mixture over chicken. Seal bag or cover bowl. Refrigerate 2 to 3 hours.

3. In 12-inch skillet, heat oil over medium heat. Remove chicken from marinade and pat dry on paper towels. Discard marinade. When oil is hot and shimmers lightly, place chicken in skillet. Cook about 3 minutes or until golden brown. Flip and cook 2 to 3 minutes longer or until golden on other side. Place chicken on plate.

4. In same skillet, cook onion over medium heat 5 minutes, stirring occasionally, until soft and lightly browned. Add garlic and cook 30 seconds or until fragrant. Add tomatoes, broth, peanut butter, granulated sugar, ground cumin, cinnamon, chocolate and chiles. Cook uncovered 3 minutes, stirring occasionally, until mixture simmers and peanut butter and chocolate are melted.

5. Reduce heat to medium-low and nestle chicken breasts in sauce. Cook uncovered 15 to 20 minutes, stirring occasionally, until sauce thickens and juice of chicken is no longer pink when center of thickest part is cut (170°F). Taste and add salt and pepper if desired. Serve immediately.

1 Serving: Calories 320 (Calories from Fat 120); Total Fat 14g (Saturated Fat 4g; Trans Fat 0g); Cholesterol 80mg; Sodium 2130mg; Total Carbohydrate 15g (Dietary Fiber 3g; Sugars 8g); Protein 33g • **% Daily Value:** Vitamin A 15%; Vitamin C 20%; Calcium 8%; Iron 15% • **Exchanges:** 1/2 Starch, 1/2 Other Carbohydrate, 4 1/2 Lean Meat • **Carbohydrate Choices:** 1

WHY IT WORKS:

COFFEE PERKS When harvested, coffee beans (actually seeds taken from the coffee fruit called a coffee cherry) have very little flavor. Their seductive aroma and taste come after the beans have been fermented and roasted. Once brewed, coffee is useful in many aspects of cooking. It makes a great marinade and braising liquid because its natural acids tenderize meat (try adding a cup to your next pot roast before cooking). Coffee-tasting experts claim coffee contains hints of cinnamon, chocolate, wine, fruit and even caramel flavors. For this reason, coffee enhances and balances the flavor of a number of savory dishes, including this mole sauce. Try replacing some of the water with coffee the next time you make beef gravy, stew or soup.

Pineapple-Glazed Spicy Chicken Breasts

PREP TIME: 15 MINUTES • START TO FINISH: 40 MINUTES

4 SERVINGS

Rub

2 tablespoons packed dark
    brown sugar

1 1/2 teaspoons salt

1 1/2 teaspoons ground coriander

1 1/2 teaspoons ground allspice

3/4 teaspoon ground cinnamon

1/2 teaspoon ground cumin

1/4 teaspoon ground red pepper
    (cayenne)

4 boneless skinless chicken breasts

2 tablespoons vegetable oil

Glaze

1/2 cup pineapple juice

1/4 cup real maple syrup

1 tablespoon lemon juice

2 tablespoons butter

2 teaspoons Dijon mustard

1. In 9-inch pie plate, mix brown sugar, salt, coriander, allspice, cinnamon, cumin and red pepper; set aside.

2. Place chicken between pieces of plastic wrap or waxed paper. Use flat side of a meat mallet, pounder or rolling pin to gently pound each chicken piece to 1/4-inch thickness.

3. Drizzle oil over chicken and work it in with your hands. Place 1 piece of chicken in spice mixture and turn over to make sure all surfaces are coated with thin layer of spices. Place chicken on plate. Repeat with remaining chicken.

4. In 1-quart saucepan, heat all glaze ingredients to boiling over medium heat. Cook uncovered about 10 minutes, stirring occasionally, until thickened and syrupy and reduced to 1/2 cup. Remove from heat. Remove 2 table-spoons glaze to brush over chicken.

5. Spray grill rack with cooking spray or brush with oil. Heat coals or gas grill for medium-high heat. (To test heat for cooking, place your hand, palm side down, about 1 inch from grill rack. Count "one-one thousand, two-one thousand, three-one thousand." When you have to remove your hand at "three," you have reached medium-high heat and are ready to cook.) Grill chicken uncovered 4 to 5 minutes per side or until juice of chicken is no longer pink when center of thickest part is cut (170°F).

6. When chicken is almost cooked through, brush with the reserved 2 table-spoons glaze. Grill 1 minute longer. Remove chicken from grill and drizzle with the remaining glaze.

1 Serving: Calories 370 (Calories from Fat 150); Total Fat 17g (Saturated Fat 5g; Trans Fat 0g); Cholesterol 90mg; Sodium 1060mg; Total Carbohydrate 26g (Dietary Fiber 0g; Sugars 23g); Protein 27g • **% Daily Value:** Vitamin A 6%; Vitamin C 4%; Calcium 6%; Iron 10% • **Exchanges:** 2 Other Carbohydrate, 4 Lean Meat, 1 Fat • **Carbohydrate Choices:** 2

WHY IT WORKS: **GRILLING HEAT** Grilling may be one of the most exciting activities of summer, but it can also be the most frustrating. The intense heat of the grill and its unpredictability (especially charcoal grills) can mean burning the outside of your food before the inside even gets warm. One of the best secrets to avoiding this problem is called "two-stage grilling." In a charcoal grill this means filling half of your grill with your normal amount of charcoal but placing only a single charcoal layer on the other half. Food can then be started on the hot side and moved to the less intense side to finish cooking. The same effect can be achieved by using the racks that some gas grills have on their lids. This method guarantees an even cook and a successful barbecue.

Pineapple-Glazed Spicy Chicken Breasts

Maple-Thyme Roasted Chicken Breasts

PREP TIME: 10 MINUTES • **START TO FINISH:** 45 MINUTES   4 SERVINGS

1/3 cup real maple syrup

2 tablespoons balsamic vinegar

1 tablespoon fresh thyme leaves or
    1 teaspoon dried thyme leaves

1/2 teaspoon salt

1 clove garlic, finely chopped

4 bone-in skin-on chicken breast
    halves with large pieces of skin
    intact (about 3 lb)

4 tablespoons firm butter, each
    tablespoon cut into smaller pieces

1 tablespoon vegetable oil

1/2 teaspoon salt

1/4 teaspoon freshly ground pepper

1. Adjust oven rack to middle position. Heat oven to 425°F. Line 13 × 9-inch pan with foil.

2. In small bowl, mix syrup, vinegar, thyme, 1/2 teaspoon salt and the garlic.

3. Starting on one side of each chicken piece, slowly work your fingers under the skin. You are trying to loosen the connection between the skin and meat, not remove the skin. Place chicken, skin sides up, in foil-lined pan. For each chicken piece, use a spoon to drizzle about 2 tablespoons of the syrup mixture under the skin and spread evenly over the meat. Dot each with 1 tablespoon of the butter pieces. Evenly replace any skin you may have displaced. Rub skin with oil, then sprinkle with 1/2 teaspoon salt and the pepper.

4. Roast chicken uncovered 30 to 35 minutes or until juice of chicken is no longer pink when thickest part is cut to bone (180°F). Remove from oven and allow to rest 5 minutes before serving to let juices reabsorb.

1 Serving: Calories 530 (Calories from Fat 260); Total Fat 28g (Saturated Fat 10g; Trans Fat 1g); Cholesterol 165mg; Sodium 780mg; Total Carbohydrate 19g (Dietary Fiber 0g; Sugars 16g); Protein 50g • **% Daily Value:** Vitamin A 10%; Vitamin C 0%; Calcium 6%; Iron 10% • **Exchanges:** 1 1/2 Other Carbohydrate, 7 Lean Meat, 1 Fat • **Carbohydrate Choices:** 1

WHY IT WORKS: **MAPLE MATCH** When pulled from a tree, maple sap is as thin as water and just about as flavorful. That may be why it takes about forty gallons of maple sap to make one gallon of maple syrup! As maple sap boils down to make syrup, the water evaporates and the sugar concentrates. The longer it cooks, the more the sugar changes as it combines with other components of the sap and caramelizes. Real maple syrup is just a little thicker than water and is complex in flavor (slightly smoky, sometimes bitter and maybe even chocolaty). Used in sweet and savory cooking, maple is the perfect partner for matching and enhancing the slight sweetness of sautéed vegetables, the smokiness of grilled meat and the floral quality of fresh herbs.

Maple-Thyme Roasted Chicken Breasts

Oven-Fried Chicken
WITH SWEET ONION–MUSHROOM GRAVY

PREP TIME: 1 HOUR 35 MINUTES • START TO FINISH: 5 HOURS 55 MINUTES   5 SERVINGS

Brine

2 tablespoons salt
1/2 cup packed brown sugar
1 tablespoon molasses
1 tablespoon paprika
2 cloves garlic, smashed
1 dried bay leaf
3 1/2 cups buttermilk

Chicken

5 boneless skinless chicken breast
    halves (about 1 1/2 lb)
5 boneless skinless chicken thighs
    (about 1 lb)

Breading

2 cups all-purpose flour
2 teaspoons freshly ground pepper
1 egg
1 1/2 teaspoons baking powder
1/4 teaspoon baking soda
1 tablespoon Dijon mustard
1/2 cup buttermilk
1/4 cup butter

Gravy

2 teaspoons vegetable oil
1 tablespoon butter
1 large sweet onion, thinly sliced
    (1 1/2 cups)
1 teaspoon packed light brown sugar
1/4 teaspoon salt
1 tablespoon butter
1/2 cup finely chopped mushrooms
1/4 cup dry white wine or
    nonalcoholic wine
2 tablespoons all-purpose flour
1 1/2 teaspoons chopped fresh sage
    leaves or 1/4 teaspoon dried sage
    leaves
1 3/4 cups chicken broth

1. In 2-gallon resealable plastic food-storage bag, mix all brine ingredients except buttermilk. Add 3 1/2 cups buttermilk and seal bag. Use your hands to knead bag to mix in salt and spices, about 2 minutes. Add chicken to bag and reseal bag. Refrigerate at least 3 hours but no more than 5 hours.

2. In 1-gallon resealable plastic food-storage bag, mix 2 cups flour and the ground pepper. Place large wire rack on 15 × 10 × 1-inch pan. Remove chicken from brine and pat dry on paper towels. Place chicken pieces, two at a time, in bag of seasoned flour; seal bag and shake well to lightly coat. Remove chicken and place on wire rack. Repeat with remaining chicken. Set bag of remaining seasoned flour aside. Discard brine. After chicken is coated, refrigerate uncovered at least 15 minutes.

3. In medium bowl, beat egg, baking powder, baking soda and mustard with wire whisk until well blended. Add 1/2 cup buttermilk and beat well until blended.

4. Dip each piece of chicken into egg mixture and return to bag of seasoned flour. Shake dipped chicken again, remove from bag and return to wire rack.

5. Adjust oven rack to middle position. Heat oven to 425°F. Place 1/4 cup butter in 15 × 10 × 1-inch pan; place in oven to melt.

6. Remove pan from oven and place chicken in melted butter in pan. Bake 20 minutes. Remove from oven and turn chicken pieces over. Bake 10 to 20 minutes longer or until coating is golden brown and crispy, and juice of chicken is no longer pink when center of thickest part is cut (170°F for breasts; 180°F for thighs).

7. As soon as chicken is in oven, in 10-inch skillet, heat oil and 1 tablespoon butter over medium heat until butter stops sizzling. Add onion, brown sugar and 1/4 teaspoon salt. Cook 20 minutes, stirring occasionally, until onion is soft and golden brown. (Do not rush by turning up the heat.) Remove onion from skillet, using slotted spoon; set onion aside.

8. Add remaining 1 tablespoon butter and the mushrooms to skillet. Cook over medium heat 4 minutes, stirring occasionally, until mushrooms lose some liquid and brown around edges. Add wine and quickly stir and scrape any browned bits of mushroom or onion that may be stuck to pan. Cook 3 minutes longer or until wine evaporates. Return onion to skillet and sprinkle 2 tablespoons flour and the sage over mushrooms and onion. Stir well and cook 2 minutes, stirring constantly.

9. Slowly stir in broth. Cook, stirring constantly, until gravy comes to a simmer. Simmer 4 to 5 minutes or until thickened. Serve gravy with chicken.

1 Serving: Calories 390 (Calories from Fat 160); Total Fat 18g (Saturated Fat 7g; Trans Fat 0.5g); Cholesterol 115mg; Sodium 2060mg; Total Carbohydrate 19g (Dietary Fiber 1g; Sugars 11g); Protein 39g • **% Daily Value:** Vitamin A 10%; Vitamin C 2%; Calcium 10%; Iron 15% • **Exchanges:** 1/2 Starch, 1 Other Carbohydrate, 5 1/2 Lean Meat • **Carbohydrate Choices:** 1

Oven-Fried Chicken with Sweet Onion–Mushroom Gravy

Spicy Chicken with Broccoli

4 boneless skinless chicken breasts
(about 1 lb)

2 teaspoons cornstarch

1/2 teaspoon salt

1/4 teaspoon white pepper

1 lb fresh broccoli

3 green onions (with tops)

1 hot green chile or 1 teaspoon
crushed red pepper

3 tablespoons vegetable oil

2 tablespoons brown bean sauce,
if desired

2 teaspoons finely chopped garlic

1 teaspoon sugar

1 teaspoon finely chopped gingerroot

1 tablespoon sesame seed, toasted

1. Cut chicken into 2 × 1/2-inch pieces. In medium bowl, toss chicken, cornstarch, salt and white pepper. (Black pepper can be used but, unlike white pepper, will add black specks.) Cover and refrigerate 20 minutes.

2. Meanwhile, peel outer layer from broccoli stems. Cut broccoli lengthwise into 1-inch stems; remove florets. Cut stems diagonally into 1/4-inch slices.

3. In 1 1/2-quart saucepan, heat 3 cups water to boiling; add broccoli florets and stems. Cover and cook 1 minute; drain. Immediately rinse in cold water; drain. (Blanching and cooling makes the broccoli a pretty deep green without overcooking it.)

4. Cut green onions diagonally into 1-inch pieces. Remove seeds and membrane from chile; cut chile into very thin slices.

5. Heat wok or 12-inch skillet until very hot. Add oil; rotate wok to coat side. Add chile, brown bean sauce if desired, garlic, sugar and gingerroot; stir-fry 10 seconds. Add chicken; stir-fry about 2 minutes or until chicken is no longer pink in center. Add broccoli and green onions; stir-fry about 1 minute or until broccoli is hot. Sprinkle with sesame seed.

1 Serving: Calories 280 (Calories from Fat 140); Total Fat 15g (Saturated Fat 2.5g; Trans Fat 0g); Cholesterol 70mg; Sodium 380mg; Total Carbohydrate 9g (Dietary Fiber 3g; Sugars 2g); Protein 28g • **% Daily Value:** Vitamin A 20%; Vitamin C 80%; Calcium 6%; Iron 10% • **Exchanges:** 2 Vegetable, 3 1/2 Very Lean Meat, 2 1/2 Fat • **Carbohydrate Choices:** 1/2

WHY IT WORKS: **SESAME SECRETS** Sesame seed—native to the Middle East—is probably best known in America for its use in Asian cooking. The seeds grow in pods that burst explosively when ripe (this is thought to be the origin of the phrase "open sesame"). Uncooked, sesame seed has a nutty, slightly bitter flavor. When toasted, its nutty flavor intensifies greatly and is especially apparent in toasted sesame oil. Like all high-fat seeds and nuts, sesame is prone to rancidity. Buy sesame seed fresh (smell it first if you can). Tightly wrap and freeze any sesame seed not used within a week.

Cheese Steak Sandwiches
WITH SAUTÉED ONIONS AND PEPPERS

3 tablespoons olive oil

2 tablespoons butter

2 medium onions, thinly sliced

2 red bell peppers, thinly sliced

2 lb beef top round (about 1 1/2 inch thick), cut lengthwise into paper-thin strips (Ask your butcher to slice the beef. However, if you prefer to slice it yourself, freeze the beef 30 to 60 minutes or until it's firm but not frozen to make it easier to slice.)

1/2 teaspoon salt

1/2 teaspoon pepper

2 teaspoons Worcestershire sauce

6 hoagie buns, split

1 1/4 cups cheese dip (from 15-oz jar)

1. In 10-inch skillet, heat 1 1/2 tablespoons of the oil and 1 tablespoon of the butter over medium heat until hot. Add onions and bell peppers. Cook about 10 minutes, stirring occasionally, until golden brown and tender. Remove skillet from heat and remove onion mixture from skillet; set aside.

2. Toss beef with salt and pepper so seasonings are evenly distributed. To the same skillet, add remaining oil and butter and increase heat to medium-high. Add one-fourth of the beef and cook 1 to 2 minutes, turning once, until beef is browned. Remove beef from skillet, and repeat to cook remaining beef.

3. Return beef to skillet with onions and bell peppers. Stir in Worcestershire sauce. Divide beef evenly among bottom halves of buns and spoon 3 table-spoons cheese dip onto each. Cover with top halves of buns. (If your cheese dip has been refrigerated, spoon it into a microwavable bowl and microwave 10 to 20 seconds on High or until warm.)

1 Sandwich: Calories 530 (Calories from Fat 220); Total Fat 24g (Saturated Fat 8g; Trans Fat 1.5g); Cholesterol 100mg; Sodium 930mg; Total Carbohydrate 41g (Dietary Fiber 3g; Sugars 6g); Protein 38g • **% Daily Value:** Vitamin A 60%; Vitamin C 70%; Calcium 15%; Iron 30% • **Exchanges:** 2 Starch, 1/2 Other Carbohydrate, 4 1/2 Medium-Fat Meat • **Carbohydrate Choices:** 3

WHY IT WORKS: **SAY CHEESE!** Everyone loves the taste of melted cheese, but making a cheese sauce can be time-consuming. And if overheated, cheese can separate. Processed cheese, made up of a combination of different types of natural cheese (usually an aged cheese for flavor and a young cheese for texture), was invented to make melting cheese fool-proof. Processed cheese manufacturers can change the color, flavor and texture of their product by starting with different cheeses. These cheeses are melted and then mixed with emulsifying salts—chemicals that stop the cheese from separating. The result? Melted cheese with no fuss.

Chinese Barbecued Flank Steak

PREP TIME: 5 MINUTES • **START TO FINISH:** 2 HOURS 20 MINUTES   4 SERVINGS

1/2 cup sake, dry white wine or
    beef broth
1/2 cup soy sauce
1/4 cup Worcestershire sauce
2 tablespoons packed dark
    brown sugar
2 tablespoons grated gingerroot
1 tablespoon lime juice
1 tablespoon balsamic vinegar
1 teaspoon dark sesame oil
2 cloves garlic, finely chopped
1 1/2 lb beef flank steak

1. In 13 × 9-inch glass baking dish, beat all ingredients except beef with wire whisk. Add beef to dish or plastic food storage bag, turning several times. Cover and refrigerate at least 2 hours but no longer than 24 hours.

2. Adjust oven rack so top of beef will be about 3 inches from heat. Set oven control to broil. Line broiler pan with foil. Remove beef from marinade; set marinade aside. Pat beef dry with paper towels and place in broiler pan. Broil 7 minutes per side or until beef is medium-rare (135°F). Remove beef from broiler. Cover with foil and allow to rest.

3. Meanwhile, in 1-quart saucepan, heat reserved marinade to boiling over high heat; boil and stir 1 minute. Reduce heat to medium and simmer 3 minutes. Remove from heat; set aside.

4. Remove foil and place beef on cutting board. Use sharp knife to cut beef against the grain into 1/4-inch slices. Serve with hot marinade.

1 Serving: Calories 260 (Calories from Fat 100); Total Fat 12g (Saturated Fat 4.5g; Trans Fat 0.5g); Cholesterol 90mg; Sodium 580mg; Total Carbohydrate 4g (Dietary Fiber 0g; Sugars 3g); Protein 35g • **% Daily Value:** Vitamin A 2%; Vitamin C 0%; Calcium 0%; Iron 20% • **Exchanges:** 1/2 Other Carbohydrate, 5 Very Lean Meat, 1 1/2 Fat • **Carbohydrate Choices:** 0

RECIPE Rx: THE INCREDIBLE SHRINKING STEAK You went to the butcher and bought a good-looking flank steak, just for this recipe. The problem is your finished steak is almost half the size it was when it was raw! No, this isn't a conspiracy by butchers to get

you to buy more meat; it is a natural property of the meat. As meat is heated, the muscle fibers start to contract and pull. In meats where the fibers all run in one direction, such as flank steak, this effect can be quite dramatic. Although this can't be completely avoided, using gentle heat can minimize it. If the heat is really high not only will the meat burn more easily but also it will shrink faster. So cook as instructed and next time buy enough meat to compensate for the shrink.

Beef Fajita Wraps

WITH PINEAPPLE SALSA

PREP TIME: 40 MINUTES • **START TO FINISH:** 40 MINUTES

4 WRAPS

Salsa

1/2 medium pineapple, cut into
    1/2-inch pieces (2 cups)
1 small red bell pepper, chopped
    (1/2 cup)
1 small serrano or jalapeño chile,
    seeded and finely chopped
1/4 cup finely chopped red onion
2 tablespoons chopped fresh cilantro
2 tablespoons lime juice

Wraps

1/2 lb beef flank steak
1/4 cup lime juice
1 1/2 teaspoons ground cumin
3/4 teaspoon salt
4 cloves garlic, finely chopped
1 large onion, thinly sliced
3 medium bell peppers (any color),
    thinly sliced
4 flour tortillas (8 inch)

1. In medium glass bowl, mix all salsa ingredients. Cover and refrigerate 30 minutes, but no longer than 1 week, to blend the flavors.

2. Meanwhile, cut steak into very thin slices across the grain. In shallow glass or plastic dish, mix 1/4 cup lime juice, the cumin, salt and garlic. Stir in steak. To marinate, cover and refrigerate at least 15 minutes but no longer than 24 hours, stirring occasionally.

3. Remove steak from marinade; set marinade aside. Pat steak dry with paper towels. Spray 12-inch skillet with cooking spray; heat over medium-high heat. Add steak; cook 3 minutes, stirring once. Stir in onion, bell peppers and marinade. Cook 5 to 8 minutes, stirring frequently, until onion and peppers are crisp-tender.

4. Place 1/4 of steak mixture on center of each tortilla. Fold one end of tortilla up about 1 inch over beef mixture; fold right and left sides over folded end, overlapping. Serve with salsa.

1 Wrap: Calories 320 (Calories from Fat 70); Total Fat 8g (Saturated Fat 2.5g; Trans Fat 0.5g); Cholesterol 30mg; Sodium 690mg; Total Carbohydrate 45g (Dietary Fiber 5g; Sugars 12g); Protein 17g • **% Daily Value:** Vitamin A 30%; Vitamin C 230%; Calcium 10%; Iron 20% • **Exchanges:** 2 Starch, 1 Other Carbohydrate, 1 1/2 Medium-Fat Meat • **Carbohydrate Choices:** 3

WHY IT WORKS: **HEAT AND MEAT** You know the scene: You're seated at a Mexican restaurant. A waitress holding a sizzling fajita platter rushes by, filling your table with the delicious aroma of frying meat. Spices and herbs aside, this smell is quite different from that of beef stew. Why? It has everything to do with temperature and time. When meat is heated above 285°F, its proteins combine with natural sugars to produce the brown color and flavor we all know and love. (Boiling meat, because of its lower temperature, won't produce this color and flavor.) This browning process, called the Maillard reaction, happens best when your meat is dry. Make sure to pat the moisture off the surface before searing your steak

Beef Fajita Wraps with Pineapple Salsa

Slow-Cooked Beef
WITH POBLANO-LIME SALSA

PREP TIME: 50 MINUTES • **START TO FINISH:** 4 HOURS   8 SERVINGS

Beef

1 tablespoon salt

1 tablespoon chili powder

2 teaspoons ground cumin

1 beef brisket (2 1/2 lb)

4 slices thick-sliced bacon, cut into
   1-inch pieces

2 medium onions, chopped (2 cups)

3 cloves garlic, finely chopped

1 can (14.5 oz) diced tomatoes,
   undrained

2 teaspoons dried oregano leaves

6 sprigs fresh parsley

4 sprigs fresh thyme

3 dried bay leaves

1 can (14 oz) low-sodium beef broth

Salsa

1/4 lb ripe plum (Roma) tomatoes,
   chopped

1 tablespoon finely chopped
   red onion

1 tablespoon finely chopped
   poblano chiles

1 tablespoon lime juice

1 clove garlic, finely chopped

1/2 small jalapeño chile, seeded
   and finely chopped

Dash of sugar

Dash of salt

Dash of ground cumin

Tortillas

8 flour tortillas (8 inch), warmed

1. Adjust oven rack to lowest position. Heat oven to 350°F.

2. In small bowl, mix 1 tablespoon salt, the chili powder and 2 teaspoons cumin. Rub mixture on beef; set aside.

3. In 4-quart ovenproof Dutch oven, cook bacon over medium heat, stirring occasionally, until crisp. Remove bacon but leave bacon drippings in pan. Increase heat to medium-high. Use long tongs to set one side of beef into hot drippings. Allow beef to brown well on one side, 3 to 5 minutes (do not move around too much or you will not get a well-browned crust). Repeat on all sides of beef. Place beef on plate; set aside.

4. Reduce heat to medium. Add 2 cups onions to Dutch oven and cook 2 minutes, stirring occasionally, until slightly soft. Add garlic, tomatoes, oregano, parsley, thyme, bay leaves, broth and bacon. Return beef to pan and heat liquid to boiling. Cover pan and place in oven. Cook 1 1/2 hours. Remove from oven and flip beef. Replace cover and bake 1 1/2 hours longer. Remove pan from oven and let stand, covered, with beef in broth.

5. In small bowl, mix all salsa ingredients; set aside.

6. Remove beef from pan to cutting board. Use 2 forks to shred beef. Return beef to pan until serving.

7. For each serving, use slotted spoon to place about 1/2 cup shredded beef on center of 1 tortilla, then top with about 2 tablespoons salsa. Roll tortilla around filling.

1 Serving: Calories 370 (Calories from Fat 120); Total Fat 13g (Saturated Fat 4.5g; Trans Fat 1g); Cholesterol 65mg; Sodium 1390mg; Total Carbohydrate 32g (Dietary Fiber 3g; Sugars 4g); Protein 30g • **% Daily Value:** Vitamin A 20%; Vitamin C 15%; Calcium 10%; Iron 25% • **Exchanges:** 2 Starch, 3 1/2 Lean Meat • **Carbohydrate Choices:** 2

WHY IT WORKS: **THE HEAT IS ON** We've all experienced the invigorating rush of mouth-numbing heat that comes from eating Mexican and Thai food. But where does this heat that makes you sweat and burns your mouth come from? A chemical called capsaicin gives chile peppers their heat. Found mostly in the seeds and inner ribs of chiles, capsaicin levels vary depending on the type of chile. Scientists measure the capsaicin in chiles using Scoville units—the higher the number, the hotter the pepper. For example, sweet bell peppers have 0 Scoville units; jalapeños can have up to 10,000. (The poblano used in this recipe has a Scoville of 1,000.) The hottest of all peppers are habaneros, with levels of up to 300,000!

Mama's Spaghetti and Meatballs

PREP TIME: 50 MINUTES • **START TO FINISH:** 50 MINUTES   4 SERVINGS

Sauce

2 tablespoons olive oil

1 large onion, chopped (1 cup)

1 small green bell pepper, chopped
   (1/2 cup)

2 large cloves garlic, finely chopped

2 cans (14 1/2 oz each) whole
   tomatoes, undrained

2 cans (8 oz each) tomato sauce

2 tablespoons chopped fresh or
   2 teaspoons dried basil leaves

1 tablespoon chopped fresh or
   1 teaspoon dried oregano leaves

1/2 teaspoon salt

1/2 teaspoon fennel seed

1/4 teaspoon pepper

Meatballs

1 lb ground chuck or lean (at least
   80%) ground beef

1/2 cup unseasoned dry bread
   crumbs

1/4 cup buttermilk

1/2 teaspoon salt

1/2 teaspoon Worcestershire sauce

1/4 teaspoon pepper

1 small onion, chopped (1/4 cup)

1 egg

Spaghetti

1 1/2 teaspoons salt, if desired

8 oz uncooked spaghetti

1. In 3-quart saucepan, heat oil over medium heat. Cook 1 cup onion, the bell pepper and garlic in oil 2 minutes, stirring occasionally. (The vegetables should soften, but not turn brown). Stir in remaining sauce ingredients, breaking up tomatoes with a fork or snipping with kitchen scissors. Heat to boiling; reduce heat. Cover and simmer 45 minutes. Stir occasionally to make sure sauce isn't sticking.

2. Meanwhile, heat oven to 400°F.

3. In large bowl, mix all meatball ingredients. Shape mixture into twenty 1 1/2-inch meatballs. (Wet your hands to make the meatballs easier to form. A small ice cream scoop is handy in shaping the meatballs.) Place in ungreased 13 × 9-inch pan.

4. Bake uncovered 20 to 25 minutes or until thoroughly cooked, when no longer pink in center and juice is clear.

5. Meanwhile, fill 5-quart Dutch oven with 3 quarts water; heat to boiling over high heat. When water is boiling, add 1 1/2 teaspoons salt if desired. When water returns to boil, add spaghetti. Stir immediately to make sure it doesn't stick to itself or pan. Boil spaghetti 8 to 10 minutes or until cooked through but still slightly firm. Drain in colander. There is no need to shake off excess moisture. Serve sauce with spaghetti and meatballs.

1 Serving: Calories 680 (Calories from Fat 210); Total Fat 24g (Saturated Fat 7g; Trans Fat 1g); Cholesterol 125mg; Sodium 1780mg; Total Carbohydrate 80g (Dietary Fiber 9g; Sugars 15g); Protein 36g • **% Daily Value:** Vitamin A 35%; Vitamin C 50%; Calcium 20%; Iron 45% • **Exchanges:** 4 Starch, 1 Other Carbohydrate, 1 Vegetable, 3 Medium-Fat Meat, 1 Fat • **Carbohydrate Choices:** 5

WHY IT WORKS: **THAT'S A TENDER MEATBALL!** A great meatball is more like a small meat loaf than a small hamburger. The meat itself is not the only star of the show. Instead, the added ingredients (eggs, bread crumbs, spices) greatly contribute to the success of the finished product. An often overlooked meatball ingredient is the liquid. Using buttermilk insures a great-tasting, tender meatball. The mild lactic acid in the buttermilk will enhance the flavor and texture of the final dish.

Creamy Tomato Lasagna

WITH MASCARPONE CHEESE

PREP TIME: 1 HOUR 35 MINUTES • **START TO FINISH:** 2 HOURS 25 MINUTES   12 SERVINGS

Meat Sauce

1/4 cup olive oil

2 medium carrots, chopped (1 cup)

2 medium stalks celery, chopped (1 cup)

1 large onion, chopped (1 cup)

3 cloves garlic, finely chopped

1/2 cup chopped fresh mushrooms (4 oz)

1/2 lb bulk Italian sausage or links (remove from casings)

1/2 lb ground chuck or lean (at least 80%) ground beef

1/2 cup white wine or nonalcoholic wine

1 cup whole milk

1 can (28 oz) diced tomatoes, drained

2 tablespoons tomato paste

1 tablespoon balsamic vinegar

2 teaspoons dried basil leaves

1/2 teaspoon ground black pepper

1/4 teaspoon crushed red pepper

1/3 cup mascarpone cheese or cream cheese, softened

1. In 3-quart saucepan, heat oil over medium heat until hot. Add carrots, celery and onion. Cook about 7 minutes, stirring occasionally, until softened. Add garlic and cook 30 seconds or until fragrant. Add mushrooms and cook about 5 minutes or until they have given up most of their juices.

2. Crumble sausage and beef into saucepan. Cook 10 minutes, breaking up and stirring occasionally, until meat is brown. Drain excess fat.

3. Increase heat to medium-high and stir in wine. Cook about 5 minutes, stirring occasionally, until wine nearly evaporates. Add 1 cup milk and cook about 15 minutes, stirring constantly, until no liquid remains. Reduce heat to low. Stir in tomatoes, tomato paste, vinegar, basil, black pepper and red pepper. Heat to simmer, then simmer 15 minutes.

4. Stir in mascarpone and remove sauce from heat. Taste and adjust seasoning if necessary. (Mixture should be saucy in order to hydrate the noodles during baking.)

5. In 2-quart saucepan, melt butter over medium heat. Stir in flour. Cook about 3 minutes, stirring constantly, until smooth and bubbly and making sure mixture does not brown. Remove from heat.

6. Gradually beat in 3 cups milk with wire whisk. Heat to boiling, stirring constantly (especially the corners), and boil 3 minutes or until thickened. (Not cooking the whole time will leave your sauce tasting floury.) Remove from heat and stir in salt, white pepper and nutmeg. Taste and adjust seasoning if necessary. (Do not add too much salt because you will be adding salty cheese.)

White Sauce

1/4 cup butter
1/4 cup all-purpose flour
3 cups whole milk
1/2 teaspoon salt
1/4 teaspoon white pepper
1/8 teaspoon freshly ground nutmeg

Cheese and Pasta

3 cups shredded mozzarella cheese
  (12 oz)
2 cups shredded Parmesan cheese
  (8 oz)
12 uncooked no-boil lasagna noodles
  (from 9- or 10-oz package)

7. Adjust oven rack to middle position. Heat oven to 425°F. Spray 13×9-inch (3-quart) glass baking dish with cooking spray.

8. In medium bowl, mix mozzarella and Parmesan; set aside.

9. Spread about 1 1/4 cups of the meat sauce evenly over bottom of baking dish (it may not completely cover the bottom); top with 3 noodles. Top noodles with 1/2 cup of the white sauce, spreading it as best as you can. Sprinkle with 1 cup of the cheese mixture. Top cheese with 1 1/4 cups of the meat sauce. Place 3 noodles on top of meat sauce. Repeat the following layers twice: 1/2 cup white sauce, 1 cup cheese mixture, 1 1/4 cups meat sauce, 3 noodles. Spread remaining white sauce over noodles and sprinkle with remaining 2 cups cheese. You will be at the top of baking dish.

10. Tear off piece of foil large enough to amply cover top of baking dish. Spray one side of foil with cooking spray. Cover lasagna with foil, sprayed side down. (Lasagna can be refrigerated up to 12 hours at this point.)

11. Bake 30 minutes (if lasagna was refrigerated, bake 40 minutes). Carefully remove foil and bake 20 minutes longer or until top is lightly brown in spots and edges are hot and bubbly.

1 Serving: Calories 510 (Calories from Fat 280); Total Fat 31g (Saturated Fat 15g; Trans Fat 1g); Cholesterol 80mg; Sodium 950mg; Total Carbohydrate 30g (Dietary Fiber 3g; Sugars 8g); Protein 29g • **% Daily Value:** Vitamin A 60%; Vitamin C 10%; Calcium 60%; Iron 15% • **Exchanges:** 1 1/2 Starch, 1/2 Other Carbohydrate, 3 1/2 High-Fat Meat • **Carbohydrate Choices:** 2

WHY IT WORKS: **INSTANT NOODLES** Saying that bread, cookie or pasta dough is "cooked" means that the starch in the flour has fully absorbed the water in the dough. Depending on the thickness of the dough, this process can take minutes (as with pasta) or almost an hour (as with bread). For traditional lasagna noodles, boiling causes the dough to absorb water and cook through. The no-boil lasagna noodles used in this recipe have been pretreated with water; they do not need to be boiled before using. The heat of baking and the moisture from the sauce cook the noodles while the lasagna bakes.

Mini Mexican Meat Loaves

WITH CHIPOTLE BARBECUE SAUCE

PREP TIME: 20 MINUTES • **START TO FINISH:** 50 MINUTES   6 SERVINGS (2 MINI LOAVES EACH)

Meat Loaves

1 1/2 lb ground chuck or lean (at least 80%) ground beef

2/3 cup milk

1/3 cup salsa

1/2 cup shredded Colby-Monterey Jack cheese blend (2 oz)

1 can (4.5 oz) chopped green chiles, drained

1 tablespoon Worcestershire sauce

1/2 teaspoon salt

1/2 teaspoon ground mustard

1/4 teaspoon pepper

1 clove garlic, finely chopped, or 1/8 teaspoon garlic powder

3 slices bread, torn into small pieces

1 small onion, chopped (1/4 cup)

1 egg

1/4 cup salsa

Sauce

1 cup barbecue sauce

2 chipotle chiles in adobo sauce (from 7-oz can), chopped

2 teaspoons adobo sauce (from can of chiles)

2 tablespoons orange marmalade

1. Heat oven to 350°F. Spray 12 regular-size muffin cups with cooking spray.

2. In large bowl, mix all meat loaf ingredients except 1/4 cup of the salsa. (Slip on a pair of disposable gloves to make mixing the beef mixture less messy.) Divide beef mixture evenly among cups (cups will be very full). Brush tops with remaining 1/4 cup of the salsa. Place muffin pan on cookie sheet to catch any spillover.

3. Bake about 30 minutes or until no longer pink in center and juice is clear (meat thermometer inserted in middle of loaves in middle of muffin pan should read 160°F; outer loaves will be done sooner).

4. Meanwhile, in 1-quart saucepan, heat all sauce ingredients to boiling; reduce heat. Simmer uncovered 5 minutes, stirring occasionally.

5. Immediately remove meat loaves from pan. Top with sauce.

1 Serving: Calories 400 (Calories from Fat 160); Total Fat 18g (Saturated Fat 7g; Trans Fat 1g); Cholesterol 115mg; Sodium 1330mg; Total Carbohydrate 32g (Dietary Fiber 2g; Sugars 18g); Protein 26g • **% Daily Value:** Vitamin A 20%; Vitamin C 8%; Calcium 15%; Iron 20% • **Exchanges:** 1 Starch, 1 Other Carbohydrate, 3 Medium-Fat Meat, 1/2 Fat • **Carbohydrate Choices:** 2

WHY IT WORKS: **CHUCK IT** Hamburgers and meat loaf are best when juicy and flavorful. The secret to this combination is choosing the right cut of meat. For these dishes you don't need a tender cut, because the meat is ground. But you do need a flavorful cut. In addition, you need some fat (the juicy richness that we enjoy in these dishes comes from a balance of fat and protein). The cut meeting both criteria is chuck. From the upper shoulder of cattle, chuck is flavorful and has just enough fat to make your burger or meat loaf juicy but not greasy.

Mini Mexican Meat Loaves with Chipotle Barbecue Sauce

Oven-Barbecued Baby Back Ribs

WITH VINEGAR-MOLASSES SAUCE

PREP TIME: 35 MINUTES • START TO FINISH: 6 HOURS 50 MINUTES   4 SERVINGS

Sauce

1 cup ketchup

1 cup tomato puree (from 15-oz can)

1 jar (7 oz) hoisin sauce (3/4 cup)

1/2 cup apple juice

1/4 cup cider vinegar

2 tablespoons packed light
   brown sugar

2 tablespoons molasses

1/2 teaspoon salt

1/2 teaspoon red pepper sauce

1/4 teaspoon onion powder

1/4 teaspoon freshly ground pepper

3 cloves garlic, smashed

Ribs

4 lb pork baby back ribs, trimmed of
   excess fat, membrane removed
   (see Recipe R$_x$ on page 91)

1/2 cup apple juice

1. In 2-quart saucepan, heat all sauce ingredients to boiling over medium heat. Reduce heat to medium-low and simmer about 20 minutes, stirring occasionally, until sauce thickens slightly. Set aside and cool completely, about 1 hour.

2. Place ribs in 2-gallon resealable plastic food-storage bag, and pour cooled sauce over the ribs. Try to cover all surfaces of ribs with sauce. Reseal bag and refrigerate at least 4 hours but no longer than 12 hours.

3. Adjust oven racks to top and bottom positions. Heat oven to 450°F. Line 2 large cookie sheets with heavy-duty foil. Remove ribs from sauce; set sauce aside. Place ribs, meaty sides up, on cookie sheets. Bake 25 minutes.

4. Remove cookie sheets from oven and remove any fat that may have accumulated. Reduce oven temperature to 300°F. Brush ribs generously with some of the reserved sauce. Cover ribs tightly with foil and return to oven. Bake 1 to 1 1/2 hours or until ribs are very tender and no longer pink next to bones.

5. Meanwhile, in 2-quart saucepan, heat reserved sauce and 1/2 cup apple juice to boiling over medium heat. Reduce heat and simmer 10 minutes or until sauce is the consistency of ketchup. Cool sauce to room temperature.

6. Remove ribs from oven and carefully peel back foil (be careful, there will be a lot of steam). Serve ribs with room-temperature sauce.

1 Serving: Calories 1160 (Calories from Fat 620); Total Fat 69g (Saturated Fat 25g; Trans Fat 0g); Cholesterol 265mg; Sodium 2290mg; Total Carbohydrate 66g (Dietary Fiber 4g; Sugars 50g); Protein 69g • **% Daily Value:** Vitamin A 40%; Vitamin C 20%; Calcium 20%; Iron 40% • **Exchanges:** 1 Starch, 3 1/2 Other Carbohydrate, 9 1/2 Medium-Fat Meat, 4 Fat • **Carbohydrate Choices:** 4 1/2

WHY IT WORKS:

STEWING IN YOUR OWN JUICES The toughest cuts of meat have the most flavor. If cooked incorrectly, though, no amount of flavor will compensate for a rubbery texture. The secret to flavorful and tender meat is time and temperature. Tough cuts of meat are full of collagen (a gluelike substance that holds meat together). If cooked for a long time at a low temperature, collagen dissolves into gelatin, making for tender meat. However, cook at too high of a temperature for too long and the meat will re-toughen. So how do you create gelatin but keep the meat tender? A good rule: Never boil meat. If the liquid surrounding the meat in a stew, soup or oven braise boils, your meat will be chewy. Remember to keep it low and slow!

RECIPE R$_x$: SAVING YOUR SKIN One of the secrets of making great ribs is removing the thin membrane located on the bony side of the slab. This membrane can stop the sauce from penetrating the meat and make your ribs less than "fall-off-the-bone" tender. Start by using a sharp knife to scrape the membrane loose from the top of the wide end of the slab. Once you have freed about 1 inch of it from the bone, use a wad of paper towels to grab hold of it and pull (it's too slippery to grab with bare hands). The membrane will probably not come off in one shot, but sometimes you get lucky. In the end, it is a simple trick for great ribs.

Oven-Barbecued Baby Back Ribs with Vinegar-Molasses Sauce

Linguine with Caramelized Onions
AND ANGRY TOMATO SAUCE

PREP TIME: 50 MINUTES • **START TO FINISH:** 50 MINUTES

6 SERVINGS (1 1/2 CUPS EACH)

2 tablespoons extra-virgin olive oil

1 tablespoon butter

1 large red onion, thinly sliced
(1 1/2 cups)

1/2 lb thick-sliced pancetta or bacon,
cut into 1/4-inch pieces

1 large clove garlic, finely chopped

1 tablespoon tomato paste

1/4 cup oil-packed sun-dried
tomatoes, drained and chopped

1 can (28 oz) crushed tomatoes,
undrained

1 teaspoon dried oregano leaves

1/4 teaspoon crushed red pepper

1 tablespoon salt, if desired

1 lb uncooked linguine

1/2 cup freshly grated Parmesan
cheese

1. Fill large pot with 5 quarts water; heat to boiling over high heat.

2. Meanwhile, in 12-inch skillet, heat oil and butter over medium heat. When butter stops sizzling, add onion and cook 15 minutes, stirring occasionally, until onion is soft and golden brown. Scatter in pancetta and cook 5 minutes longer or until brown and crisp. Add garlic and cook about 30 seconds or until fragrant.

3. Use spatula to clear a spot in center of skillet. Add tomato paste and smear it on skillet bottom. Immediately scrape tomato paste off skillet. Paste should become even darker red, maybe even browned. If not, repeat until you see a color change. Stir tomato paste into onion mixture.

4. Add sun-dried tomatoes and crushed tomatoes to skillet. Scrape bottom of skillet to dislodge any stuck bits. Stir in oregano and red pepper. Heat to a simmer and reduce heat to low, stirring occasionally, while you prepare pasta.

5. When water in pot is boiling, add salt if desired. When water returns to a boil, add linguine. Stir immediately to make sure it doesn't stick to itself or pan. Boil linguine 8 to 10 minutes or until cooked through but still slightly firm. Drain in colander. There is no need to shake off excess moisture.

6. Return linguine to pot and stir in sauce. Cook over medium heat 2 minutes, stirring occasionally, until sauce thickens slightly. Sprinkle with cheese; stir to combine. Serve with additional cheese if desired.

1 Serving: Calories 510 (Calories from Fat 150); Total Fat 16g (Saturated Fat 5g; Trans Fat 0g); Cholesterol 20mg; Sodium 570mg; Total Carbohydrate 71g (Dietary Fiber 7g; Sugars 6g); Protein 19g • **% Daily Value:** Vitamin A 15%; Vitamin C 20%; Calcium 20%; Iron 25% • **Exchanges:** 4 Starch, 1/2 Other Carbohydrate, 1 High-Fat Meat, 1 Fat • **Carbohydrate Choices:** 5

WHY IT WORKS: **TOMATO PASTE** The Old World method of preserving the flavor of summer's bounty was to peel, grind and dry tomatoes in the warmth of the southern sun. Tomato paste is still a powerful ingredient in your kitchen pantry—just as it was in Italy centuries ago—if used correctly. Used in excess, it gives an overly sweet and fruity flavor to sauces and gravies. For best results, combine tomato paste with fresh or canned tomatoes. A small amount, about 1 tablespoon to a pot of spaghetti sauce, deepens the tomato flavor without overwhelming other ingredients. To increase the flavor even more, cook the paste along with the onions at the beginning of your recipe.

Linguine with Caramelized Onions and Angry Tomato Sauce

Crispy Fish Tacos

WITH SPICY SWEET-AND-SOUR SAUCE

PREP TIME: 15 MINUTES • START TO FINISH: 40 MINUTES   6 TACOS

Sauce

1 cup sour cream
1 tablespoon chopped fresh cilantro
1 tablespoon lime juice
1 teaspoon packed light brown sugar
1 chipotle chile in adobo sauce
    (from 7-oz can), chopped

Fish

1 cup all-purpose flour
1/2 teaspoon salt
1/2 teaspoon ground cumin
1/4 teaspoon baking powder
1/4 teaspoon garlic powder
3/4 cup beer or nonalcoholic beer
1/4 cup ice-cold water
Vegetable oil
1 lb halibut, flounder or cod fillets,
    skin removed and fish cut into
    5 × 3/4-inch strips
6 flour tortillas (10 inch)

Toppings

2 cups shredded lettuce
3/4 cup salsa
1 avocado, pitted, peeled and sliced
1 cup shredded Monterey Jack
    cheese (4 oz)
1 lime, cut into 6 wedges
Fresh cilantro

1. In small bowl, mix all sauce ingredients well; set aside.

2. In large bowl, beat flour, salt, cumin, baking powder and garlic powder with wire whisk. Stir in beer and water until no dry flour mixture is visible.

3. Heat oven to 200°F (or set to warm). Line cookie sheet with foil. Place wire rack on lined cookie sheet and place in oven.

4. In 4-quart Dutch oven or deep fryer, heat 1 1/2 inches oil to 375°F. Dip fish strips in batter and remove with tongs, holding fish strips over bowl so excess batter drips off. Lower fish strips into hot oil. Repeat with remaining fish strips. (Do not crowd pan; cook only as many fish strips at once that will fit in pan without touching each other.) Cook fish strips 4 minutes on one side until golden brown. Turn fish (flip fish away from you to avoid being spattered with hot oil) and cook 3 minutes on other side until golden. Remove fish from pan and place on wire rack on cookie sheet. Keep fish warm in oven while you prepare remaining strips.

5. To assemble tacos, place 1 or 2 fish strips on center of each tortilla. Top with about 2 tablespoons sauce, the lettuce, salsa, avocado, cheese, a squirt of lime juice and the cilantro.

1 Taco: Calories 520 (Calories from Fat 210); Total Fat 24g (Saturated Fat 10g; Trans Fat 1g); Cholesterol 85mg; Sodium 800mg; Total Carbohydrate 50g (Dietary Fiber 5g; Sugars 5g); Protein 27g • **% Daily Value:** Vitamin A 20%; Vitamin C 10%; Calcium 30%; Iron 20% • **Exchanges:** 3 Starch, 1/2 Other Carbohydrate, 2 1/2 Medium-Fat Meat, 1 1/2 Fat • **Carbohydrate Choices:** 3

WHY IT WORKS:

THE RIGHT OIL FOR FRYING There has been much talk lately about health and flavor differences among oils, but oils also differ in frying behavior. As oil is exposed to the high heat of frying, it begins to break down. If heated to too high a temperature, oil quickly begins to smoke and break down; this temperature is called its "smoke point." Every time oil is heated, its smoke point is lowered. For example, a fresh pan of peanut oil may begin to smoke at 450°F, but after the oil is used two or three times, it may smoke at 375°F. Oil at its smoke point can be dangerous because it can catch fire. It may also give off-flavors to foods. Keep it safe by only using an oil a few times to deep-fry. Also choose oils that have a high smoke point when fresh. The best oils for deep-frying are soybean (vegetable), corn, sunflower, peanut and canola.

Crispy Fish Tacos with Spicy Sweet-and-Sour Sauce

California Black Bean Burgers

WITH HORSERADISH SAUCE

PREP TIME: 15 MINUTES • **START TO FINISH:** 1 HOUR 25 MINUTES   6 SANDWICHES

Sauce

1 cup sour cream
2 tablespoons mayonnaise or
   salad dressing
2 tablespoons coarse-grained
   mustard
2 tablespoons prepared horseradish

Burgers

1 can (15 oz) black beans, undrained
1 can (4.5 oz) chopped green chiles,
   undrained
1 cup unseasoned dry bread crumbs
1 teaspoon chili powder
1 egg, beaten
1/4 cup yellow cornmeal
2 tablespoons vegetable oil
6 burger buns, toasted
1 1/4 cups shredded lettuce
3 tablespoons chunky-style salsa

1. In small bowl, mix all sauce ingredients. Cover and refrigerate at least 1 hour to blend the flavors.

2. Place beans in food processor or blender. Cover and process until slightly mashed; remove from food processor. In medium bowl, mix beans, chiles, bread crumbs, chili powder and egg.

3. Place cornmeal in pie plate or shallow dish. Shape mixture into 6 patties, each about 1/2 inch thick. (If mixture is too sticky to form patties easily, coat your hands with about 1 teaspoon of oil or spray your hands with cooking spray.) Coat each patty with cornmeal.

4. In 10-inch skillet, heat oil over medium heat. Cook patties in oil 5 to 10 minutes, turning once, until crisp and thoroughly cooked on both sides. Do not crowd pan. If necessary, cook patties in two batches.

5. Spread bottom halves of buns with sauce. Top with lettuce, patties, salsa and tops of buns.

1 Sandwich: Calories 480 (Calories from Fat 180); Total Fat 21g (Saturated Fat 7g; Trans Fat 0.5g); Cholesterol 65mg; Sodium 960mg; Total Carbohydrate 60g (Dietary Fiber 6g; Sugars 7g); Protein 14g • **% Daily Value:** Vitamin A 10%; Vitamin C 6%; Calcium 20%; Iron 25% • **Exchanges:** 3 Starch, 1/2 Other Carbohydrate, 1 Vegetable, 1/2 Medium-Fat Meat, 3 Fat • **Carbohydrate Choices:** 4

WHY IT WORKS: **WHERE'S THE MEAT?** Typically, vegetarian dishes contain starch (such as beans, potatoes or pasta) which often doesn't have much flavor. Starch, as with most carbohydrates, tends to dull the impact of certain flavors as it literally gets in the way of your taste buds. A solution is found in the classic cooking of vegetarian cuisines, such as Indian or Mexican: Use strong flavors to help build complexity. Another way to build complexity when making a vegetarian casserole is to roast the vegetables to enhance their sweetness and create a subtle smoky flavor. Or, consider a sharp or spicy condiment, like the horseradish sauce in this recipe. The powerful flavor of the condiment will be balanced by the mellowness of the bean burgers.

California Black Bean Burgers with Horseradish Sauce

Parmesan Pasta with Beef Ragu

PREP TIME: 45 MINUTES • **START TO FINISH:** 1 HOUR 30 MINUTES   6 SERVINGS (2 CUPS EACH)

Ragu

3 tablespoons olive oil

2 medium carrots, finely chopped (1 cup)

1 medium onion, finely chopped (1 cup)

3 cloves garlic, finely chopped

1/2 lb bulk Italian sausage or links (remove from casing)

1/2 lb ground chuck or lean (at least 80%) ground beef

2/3 cup dry red wine or beef broth

1 can (14 oz) beef broth

1 can (14 oz) chicken broth

1/2 cup half-and-half

1 can (28 oz) crushed tomatoes, undrained

1/2 teaspoon ground fennel seed

Pasta

1 tablespoon salt, if desired

1 lb uncooked penne pasta

2 tablespoons olive oil

3/4 cup grated Parmesan cheese

1. In 3-quart saucepan, heat 3 tablespoons oil over medium heat until fragrant. Add carrots and onion. Cook 7 minutes, stirring constantly, until vegetables soften but do not brown. Add garlic and cook about 30 seconds or until fragrant.

2. Crumble sausage and beef into saucepan. Cook 8 to 10 minutes, breaking up and stirring occasionally, until meat is brown. Drain fat.

3. Increase heat to high. Add wine to meat mixture and stir and scrape bottom of pan as wine boils. Allow wine to evaporate, about 7 minutes or until pan bottom is dry. Add beef broth and chicken broth and return to boiling. Allow mixture to evaporate just as wine did, stirring occasionally, about 25 minutes.

4. Add half-and-half to nearly dry pan. Cook 10 minutes, stirring constantly, until there is only a glaze left on bottom of pan (be careful—half-and-half can scorch, so stir well).

5. Add tomatoes and fennel and heat mixture to a simmer. Reduce heat to medium-low and cook about 20 minutes or until flavors are blended.

6. Meanwhile, fill large pot with 5 quarts water; heat to boiling over high heat. When water is boiling, add salt if desired. When water returns to boil, add pasta. Stir immediately to make sure it doesn't stick to itself or pan. Boil pasta 9 to 10 minutes or until cooked through but still slightly firm. Drain in colander. There is no need to shake off excess moisture.

7. In 12-inch skillet, heat 2 tablespoons oil over medium heat until hot. Add pasta (be careful—leftover water can make oil spatter). Cook 4 minutes, stirring occasionally, until edges of pasta turn slightly brown. Divide pasta evenly among 6 warmed pasta bowls. Sprinkle each with 2 tablespoons cheese. Top each with about 1 cup sauce.

1 Serving: Calories 690 (Calories from Fat 280); Total Fat 31g (Saturated Fat 10g; Trans Fat 0.5g); Cholesterol 60mg; Sodium 1290mg; Total Carbohydrate 71g (Dietary Fiber 7g; Sugars 7g); Protein 32g • **% Daily Value:** Vitamin A 90%; Vitamin C 20%; Calcium 30%; Iron 30% • **Exchanges:** 4 Starch, 1/2 Other Carbohydrate, 1 Vegetable, 2 1/2 High-Fat Meat, 1 1/2 Fat • **Carbohydrate Choices:** 5

WHY IT WORKS: **GOT MILK?** This ragu calls for the unusual step of adding half-and-half to the ground meat mixture. Cooking meat with dairy products (milk is common) is a very old technique used throughout the Middle East and medieval Europe. Cooking meat in milk does two things: First, because the meat is cooking in a liquid, and not oil, the temperature of the meat cannot rise above that of boiling milk (somewhere around 212°F). This means the meat will be moist but not brown. A second benefit is flavor. As milk heats, its flavors are radically changed (compare the flavor of evaporated milk with fresh milk). These new flavors enhance the meat's flavor, making it even more rich and complex.

Penne

WITH CARAMELIZED ONION–GORGONZOLA CHEESE SAUCE

PREP TIME: 15 MINUTES • **START TO FINISH:** 1 HOUR 30 MINUTES   6 SERVINGS (ABOUT 1 1/2 CUPS EACH)

2 tablespoons butter

1 large sweet onion, thinly sliced
(1 1/2 cups)

1 clove garlic, thinly sliced

1 tablespoon salt, if desired

1 lb uncooked penne pasta

1 3/4 cups whipping (heavy) cream

1/4 cup butter

4 oz Gorgonzola cheese (preferably
Gorgonzola dolce, or sweet
Gorgonzola), crumbled (1 cup)

1/4 teaspoon salt

1/8 teaspoon pepper

Dash of freshly grated nutmeg or
ground nutmeg

1. In 10-inch nonstick skillet, melt 2 tablespoons butter over medium-high heat. Stir in onion and garlic to coat with butter. Cook uncovered about 5 minutes, stirring occasionally, until onion is softened. Reduce heat to medium-low. Cook uncovered 35 to 40 minutes, stirring occasionally, until onion is light golden brown. Do not let onion or garlic burn. (Onions will shrink during cooking.)

2. Meanwhile, fill large pot with 5 quarts water; heat to boiling over high heat. When water is boiling, add 1 tablespoon salt if desired. When water returns to boil, add pasta. Stir immediately to make sure it doesn't stick to itself or pan. Boil pasta 9 to 10 minutes or until cooked through but still slightly firm. Drain in colander. There is no need to shake off excess moisture.

3. Add onion mixture to pot. Increase heat to medium and add 1 cup of the whipping cream and 1/4 cup butter. Cook, stirring occasionally, until butter melts and cream simmers. Stir in cheese, salt, pepper and nutmeg. Add drained pasta and remaining 3/4 cup whipping cream. Cook and stir until pasta is coated and sauce is hot.

1 Serving: Calories 680 (Calories from Fat 360); Total Fat 40g (Saturated Fat 23g; Trans Fat 1.5g); Cholesterol 120mg; Sodium 470mg; Total Carbohydrate 64g (Dietary Fiber 5g; Sugars 5g); Protein 16g • **% Daily Value:** Vitamin A 30%; Vitamin C 0%; Calcium 15%; Iron 15% • **Exchanges:** 4 Starch, 1/2 High-Fat Meat, 7 Fat • **Carbohydrate Choices:** 4

WHY IT WORKS: SLOW AND STEADY WITH CHEESE

All cheese starts out looking like the curds and whey of cottage cheese. But with time, pressure and the help of friendly bacteria, we get the enormous variety of cheese available in your grocery store. All cheese is made up of fat and protein—two components that do not typically mix well. As it ages and loses moisture, cheese becomes concentrated in flavor. This means that the fat and protein in cheese also become concentrated. If they become too concentrated, it may lead to disaster as you try to melt cheese into sauces. Excess heat will change the protein's shape and melt the fat, leaving an oil slick on top of your sauce. To play it safe when using aged cheese like Gorgonzola, use a small amount near the end of cooking and do not heat it to boiling. To be extra safe, remove your sauce from the heat before adding the cheese.

Company's Coming

ENTERTAINING

WITH EASE

Braised Chicken
WITH WILD MUSHROOMS AND THYME

PREP TIME: 55 MINUTES • **START TO FINISH:** 2 HOURS 30 MINUTES   4 SERVINGS

1 cup boiling water
1/2 oz dried porcini mushrooms
1 tablespoon butter
1 tablespoon olive oil
1 cut-up broiler-fryer chicken
    (3 to 3 1/2 lb)
2 large onions, chopped (2 cups)
5 cloves garlic, finely chopped
6 medium button mushrooms, sliced
2 medium carrots, chopped (1 cup)
2 medium stalks celery, chopped
    (1 cup)
2 dried bay leaves
2 fresh thyme sprigs or 1 teaspoon
    dried thyme leaves
5 tablespoons chopped fresh parsley
1 cup chicken broth
1/2 cup dry white wine or
    chicken broth
1 can (14.5 oz) diced tomatoes,
    undrained
1/4 teaspoon salt
1/4 teaspoon freshly ground pepper

1. Adjust oven rack to middle position. Heat oven to 300°F.

2. In small bowl, pour boiling water over dried mushrooms. Let stand 30 minutes to allow mushrooms to rehydrate (if mushrooms float to surface, place small saucer in bowl to keep them submerged). Use slotted spoon to remove rehydrated mushrooms from water; set aside. Reserve mushroom water.

3. In 4- or 5-quart ovenproof Dutch oven, heat butter and oil over medium-high heat until butter is melted. Add half of the chicken pieces and cook 6 minutes, turning occasionally, until chicken is deep golden brown (you are not cooking the chicken, just giving it color). Remove chicken from Dutch oven and place on plate. Repeat with remaining chicken.

4. Reduce heat to medium and add onions and garlic. Cook 5 minutes, stirring occasionally, until soft. Add rehydrated and sliced button mushrooms, carrots, celery, bay leaves, thyme and 3 tablespoons of the parsley. Cook 5 minutes, stirring occasionally, until vegetables are softened and mushrooms give up their juices.

5. Add reserved mushroom water and heat to a simmer. Simmer uncovered 10 minutes (you are trying to concentrate the flavor of the liquid). Add chicken (along with any juices that may have accumulated on plate), broth, wine, tomatoes, salt and pepper.

6. Cover pan and place in oven. Bake 1 1/2 hours or until chicken is very tender and there is a good amount of broth. Remove and discard bay leaves and thyme sprig. Place 2 pieces chicken into each of 4 large, flat serving bowls and ladle broth over. Sprinkle with remaining 2 tablespoons parsley.

1 Serving: Calories 410 (Calories from Fat 150); Total Fat 17g (Saturated Fat 5g; Trans Fat 0.5g); Cholesterol 125mg; Sodium 730mg; Total Carbohydrate 21g (Dietary Fiber 5g; Sugars 9g); Protein 43g • **% Daily Value:** Vitamin A 130%; Vitamin C 25%; Calcium 10%; Iron 20% • **Exchanges:** 1 Starch, 1 Vegetable, 5 1/2 Lean Meat • **Carbohydrate Choices:** 1 1/2

WHY IT WORKS: FLAVOR VARIATIONS OF MUSHROOMS

Mushrooms are one of the most misunderstood foods in the produce section. First, many people call them a vegetable when they are really a fungus. (A fungus gets energy from the plants they grow on rather than the sun.) It is also assumed that all mushrooms taste like the common button mushroom; in reality, their flavors vary widely. Shiitake mushrooms are slightly smoky, morels are nutty and chanterelles taste distinctly like apricots. Adding mushrooms will also enhance the flavor of your dish, as these fungi are the natural source of the flavor enhancer MSG.

Braised Chicken with Wild Mushrooms and Thyme

Lemon-Rosemary Roasted Chicken

WITH WHITE WINE SAUCE

PREP TIME: 35 MINUTES • **START TO FINISH:** 1 HOUR 40 MINUTES   6 SERVINGS

Chicken

1/4 cup olive oil

1 1/2 tablespoons fresh lemon juice

2 tablespoons chopped fresh
    rosemary leaves

1 teaspoon salt

1/2 teaspoon freshly ground pepper

3 cloves garlic, finely chopped

1 whole broiler-fryer chicken
    (3 to 3 1/2 lb)

2 small lemons, each cut into quarters

1 head garlic, unpeeled and cut
    in half crosswise

1 cup chicken broth, more if needed

Sauce

2 shallots, finely chopped

1 1/3 cups chicken broth

3/4 cup dry white wine or
    chicken broth

1 fresh rosemary sprig

1/4 cup cold firm butter, cut into
    4 pieces

1 teaspoon fresh lemon juice

1/4 teaspoon salt

1/4 teaspoon freshly ground pepper

1. Heat oven to 425°F. Roasting chicken at a high temperature results in moist, evenly browned chicken. Position V-shaped rack in heavy roasting pan. Spray rack with cooking spray.

2. In small bowl, mix oil, 1 1/2 tablespoons lemon juice, 2 tablespoons rosemary, 1 teaspoon salt, 1/2 teaspoon pepper and the chopped garlic.

3. Rinse cavity of chicken and pat dry with paper towels. Use your fingers to loosen connection between skin and breast meat, slowly working your way under skin. Continue over entire chicken. Generously spread oil mixture under skin, working it over the thighs, breast and drumsticks.

4. Spread thin coat of oil mixture over outside of skin. Place lemon quarters and garlic halves in cavity of chicken. Use kitchen twine to tie legs of chicken tightly together. Place chicken, breast side down, on oiled rack. Pour 1 cup broth into bottom of pan. Insert meat thermometer so tip is in thickest part of inside thigh and does not touch bone.

5. Roast chicken uncovered 30 minutes. Use kitchen tongs or two long-handled wooden spoons to turn chicken breast side up. Check to see if there is still liquid in bottom of pan. If not, add 1/4 cup broth. Roast 30 to 35 minutes longer or until thermometer reads 180°F, juice is no longer pink when center of thigh is cut, and legs move easily when lifted or twisted. Remove chicken from rack and place on platter. Cover tightly with foil; set aside.

6. Remove V-shaped rack from pan. Place pan over two burners and heat to boiling over medium-high heat. Boil any remaining liquid in pan until dry. Add shallots and cook 2 minutes, stirring frequently, until soft. Pour 1 1/3 cups broth into pan and heat to boiling, scraping any browned bits from bottom of pan.

7. Add wine and rosemary sprig to pan. Heat to boiling, stirring occasionally. Boil 5 minutes, stirring occasionally, until sauce is reduced to a little less than 1 cup. Remove from heat. Beat in butter, 1 piece at a time, with wire whisk, adding the next piece only after the first has been completely beaten in and melted. Stir in 1 teaspoon lemon juice, 1/4 teaspoon salt and 1/4 teaspoon pepper. Remove lemon quarters and garlic halves from cavity of chicken. Serve chicken with sauce.

1 Serving: Calories 360 (Calories from Fat 230); Total Fat 26g (Saturated Fat 8g; Trans Fat 1g); Cholesterol 105mg; Sodium 660mg; Total Carbohydrate 4g (Dietary Fiber 0g; Sugars 0g); Protein 28g • **% Daily Value:** Vitamin A 10%; Vitamin C 8%; Calcium 4%; Iron 10% • **Exchanges:** 4 Medium-Fat Meat, 1 Fat • **Carbohydrate Choices:** 0

WHY IT WORKS:

HITTING THE SAUCE Sauces are one of the cleverest inventions in the kitchen. Although many people think sauces are only for masking a poorly cooked dish, their true purpose is extending the flavor of your meat. When you fry meat and vegetables, especially when the pan is not nonstick, crispy bits of meat juices collect and glaze the bottom of the pan. This glaze, called the "fond" (French for bottom), contains concentrated meat flavor. To release the fond, deglaze the pan by adding liquid such as stock, wine or juice. This simple sauce can now be thickened, concentrated (by boiling) or enriched by adding butter.

Grilled Moroccan Spiced Chicken Breasts
STUFFED WITH COUSCOUS AND PINE NUTS

PREP TIME: 20 MINUTES • START TO FINISH: 40 MINUTES   4 SERVINGS

Stuffing

1/4 cup uncooked couscous

1/4 cup plus 2 tablespoons
   chicken broth

2 tablespoons butter

1/2 teaspoon ground coriander

1/2 teaspoon ground cumin

1/4 teaspoon salt

1/4 teaspoon ground turmeric

1 teaspoon grated lemon peel

2 tablespoons fresh lemon juice

1 tablespoon dried cranberries

1 tablespoon pine nuts

Dash of red pepper sauce or to taste

Chicken

4 boneless skinless chicken breasts
   (about 1 1/4 lb)

1 tablespoon vegetable oil

1/2 teaspoon salt

1/2 teaspoon ground cumin

1/4 teaspoon freshly ground pepper

1. In small bowl, place couscous; set aside.

2. In 1-quart saucepan, heat broth, butter, coriander, 1/2 teaspoon cumin, 1/4 teaspoon salt and the turmeric to boiling.

3. Pour hot broth over couscous, stir well and cover with foil. Let stand 5 minutes to allow liquid to be absorbed. Uncover and fluff couscous with fork. Stir in lemon peel, lemon juice, cranberries, pine nuts and pepper sauce; set aside.

4. Meanwhile, place 1 chicken breast on work surface. Notice it has a thick end and a thin end. To create a pocket for the stuffing, insert long, thin knife (a boning knife is ideal) into middle of thick end, parallel to work surface. Slide knife in until it reaches middle of chicken. Move knife up and down within the chicken to form a pocket. You want to have a smaller opening where knife entered the chicken and a larger pocket within the chicken to stuff with couscous mixture. Repeat with remaining chicken breasts.

5. Spray grill rack with cooking spray or brush with oil. Heat coals or gas grill for medium heat. (Check the temperature of the coals by placing your hand, palm side down, near but not touching the cooking grill rack. If you can keep your hand there for 2 seconds [one-thousand one, one-thousand two], the temperature is high; 3 seconds is medium-high; 4 seconds is medium; 5 seconds is low.)

6. Use one hand to hold chicken with thick end up. With other hand, stuff 1/4 cup of the couscous into pocket. Repeat with remaining chicken. Brush chicken with oil.

7. In small bowl, mix 1/2 teaspoon salt, 1/2 teaspoon cumin and the pepper. Sprinkle mixture evenly over chicken breasts.

8. Grill chicken covered 15 to 20 minutes, turning occasionally, until juice of chicken is no longer pink when center of thickest part is cut (170°F) and stuffing is hot. To serve, slice each breast and layer on plate so stuffing is visible.

WHY IT WORKS: **CREATING COUSCOUS** Although it may look like a seed or a grain, couscous is actually pasta. Unlike spaghetti or macaroni, couscous is not extruded or rolled out and cut into pieces. Instead, couscous is made by hand. Native to the North African countries of Morocco, Algeria and Tunisia, couscous is one of the world's first pastas. To make it, durum semolina flour (a harder, coarser wheat than used in regular wheat flour) is mixed with water and rolled between the palms of the hand. With time and a great deal of patience, small pellets of pasta are formed, steamed and finally dried. Traditionally, couscous is steamed in a large pot (called a couscousiere) above simmering stews called tagines. The boxed couscous available in stores is much easier to prepare because it has already been steamed and dried so it is ready to cook.

1 Serving: Calories 320 (Calories from Fat 140); Total Fat 15g (Saturated Fat 5g; Trans Fat 0g); Cholesterol 100mg; Sodium 660mg; Total Carbohydrate 11g (Dietary Fiber 1g; Sugars 2g); Protein 34g • **% Daily Value:** Vitamin A 6%; Vitamin C 2%; Calcium 2%; Iron 10% **Exchanges:** 1 Starch, 4 1/2 Lean Meat • **Carbohydrate Choices:** 1

Chicken with Chipotle-Peach Glaze

PREP TIME: 10 MINUTES • START TO FINISH: 30 MINUTES   8 SERVINGS

1/2 cup peach preserves

1/4 cup lime juice

1 chipotle chile in adobo sauce
(from 7-oz can), seeded
and chopped

1 teaspoon adobo sauce
(from can of chiles)

2 tablespoons chopped fresh cilantro

1 teaspoon garlic-pepper blend

1/2 teaspoon ground cumin

1/2 teaspoon salt

8 boneless skinless chicken breasts
(about 2 1/2 lb)

4 ripe peaches, cut in half and pitted

Cilantro sprigs, if desired

1. Heat coals or gas grill for medium heat. (Check the temperature of the coals by placing your hand, palm side down, near but not touching the cooking grill rack. If you can keep your hand there for 2 seconds [one-thousand one, one-thousand two], the temperature is high; 3 seconds is medium-high; 4 seconds is medium; 5 seconds is low.)

2. In 1-quart saucepan, mix preserves, lime juice, chile and adobo sauce. Heat over low heat, stirring occasionally, until preserves are melted. Stir in chopped cilantro; set aside.

3. Mix garlic-pepper, cumin and salt together. Sprinkle both sides of chicken with mixture.

4. Grill chicken covered 15 to 20 minutes, turning once or twice and brushing with preserves mixture during last 2 minutes of grilling, until juice of chicken is no longer pink when center of thickest part is cut (170°F). Add peach halves to grill for last 2 to 3 minutes of grilling just until heated.

5. In 1-quart saucepan, heat any remaining preserves mixture to boiling; boil and stir 1 minute. Serve with chicken and peaches. Garnish with cilantro sprigs if desired.

1 Serving: Calories 250 (Calories from Fat 45); Total Fat 5g (Saturated Fat 1.5g; Trans Fat 0g); Cholesterol 85mg; Sodium 270mg; Total Carbohydrate 20g (Dietary Fiber 2g; Sugars 14g); Protein 32g • **% Daily Value:** Vitamin A 4%; Vitamin C 6%; Calcium 2%; Iron 8% • **Exchanges:** 1/2 Fruit, 1 Other Carbohydrate, 4 1/2 Very Lean Meat, 1/2 Fat • **Carbohydrate Choices:** 1

WHY IT WORKS: **CHIPOTLE CHILES** Of all of the peppers introduced to America in the last few decades, none has been as widely received as chipotle. Sweet, hot and smoky, chipotle complements everything from barbecue sauce to mayonnaise and has found its way into breads, biscuits and even stuffing recipes. Chipotle chiles are made by smoking jalapeño peppers (usually red jalapeños). The result is a leathery, brick-red chile that in Mexico is jokingly compared to a cigar butt in size and shape. Dried chipotles are not commonly found in American grocery stores. Instead they are usually mixed with a tomato-vinegar sauce called adobo and sold in small cans. When working with canned chipotle in adobo use caution and rubber gloves. One pepper is often more than enough to heat your whole dish; the remainder can be transferred to another container, covered and refrigerated.

Chicken with Chipotle-Peach Glaze

Thyme-Infused Chicken Breasts
WITH POMEGRANATE SAUCE

PREP TIME: 30 MINUTES • **START TO FINISH:** 1 HOUR 20 MINUTES   4 SERVINGS

Chicken

2 quarts (8 cups) cold water
1/2 cup salt (preferably non-iodized)
5 black peppercorns
4 cloves garlic, smashed
3 fresh thyme sprigs
4 bone-in skin-on chicken breasts
    (about 3 lb)
2 tablespoons vegetable oil

Sauce

2 tablespoons butter, softened
2 tablespoons all-purpose flour
2 tablespoons finely chopped onion
1 clove garlic, finely chopped
2 teaspoons tomato paste
1/2 cup white wine or chicken broth
1/2 cup chicken broth
1 fresh thyme sprig
1/2 cup pomegranate juice or
    cranberry juice
2 teaspoons packed brown sugar

1. In large bowl, mix cold water, salt, peppercorns, smashed garlic and 3 thyme sprigs until salt is dissolved. Add chicken and stir well. Cover with plastic wrap and refrigerate at least 30 minutes but no more than 3 hours.

2. Remove chicken from brine and pat dry with paper towels.

3. In 10-inch skillet, heat oil over medium-high heat until shimmering and hot. Add chicken, skin sides down, and cook 5 minutes or until golden brown. Use long-handled tongs to turn chicken and cook 5 minutes longer or until golden. Reduce heat to low.

4. Simmer uncovered about 20 minutes, without turning, until juice of chicken is no longer pink when thickest part is cut to bone (170°F). Remove chicken from skillet and place on plate, reserving drippings in skillet. Cover tightly with foil; set aside.

5. Meanwhile, in small bowl, mix butter and flour with your fingers or a spoon. Knead mixture until it is a smooth paste; set aside.

6. Pour out all but 1 tablespoon drippings from skillet. Place skillet over medium heat and stir in onion. Cook 3 minutes, stirring occasionally, or until soft. Add finely chopped garlic and cook 30 seconds, stirring constantly, until fragrant. Stir in tomato paste and cook 1 minute longer.

7. Add wine and increase heat to high. Heat to boiling, scraping any browned bits off bottom of skillet. Boil wine 5 minutes or until reduced to about 2 tablespoons.

8. Add broth and 1 thyme sprig to skillet. Boil 5 minutes, stirring occasionally, or until reduced by half. Add pomegranate juice and brown sugar. Heat to boiling, stirring pomegranate mixture with wire whisk.

9. Pinch off about half of the butter-flour paste. Drop this into boiling sauce and quickly beat in with wire whisk. Repeat with remaining paste, stirring constantly. Heat sauce to boiling and boil 2 minutes, stirring constantly. Serve sauce with chicken.

1 Serving: Calories 490 (Calories from Fat 240); Total Fat 26g (Saturated Fat 8g; Trans Fat 0.5g); Cholesterol 150mg; Sodium 3840mg; Total Carbohydrate 12g (Dietary Fiber 0g; Sugars 7g); Protein 51g • **% Daily Value:** Vitamin A 10%; Vitamin C 8%; Calcium 4%; Iron 15% • **Exchanges:** 1 Other Carbohydrate, 7 Lean Meat, 1 Fat • **Carbohydrate Choices:** 1

WHY IT WORKS: **FLOUR POWER** Flour is a good sauce thickener because it contains starch. However, the thickening power of flour's starch is released only when heated. Mixing flour with a little cold water results in a thick paste or dough. Mixing it with a lot of water and heating it to boiling gives you a smooth sauce. Why? When heated, starch (which usually looks like a little ball) breaks down into tiny pieces. These pieces now absorb great quantities of liquid and thicken your sauce.

Thyme-Infused Chicken Breasts with Pomegranate Sauce

Sautéed Turkey Cutlets
WITH ASPARAGUS AND RED BELL PEPPERS

PREP TIME: 20 MINUTES • **START TO FINISH:** 20 MINUTES   4 SERVINGS

1 turkey tenderloin (1 lb)
1/4 teaspoon salt
1/4 teaspoon freshly ground pepper
1/2 cup all-purpose flour
3 tablespoons olive oil
12 thin asparagus spears
1/2 large red bell pepper, cut into
    thin strips and strips cut in half
1/2 cup chicken broth
1 teaspoon grated lemon peel
3 tablespoons fresh lemon juice
2 tablespoons cold firm butter,
    cut into 3 pieces
2 tablespoons chopped fresh parsley

1. Cut turkey into 4 pieces. Place 1 piece, cut side up, between pieces of plastic wrap or waxed paper. Use flat side of meat mallet, pounder or rolling pin to gently pound each turkey piece to 1/4-inch thickness. Repeat with remaining turkey pieces.

2. Sprinkle turkey with salt and pepper. Place flour in shallow bowl. Coat turkey lightly with flour, dusting off excess.

3. In 10-inch skillet, heat 2 tablespoons of the oil over medium-high until shimmering and hot. Add turkey and cook about 3 minutes or until lightly browned. Flip and cook 1 minute longer. Remove turkey from skillet and place on plate. Cover tightly with foil.

4. Add remaining 1 tablespoon oil to skillet and stir in asparagus and bell pepper. Sauté 1 minute. Add broth and heat to boiling. Boil uncovered 2 minutes. Stir in lemon peel and lemon juice. When liquid returns to boiling, remove from heat. Beat in butter, 1 piece at a time, with wire whisk, adding the next piece only after the first has been completely beaten in and melted. When all of the butter has been beaten in, stir in parsley.

5. Place 1 turkey piece on each serving plate. Use kitchen tongs to remove asparagus and pepper strips from sauce and place next to cutlet. Spoon sauce over turkey and vegetables.

1 Serving: Calories 340 (Calories from Fat 160); Total Fat 17g (Saturated Fat 4.5g; Trans Fat 0g); Cholesterol 90mg; Sodium 370mg; Total Carbohydrate 16g (Dietary Fiber 2g; Sugars 2g); Protein 30g • **% Daily Value:** Vitamin A 40%; Vitamin C 45%; Calcium 4%; Iron 15% • **Exchanges:** 1 Starch, 4 Lean Meat, 1 Fat • **Carbohydrate Choices:** 1

WHY IT WORKS:

SAUTÉING IS SIMPLE Although it may sound like a fancy gourmet technique, sautéing is very simple to learn and extremely useful. The word *sauté* is a French term meaning "to jump." As the food cooks it is often stirred, shaken or flipped (jumped) to ensure even cooking. When sautéing, the pan is coated with a thin layer of oil and placed over fairly high heat. The main goal of sautéing is to quickly cook or brown; therefore, vegetables and meats are cut or pounded thin, like the turkey cutlets in this recipe. Choose to sauté when you have meats and vegetables that are naturally tender. The speed of the cooking process is too brief to soften tough or fibrous foods.

Sautéed Turkey Cutlets with Asparagus and Red Bell Peppers

Braised Chicken and Potatoes
WITH COCONUT-CURRY SAUCE

PREP TIME: 40 MINUTES • **START TO FINISH:** 1 HOUR 20 MINUTES   4 SERVINGS

2 teaspoons cumin seed

1 teaspoon coriander seed

1 teaspoon ground turmeric

1/2 teaspoon ground fenugreek

1/4 cup vegetable oil

4 whole cloves

4 green cardamom pods

1 cinnamon stick

2 medium onions, chopped (1 cup)

2 tablespoons grated gingerroot

4 cloves garlic, finely chopped

2 dried bay leaves

1 jalapeño chile, seeded and finely chopped

1 cup canned coconut milk (not cream of coconut)

8 boneless skinless chicken thighs (2 lb)

3 medium Yukon Gold potatoes (1 lb), cut into 1 1/2-inch chunks

1 can (14.5 oz) diced tomatoes, undrained

1 1/2 teaspoons salt

2 cups packed fresh spinach leaves

1. In 8-inch skillet, heat cumin and coriander seed over medium-high heat 5 minutes, stirring constantly, until fragrant and some seed pops. Remove seed from skillet to a plate and cool completely.

2. In spice or coffee grinder (used for grinding spices only), grind roasted seed to a fine powder. (If you don't have a grinder, place seed in resealable plastic food-storage bag and pound with flat side of meat mallet; mixture will be not as finely ground but will still be delicious.) Stir in turmeric and fenugreek; set aside.

3. In 12-inch skillet, heat oil over medium-high heat until shimmering and hot. Add cloves, cardamom pods and cinnamon stick. Cook 4 minutes, stirring occasionally, until cinnamon stick uncurls. Use slotted spoon to remove spices from oil; discard spices.

4. Add onions to oil and cook, stirring occasionally, until soft and slightly brown. Add gingerroot, garlic, bay leaves and chile and cook 3 minutes. Add coconut milk, chicken, potatoes, tomatoes, dry spice blend and salt. Reduce heat to medium. Cover and simmer 25 to 35 minutes or until potatoes are tender and juice of chicken is no longer pink when center of thickest part is cut (180°F). Remove and discard bay leaves.

5. Simmer uncovered 5 minutes longer to reduce sauce a bit. Add spinach and cook uncovered 1 minute or just until spinach is wilted.

1 Serving: Calories 750 (Calories from Fat 380); Total Fat 43g (Saturated Fat 17g; Trans Fat 0g); Cholesterol 140mg; Sodium 1210mg; Total Carbohydrate 38g (Dietary Fiber 7g; Sugars 9g); Protein 54g • **% Daily Value:** Vitamin A 40%; Vitamin C 30%; Calcium 15%; Iron 40% • **Exchanges:** 1 1/2 Starch, 1/2 Other Carbohydrate, 1 Vegetable, 6 1/2 Medium-Fat Meat, 2 Fat • **Carbohydrate Choices:** 2 1/2

WHY IT WORKS: **HEATING SPICES** To best retain the flavor of spices and herbs, water is removed and spices and herbs are dried. This can be a problem as adding dried basil to a boiling soup or ground cinnamon to muffins may release only some of the herb's or spice's flavor. The secret to getting the most out of your spice cabinet? Preheat your herbs and whole spices by dry roasting or frying. Heating releases the trapped essential oils, allowing them to more easily flavor your dish. To experiment, try heating whole spices like cumin, peppercorn or cinnamon in a small skillet over medium-low heat. Within minutes you will smell the essential oils reawaken! Allow them to cool on a plate before grinding and adding to your dish. You will be surprised by the intensity of the flavor.

Blue Cheese–Stuffed Pork Tenderloin

2 tablespoons butter

1 small onion, finely chopped (1/3 cup)

1 clove garlic, finely chopped

1 cup (4 oz) crumbled blue cheese (preferably an aged Gorgonzola)

3 tablespoons coarsely chopped dried cherries

3 tablespoons chopped pecans

2 teaspoons chopped fresh or 1 teaspoon dried thyme leaves

2 pork tenderloins (1 lb each)

1/4 teaspoon salt

1/4 teaspoon pepper

1 tablespoon vegetable oil

1. Adjust oven rack to middle position. Heat oven to 400°F.

2. In 8-inch skillet, heat butter over medium heat until melted. Add onion and cook 3 minutes, stirring occasionally, until soft. Add garlic and cook 30 seconds. Remove from heat and cool about 5 minutes.

3. In medium bowl, stir cheese vigorously with spoon. Stir in cooled onion mixture, cherries, pecans and thyme; set aside.

4. Place 1 pork piece on work surface with short side facing you. Use knife to slit in half lengthwise without going all the way through. Open pork like a book. Repeat with remaining pork. Spread half of the cheese mixture in center of each pork piece. Close up pork and tie with kitchen twine to secure. Season outside with salt and pepper.

5. In 12-inch ovenproof skillet, heat oil over medium-high heat until shimmering and hot. Add pork and cook about 4 minutes or until browned. Flip, being careful not to open them up, and cook about 4 minutes longer. Insert ovenproof meat thermometer so tip is in the thickest part of pork.

6. Place skillet in oven and roast 10 to 15 minutes or until meat thermometer inserted in center reads 155°F. Remove from oven and allow to rest, loosely covered with foil, about 5 minutes (temperature will continue to rise to 160°F). Slice each pork piece into 6 pieces. (If you don't have an ovenproof skillet, after browning pork in skillet, carefully place them in foil-lined 13 × 9-inch pan and then place in oven.)

1 Serving: Calories 340 (Calories from Fat 180); Total Fat 20g (Saturated Fat 8g; Trans Fat 0g); Cholesterol 115mg; Sodium 450mg; Total Carbohydrate 5g (Dietary Fiber 0g; Sugars 3g); Protein 37g • **% Daily Value:** Vitamin A 8%; Vitamin C 0%; Calcium 10%; Iron 10% • **Exchanges:** 1/2 Other Carbohydrate, 5 Lean Meat, 1 Fat • **Carbohydrate Choices:** 1/2

WHY IT WORKS: **A RAINBOW OF COLORS** Just as plants owe their green color to chlorophyll, meat is red because of a pigment called myoglobin. Myoglobin is a sensitive chemical, readily changing color when exposed to light or air. For example, without air (before slaughter or when packaged in the airtight packages often found at warehouse clubs) myoglobin colors meat a dark purple. When exposed to oxygen, myoglobin changes meat to its characteristic cherry red. Too much oxygen, combined with the florescent lights in the grocery store, can make the meat turn brown. Although this brown is unattractive, it doesn't always mean the meat is spoiled—just handled improperly. The one color to watch out for is green; it signals bacteria growth and bad meat.

Cuban Grilled Mojito Pork Tenderloins

PREP TIME: 25 MINUTES • **START TO FINISH:** 1 HOUR 10 MINUTES   6 SERVINGS

Pork

1/2 cup packed light brown sugar
1/2 cup fresh mint leaves
2 tablespoons salt (preferably non-iodized)
3 cups cold water
1/2 cup white rum
1/2 cup lime juice
2 pork tenderloins (1 lb each)
1 tablespoon vegetable oil

Dry Rub

2 tablespoons cumin seed
2 tablespoons coriander seed
2 teaspoons packed light brown sugar
1 teaspoon ground mustard

1. In medium metal bowl, mix 1/2 cup brown sugar, the mint and salt. Use handle of wooden spoon to crush mint into the brown sugar and salt. You are bruising (or muddling) the leaves to release flavor. When mint is fragrant and leaves are slightly crushed, add cold water, rum and lime juice. Stir well to dissolve salt and sugar.

2. Pour mint marinade into 1-gallon resealable plastic food-storage bag. Add pork and seal bag. Refrigerate at least 30 minutes but no longer than 8 hours.

3. Spray grill rack with cooking spray or brush with oil. Heat coals or gas grill for medium-high heat. (Check the temperature of the coals by placing your hand, palm side down, near but not touching the cooking grill rack. If you can keep your hand there for 2 seconds [one-thousand one, one-thousand two], the temperature is high; 3 seconds is medium-high; 4 seconds is medium; 5 seconds is low.)

4. Meanwhile, in 8-inch skillet, heat cumin and coriander seed over medium heat 3 minutes, stirring constantly, until fragrant (you are dry-roasting the spices, so there is no need for oil). Remove seed from skillet to a plate and cool completely. (If left in skillet, seed will continue to cook and may burn.)

5. In spice or coffee grinder (used for grinding spices only), grind roasted seed, brown sugar and mustard to a fine powder. (If you don't have a grinder, place seed in resealable plastic food-storage bag and pound with flat side of meat mallet; mixture will be not as finely ground but will still be delicious.)

6. Remove pork from marinade and pat dry with paper towels. Rub pork with oil and coat each with half of the dry rub.

7. Grill pork covered about 20 minutes, turning to brown all sides. Remove pork from grill when still slightly pink in center and meat thermometer inserted in center reads 155°F. Allow pork to rest 5 minutes (temperature will continue to rise to 160°F). Slice pork to serve. (To broil, line broiler pan with foil. Spray broiler rack with cooking spray or brush with oil. Broil pork 4 to 5 inches from heat as directed above.)

WHY IT WORKS:

HERB HOW-TO What is the difference between an herb and a spice? Herbs are generally leaves and come from subtropical or non-tropical plants (basil, rosemary or thyme, for example). Spices include just about everything else that is not a leaf: roots (ginger), flower buds (cloves), bark (cinnamon) and seeds (nutmeg). Spice preparation usually includes some form of grating or grinding. Herbs, especially fresh ones, need a lighter approach. Once the leaves of fresh herbs are damaged (crushed, sliced or torn) they begin to break down and release flavor. For this reason, add fresh herbs toward the end of cooking.

1 Serving: Calories 240 (Calories from Fat 80); Total Fat 9g (Saturated Fat 2.5g; Trans Fat 0g); Cholesterol 90mg; Sodium 660mg; Total Carbohydrate 8g (Dietary Fiber 0g; Sugars 6g); Protein 33g • **% Daily Value:** Vitamin A 0%; Vitamin C 2%; Calcium 4%; Iron 20% • **Exchanges:** 1/2 Other Carbohydrate, 5 Very Lean Meat, 1 Fat • **Carbohydrate Choices:** 1/2

Cuban Grilled Mojito Pork Tenderloins

Pan-Roasted Pork Chops

WITH APRICOT-CARAMEL SAUCE

PREP TIME: 1 HOUR • **START TO FINISH:** 1 HOUR 　　　　　　　　　　　　　　　　　　　　　　4 SERVINGS

Sauce

1/4 cup sugar

1 tablespoon water

1 medium Golden Delicious apple
or other sweet crisp apple,
finely chopped (1 cup)

1 medium onion, finely chopped
(1/2 cup)

2 cloves garlic, finely chopped

1/4 teaspoon ground cinnamon

3 tablespoons cider vinegar

1 3/4 cups apple cider

3/4 cup chicken broth

2 dried bay leaves

1 fresh thyme sprig

1/2 cup apricot preserves

3 tablespoons cold firm butter,
cut into 3 pieces

Pork Chops

3 slices thick-cut bacon

4 pork loin or rib chops, about
1 1/4 inches thick (1 1/2 lb)

1/4 teaspoon salt

1/4 teaspoon freshly ground pepper

2 tablespoons chopped fresh parsley

1. In 10-inch skillet (preferably nonstick), mix sugar and water with wooden spoon. Heat over medium-high heat 5 to 7 minutes, without stirring, until sugar turns dark golden brown and just begins to smoke (do not allow to burn). Remove from heat.

2. Add apple, onion, garlic and cinnamon to skillet and stir to coat (sugar may clump and harden at first but will melt again when heated). Return to heat and cook 3 minutes, stirring occasionally, until some liquid escapes from mixture.

3. Remove from heat and add vinegar (avert your head; the fumes from the vinegar can take your breath away). Stir and return to heat. Slowly stir in apple cider and broth (sugar may clump—that is okay, it will melt). When all liquids have been added, add bay leaves and thyme.

4. Heat to boiling. Reduce heat to medium. Simmer uncovered 20 to 30 minutes, stirring occasionally, until reduced by half.

5. Meanwhile, heat oven to 375°F. In 10-inch ovenproof skillet, cook bacon over medium-high heat until crisp and brown. Remove bacon from skillet; drain on paper towels, crumble and set aside. There should be about 1 tablespoon bacon drippings remaining in pan. If there is more, pour off excess; if there is less, add a little vegetable oil.

6. Sprinkle pork with salt and pepper. Place pork in bacon drippings in skillet and cook 4 minutes or until brown. Flip and brown on other side, about 4 minutes longer. Cover skillet with lid or foil and place in oven. Roast 8 minutes or until slightly firm when touched and meat thermometer inserted in center reads 155°F (pork will continue to cook to 160°F when removed from oven). Remove pork from skillet and place on plate. Cover tightly with foil; set aside.

7. The skillet used to cook the pork should have some cooking liquid in it. Place this skillet over medium heat. Pour the reduced sauce into skillet and stir to combine. Stir in apricot preserves and heat sauce to boiling. Boil 5 minutes, stirring occasionally, until slightly thickened. Remove skillet from heat. Beat in butter, 1 piece at a time, with wire whisk, adding the next piece only after the first has been completely beaten in and melted. When all of the butter has been beaten in, taste sauce and season with salt and pepper if desired. Remove and discard bay leaves and thyme sprig.

8. Place pork on warm serving plates and top with sauce. Sprinkle with crumbled bacon and the parsley.

1 Serving: Calories 580 (Calories from Fat 210); Total Fat 23g (Saturated Fat 9g; Trans Fat 0.5g); Cholesterol 105mg; Sodium 600mg; Total Carbohydrate 62g (Dietary Fiber 2g; Sugars 48g); Protein 31g • **% Daily Value:** Vitamin A 15%; Vitamin C 10%; Calcium 4%; Iron 15% • **Exchanges:** 4 Other Carbohydrate, 4 1/2 Medium-Fat Meat • **Carbohydrate Choices:** 4

RECIPE Rx: JUST ADD WATER Some recipes for caramelized sugar have you start with dry sugar in a pan while others, such as this one, have you add a little water. Why? Surprisingly, in order for sugar to caramelize it must be heated until all of the water is evaporated

off. Therefore it seems like a step in the wrong direction to add water. Actually, the small amount of water added in this recipe is really more for security than anything else. If we just heated the sugar itself it might heat unevenly, parts of it caramelizing before the rest even heated up. The water evens out the heat by making the sugar into a syrup. That doesn't mean that you can take your eye off the pan. The process happens very fast, going from delicious caramel to bitter blackjack (the pastry name for burnt sugar), so watch carefully.

Pan-Roasted Pork Chops with Apricot-Caramel Sauce

Cashew-Breaded Pork Loin Chops

WITH SPICED PEACH CHUTNEY

PREP TIME: 1 HOUR • START TO FINISH: 1 HOUR   4 SERVINGS

Chutney

1 tablespoon vegetable oil

1 small onion, chopped (1/3 cup)

1 tablespoon grated gingerroot

1 clove garlic, finely chopped

1 jalapeño chile, seeded and
    finely chopped

1/2 bag (16-oz size) frozen sliced
    peaches (1 cup)

1/2 cup fresh or frozen cranberries

1/2 cup packed light brown sugar

2 tablespoons cider vinegar

1/2 teaspoon curry powder

1/4 teaspoon salt

Pork

1/2 cup panko (Japanese bread
    crumbs)

1/2 cup finely chopped cashews

1 egg

1 egg white

1/2 cup all-purpose flour

1/2 teaspoon salt

1/2 teaspoon freshly ground pepper

1/4 cup vegetable oil

4 boneless pork loin chops,
    1/2 inch thick (1 lb)

1. In 3-quart saucepan, heat 1 tablespoon oil over medium heat until shimmering and hot. Add onion and cook 3 minutes, stirring occasionally, until soft. Stir in gingerroot, garlic and chile and cook about 1 minute, stirring constantly.

2. Stir in peaches, cranberries, brown sugar, vinegar, curry powder and 1/4 teaspoon salt. Cook uncovered 20 minutes, stirring occasionally, until peaches begin to fall apart and cranberries soften and burst. Remove from heat and keep warm. (Chutney can be covered and refrigerated up to 1 week.)

3. In shallow bowl, mix bread crumbs and cashews. In another shallow bowl, beat egg and egg white with wire whisk. In pie plate or shallow bowl, mix flour, 1/2 teaspoon salt and the pepper. Place wire rack on cookie sheet.

4. First, lightly coat 1 pork chop with seasoned flour; shake off excess. Next, place in egg mixture; allow excess to drip off. Finally, place pork in bread crumb mixture and coat well. Place on wire rack while you coat remaining pork.

5. In 12-inch skillet, heat 1/4 cup oil over medium heat until shimmering and hot. Place pork in skillet and cook 3 minutes or until golden and crisp on one side. Flip and cook other side, about 3 minutes longer or until slightly pink in center.

6. Serve pork with warm chutney.

1 Serving: Calories 700 (Calories from Fat 300); Total Fat 33g (Saturated Fat 7g; Trans Fat 0g); Cholesterol 105mg; Sodium 640mg; Total Carbohydrate 73g (Dietary Fiber 4g; Sugars 44g); Protein 27g • **% Daily Value:** Vitamin A 6%; Vitamin C 50%; Calcium 8%; Iron 25% • **Exchanges:** 2 Starch, 3 Other Carbohydrate, 3 Medium-Fat Meat, 3 Fat • **Carbohydrate Choices:** 5

WHY IT WORKS: **THE RIGHT PAN FOR THE JOB** Not all cooking equipment is created equal. When sautéing the pork chops for this recipe it is essential that your pan heats up evenly to efficiently conduct the range top's heat to the pork. Copper and aluminum—the best heat conductors—make poor pans as they react easily with food. Instead, use a pan made with stainless steel (a nonreactive metal) coating a copper or aluminum core. This makes a heavy pan that heats slowly, but maintains even heat on the pan bottom.

Filet of Beef
WITH MUSTARD-HERB CRUST

PREP TIME: 30 MINUTES • **START TO FINISH:** 1 HOUR   4 SERVINGS

Topping

1 1/2 cups fine soft bread crumbs
   (about 3 slices bread)
1/4 cup olive oil
1/4 cup finely chopped fresh parsley
2 tablespoons finely chopped fresh
   mint leaves
1/2 teaspoon salt
1/2 teaspoon freshly ground pepper

Beef

4 center-cut beef filets mignons,
   1 3/4 inch thick (8 oz each)
Salt and pepper, if desired
1 tablespoon olive oil
1 tablespoon butter
3 tablespoons Dijon mustard

1. In small bowl, mix bread crumbs, 1/4 cup oil, the parsley, mint, 1/2 teaspoon salt and 1/2 teaspoon pepper; set aside.

2. Adjust oven rack so top of beef will be 4 to 6 inches from heat. Set oven control to broil.

3. Sprinkle beef with salt and pepper if desired. In 10-inch ovenproof skillet, heat 1 tablespoon oil and the butter over medium-high heat until butter is melted and no longer sizzles. Cook beef in oil mixture 5 minutes or until browned. Flip and cook 10 minutes longer or until brown and meat thermometer inserted in center of beef reads 145°F (medium-rare).

4. Divide mustard among beef, spreading evenly over tops. Spoon about 1/4 cup topping evenly over each filet. Use pancake turner to press down on topping so it sticks to filets. Broil 2 minutes or until bread crumbs are lightly browned.

5. Remove beef from oven and allow to stand 5 minutes before serving.

1 Serving: Calories 640 (Calories from Fat 330); Total Fat 36g (Saturated Fat 10g; Trans Fat 1g); Cholesterol 120mg; Sodium 1040mg; Total Carbohydrate 31g (Dietary Fiber 1g; Sugars 3g); Protein 48g • **% Daily Value:** Vitamin A 15%; Vitamin C 4%; Calcium 10%; Iron 35% • **Exchanges:** 2 Starch, 6 Medium-Fat Meat, 1 High-Fat Meat • **Carbohydrate Choices:** 2

WHY IT WORKS:
THE HEAT IS ON Mustard seed, which is ground to make the yellow ballpark condiment as well as the fancy brown variety, is a member of the cabbage family. Like its relatives, broccoli and Brussels sprouts, mustard can be quite potent if not prepared correctly. The offending ingredient responsible for its notorious smell—isothiocyanate—is activated by heat and water. This chemical is released when ground mustard is mixed with hot water or when cabbage is overcooked. Although pleasantly sharp in small amounts, mustard can be chokingly strong if too much is used. To avoid overpowering your guests, remember that once heated, ground mustard or crushed mustard seed gets hotter as it stands.

Thai Glazed Beef

WITH CHILE-LEMON GRASS SAUCE

PREP TIME: 40 MINUTES • **START TO FINISH:** 1 HOUR 10 MINUTES   4 SERVINGS

Beef

4 tablespoons peanut or vegetable oil

3 cloves garlic, finely chopped

1 tablespoon grated gingerroot

1 1/2 teaspoons freshly ground pepper

2 teaspoons ground coriander

1/2 lb beef tenderloin, cut into 1-inch pieces

1/4 cup sugar

3 tablespoons lime juice

2 tablespoons fish sauce

1 tablespoon balsamic vinegar

Sauce

1 medium onion, finely chopped (1/2 cup)

1/4 cup finely chopped lemon grass

2 cloves garlic, finely chopped

1 small jalapeño chile, seeded and chopped

1/2 cup chicken broth

2 tablespoons fish sauce

2 tablespoons oyster sauce

Rice

4 cups hot cooked jasmine rice

1. In medium bowl, mix 1 tablespoon of the oil, the garlic, gingerroot, pepper, coriander and beef. Cover and refrigerate 30 minutes or up to 8 hours.

2. In 12-inch skillet (preferably nonstick), heat remaining 3 tablespoons oil over medium-high heat until shimmering and hot. Add marinated beef. Cook 6 to 8 minutes, stirring constantly so garlic doesn't burn, until beef is browned and cooked through. Drain fat.

3. In small bowl, mix sugar, lime juice, 2 tablespoons fish sauce and the vinegar. Add mixture to skillet with beef. Stir and heat to boiling. Watch carefully as liquid evaporates to avoid scorching. When only about 1 tablespoon liquid is left, use slotted spoon to remove beef to bowl; cover to keep warm.

4. Add onion to skillet and cook 1 minute, stirring frequently. Stir in lemon grass, garlic and chile. Cook 30 seconds, stirring constantly. Add broth, 2 tablespoons fish sauce and the oyster sauce. Heat to boiling, stirring occasionally. Reduce heat to medium and simmer 1 minute longer. Return beef to skillet and cook 30 seconds, stirring constantly. Serve with rice.

1 Serving: Calories 480 (Calories from Fat 150); Total Fat 16g (Saturated Fat 3.5g; Trans Fat 0g); Cholesterol 30mg; Sodium 1770mg; Total Carbohydrate 63g (Dietary Fiber 2g; Sugars 16g); Protein 19g • **% Daily Value:** Vitamin A 2%; Vitamin C 6%; Calcium 4%; Iron 20% • **Exchanges:** 2 Starch, 2 Other Carbohydrate, 2 Lean Meat, 2 Fat • **Carbohydrate Choices:** 4

WHY IT WORKS: **LOOK TO LEMON GRASS** Once a mysterious ingredient in Thai restaurants, lemon grass is now available in many supermarkets. Resembling a green reed, lemon grass is an ancient herb of Southeast Asia. Its flavor is reminiscent of citrus, bay leaves and pepper, and cuts through the more pungent ingredients of Thai cooking. As with lots of herbs, it's the oils in the lemon grass that hold all the flavor, so you may want to crush the stalk before you chop it in this recipe.

RECIPE R_X: CUTTING THE GRASS At first, lemon grass doesn't even look edible. However, with a few easy steps it will be ready for this recipe. First, pick a stalk that is thick, heavy and not overly woody and has no brown discoloration. Make sure it has a delicate citrus perfume and the bulb is tightly bound together. Next, use a knife or your fingernails to remove the thick outer leaves. You should see a tender white/yellow inner stalk. Slice this stalk into very thin circles and then use the side of your knife to lightly crush the slices. The tough outer leaves can be cleaned and added to broths for a Thai accent; just remember to discard before eating.

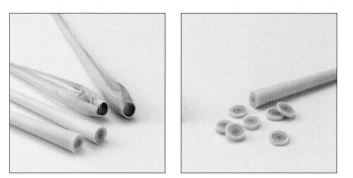

Thai Glazed Beef with Chile-Lemon Grass Sauce

Texas T-Bones

4 beef T-bone steaks, about 3/4 inch thick (10 to 12 oz each)
2 cloves garlic, cut in half
4 teaspoons black peppercorns, crushed
1/4 cup butter, softened
1 tablespoon Dijon mustard
1/2 teaspoon Worcestershire sauce
1/4 teaspoon lime juice
Salt and pepper, if desired

1. Heat coals or gas grill for medium heat. (Check the temperature of the coals by placing your hand, palm side down, near but not touching the cooking grill rack. If you can keep your hand there for 2 seconds [one-thousand one, one-thousand two], the temperature is high; 3 seconds is medium-high; 4 seconds is medium; 5 seconds is low.)

2. Trim fat on steaks to 1/4-inch thickness. Rub garlic on steak. Press peppercorns into steak. (An easy way to smash peppercorns is to place them in a resealable plastic food-storage bag or between 2 layers of paper towels and crush them with a heavy skillet, rolling pin or the flat side of a meat mallet.)

3. In small bowl, mix remaining ingredients except salt and pepper until a soft paste is formed. Place this mixture onto square of plastic wrap and shape into a roll. Refrigerate while you make the steak.

4. Grill steak covered 10 to 14 minutes for medium doneness, turning once. Sprinkle with salt and pepper if desired. Remove butter from plastic wrap and slice into 4 pieces. Top each steak with butter slice.

1 Serving: Calories 370 (Calories from Fat 210); Total Fat 24g (Saturated Fat 10g; Trans Fat 1g); Cholesterol 125mg; Sodium 260mg; Total Carbohydrate 2g (Dietary Fiber 0g; Sugars 0g); Protein 37g • **% Daily Value:** Vitamin A 10%; Vitamin C 0%; Calcium 2%; Iron 20% • **Exchanges:** 5 Medium-Fat Meat • **Carbohydrate Choices:** 0

WHY IT WORKS: **SUCCESSFUL STEAK SHOPPING** Choosing a good steak is like choosing a good car. The package and price might be right, but there is no guarantee of what is inside. At least with a steak there are a few clues to perfection. When choosing a steak to grill, look for cuts with flavor and tenderness, such as fillet, tenderloin, top loin (New York Strip) or T-Bone. These steaks are from the short loin, or middle, of the steer's back. Because they get little exercise, they tend to be very tender. Next, look at the grade. The top three grades of beef are Prime, Choice and Select. Grades are given based on the amount of fat within the meat, not on the edges. This internal fat, called marbling, is important for flavor and cooking. Prime steaks (most of which are sold to restaurants) have a higher fat content than Choice or Select, so they can withstand the heat of the grill without drying out. Finally, make sure the package is empty of liquid, which can indicate that the meat has been frozen.

Beef Tenderloin

WITH ROSEMARY-BALSAMIC REDUCTION

PREP TIME: 30 MINUTES • START TO FINISH: 45 MINUTES   6 SERVINGS

Beef

1 beef tenderloin (3 lb), trimmed
   of fat and trussed with twine
   (have butcher do this)
2 tablespoons olive oil
1/2 teaspoon salt

Sauce

1 tablespoon olive oil
2 tablespoons finely chopped shallots
1/2 cup dry red wine or beef broth
1/4 cup balsamic vinegar
1 cup low-sodium beef broth
1/3 cup dried cranberries
1 fresh rosemary sprig
2 tablespoons cold firm butter,
   cut into 3 pieces

1. Adjust oven rack to the middle position. Heat oven to 450°F.

2. Rub beef with 2 tablespoons oil and sprinkle with salt. Heat 12-inch oven-proof skillet over high heat until hot. Add beef and sear on all sides until well browned.

3. Place skillet in oven and roast beef 15 minutes. (If you don't have an oven-proof skillet, place beef in shallow roasting pan.) Remove from oven and flip beef. Roast 10 to 15 minutes longer or until meat thermometer inserted in center reads 135°F. Remove beef from skillet and place on warm platter. Cover tightly with foil (temperature will rise to 145°F for medium-rare).

4. Place skillet (or roasting pan) over medium-high heat. Add 1 tablespoon oil and the shallots. Cook 1 to 2 minutes, stirring occasionally, until shallots brown slightly.

5. Increase heat to high and add wine and vinegar. Heat to boiling. Boil uncovered 5 minutes, stirring occasionally, until reduced so about 1/4 cup liquid remains. Scrape up any browned bits from bottom of skillet, then add broth, cranberries and rosemary. Heat to boiling. Boil 5 to 7 minutes, stirring occasionally, until slightly thickened. Remove from heat and remove and discard rosemary sprig. Beat in butter, 1 piece at a time, with wire whisk, adding the next piece only after the first has been completely beaten in and melted.

6. To serve, cut beef into 1 1/2-inch slices. Divide sauce among serving plates and layer slices of beef on top.

1 Serving: Calories 420 (Calories from Fat 220); Total Fat 25g (Saturated Fat 8g; Trans Fat 1g); Cholesterol 120mg; Sodium 350mg; Total Carbohydrate 7g (Dietary Fiber 0g; Sugars 5g); Protein 43g • **% Daily Value:** Vitamin A 6%; Vitamin C 0%; Calcium 2%; Iron 20% • **Exchanges:** 1/2 Other Carbohydrate, 6 Lean Meat, 1 Fat • **Carbohydrate Choices:** 1/2

WHY IT WORKS: **THE LIFE OF VINEGAR** Vinegar is wine that went too far. Grape juice, with its high sugar content, is a favored home for friendly yeast. As the yeast eats the juice's sugar, alcohol is produced, turning the juice into wine. Usually the vintner, not wanting to lose money on a good bottle, stops the yeast either by adding sulfites, heating the wine to kill the yeast, or separating the yeast out. However, if allowed to continue eating the wine's sugar, yeast will stop producing alcohol and produce acid instead. Voilà! Vinegar is born. Typical vinegars have around 4% to 5% acidity.

Flank Steak

WITH CHIMICHURRI SAUCE

PREP TIME: 15 MINUTES • START TO FINISH: 4 HOURS 30 MINUTES   4 SERVINGS

Steak

1 beef flank steak (1 1/2 lb)

Sauce

1/4 cup chopped fresh parsley
1 cup vegetable oil
1/2 cup white wine vinegar
1/2 cup lemon juice
1 teaspoon crushed red pepper
4 cloves garlic, finely chopped

1. Make cuts about 1/2 inch apart and 1/8 inch deep in diamond pattern in both sides of beef. Place beef in shallow glass or plastic dish or resealable plastic food-storage bag.

2. In tightly covered container, shake all sauce ingredients. Pour 1 cup of the sauce over beef; turn beef to coat with sauce. To marinate, cover dish or seal bag and refrigerate at least 4 hours but no longer than 24 hours, turning beef occasionally. Cover remaining sauce and set aside to serve with beef.

3. Spray grill rack with cooking spray or brush with oil. Heat coals or gas grill for medium heat. (Check the temperature of the coals by placing your hand, palm side down, near but not touching the cooking grill rack. If you can keep your hand there for 2 seconds [one-thousand one, one-thousand two], the temperature is high; 3 seconds is medium-high; 4 seconds is medium; 5 seconds is low.)

4. Remove beef from marinade; set marinade aside. Grill beef uncovered 12 to 16 minutes for medium doneness, brushing with marinade and turning once. Discard any remaining marinade. Cut beef diagonally across grain into thin slices. Serve with remaining sauce.

1 Serving: Calories 750 (Calories from Fat 590); Total Fat 66g (Saturated Fat 12g; Trans Fat 0.5g); Cholesterol 90mg; Sodium 90mg; Total Carbohydrate 5g (Dietary Fiber 0g; Sugars 2g); Protein 35g • **% Daily Value:** Vitamin A 15%; Vitamin C 10%; Calcium 2%; Iron 20% • **Exchanges:** 1/2 Starch, 5 High-Fat Meat, 5 Fat • **Carbohydrate Choices:** 1/2

WHY IT WORKS: **KEEPING IT SAFE** Grilling is one of the best ways to cook meat; the flavors are brighter and aromas are outstanding. However, anytime you are dealing with raw meat, care must be taken. All meat, no matter how fresh, clean or organic it is, naturally has bacteria on it. Once meat is cooked to the correct temperature (for cuts of beef at least 145°F), bacteria is destroyed and there is no more danger. The problem arises when surfaces (like cutting boards) and liquids (like marinades) come into contact with food that will not be heated to this safe temperature. In this recipe, make sure that you do not use the marinade from the meat as a sauce, because it probably contains bacteria. Also, wash all areas that come into contact with the raw meat. Understanding food safety is the best way not to get sick.

Beef Tagine with Honey, Prunes and Almonds

PREP TIME: 30 MINUTES • START TO FINISH: 1 HOUR 50 MINUTES   4 SERVINGS

1 boneless beef chuck roast (2 lb),
   cut into 1-inch cubes
1 1/2 teaspoons salt
1 tablespoon vegetable oil
1 medium onion, chopped (1/2 cup)
2 cloves garlic, finely chopped
3 1/2 cups chicken broth
1 teaspoon ground ginger
1 teaspoon freshly ground pepper
1/2 teaspoon saffron threads,
   if desired, crushed between
   fingers to a powder
1 cup pitted prunes
1/4 cup honey
3/4 teaspoon ground cinnamon
1/2 teaspoon ground cumin
1/4 cup slivered almonds
Juice of 1 lemon (3 tablespoons)
1/2 teaspoon orange flower water,
   if desired
2 tablespoons chopped fresh parsley
Hot cooked couscous or brown rice,
   if desired

1. Sprinkle beef with 1/2 teaspoon of the salt.

2. In 4- or 5-quart Dutch oven or heavy pot, heat oil over medium-high heat until shimmering and hot. Add half of the beef and cook 4 minutes, stirring occasionally, until evenly browned. Use slotted spoon to remove beef and place in bowl. Repeat with remaining beef.

3. Add additional oil to pan if necessary. Add onion and cook 4 minutes, stirring constantly, until soft. Add garlic and cook 30 seconds, stirring constantly.

4. Return beef to pan. Stir in broth, ginger, pepper, remaining 1 teaspoon salt and the saffron if desired. Heat to boiling, stirring occasionally. Reduce heat to low. Gently simmer uncovered 1 hour, stirring occasionally.

5. Stir in prunes, honey, cinnamon and cumin. Cook uncovered 20 to 25 minutes, stirring occasionally, until beef is tender and prunes are plumped but not falling apart.

6. Stir in almonds, lemon juice and orange flower water if desired. Sprinkle with parsley and serve over couscous if desired.

1 Serving: Calories 560 (Calories from Fat 220); Total Fat 24g (Saturated Fat 7g; Trans Fat 0.5g); Cholesterol 85mg; Sodium 1850mg; Total Carbohydrate 51g (Dietary Fiber 5g; Sugars 36g); Protein 35g • **% Daily Value:** Vitamin A 8%; Vitamin C 8%; Calcium 8%; Iron 30% • **Exchanges:** 1 1/2 Fruit, 2 Other Carbohydrate, 5 Lean Meat, 2 Fat • **Carbohydrate Choices:** 3 1/2

WHY IT WORKS:

BUSY BEES Honey begins its life in much the same way as maple syrup, as slightly sweet vegetable sap. But unlike maple syrup, whose sap is collected from trees, the sap of honey—called nectar—is collected from flowers. As the bee carries nectar from flowers to the hive, its body breaks down the nectar's complex sugars into simpler parts. At the hive, the nectar is stored in a very thin layer on the honeycomb to speed up evaporation of water, concentrating, or "ripening," the honey. By the time beekeepers remove the comb from the hive, honey can be over 80% sugar.

Shrimp Pilaf Florentine

PREP TIME: 15 MINUTES • START TO FINISH: 30 MINUTES   4 SERVINGS

1 tablespoon olive oil

1 1/2 cups uncooked orzo or
   rosamarina pasta (8 oz)

1 small red bell pepper,
   chopped (1/2 cup)

2 medium green onions, sliced
   (2 tablespoons)

2 cloves garlic, finely chopped

2 teaspoons fresh chopped or
   1/2 teaspoon dried dill weed

1 teaspoon grated lemon peel

1/2 teaspoon salt

1 can (14 oz) chicken broth

1 cup water

2 cups shredded spinach

1 package (8 oz) frozen cooked
   medium shrimp (1 1/2 cups),
   thawed and tails peeled

1/4 cup grated Parmesan cheese

1. In 12-inch skillet, heat oil over medium-high heat. Cook pasta, bell pepper, green onions and garlic in oil 2 to 3 minutes, stirring constantly, until vegetables are crisp-tender.

2. Stir in dill weed, lemon peel, salt, broth and water. Heat to boiling; reduce heat. Cover and simmer 8 to 10 minutes or until pasta is tender.

3. Stir in spinach and shrimp. Cook 2 to 3 minutes or until shrimp are tender. Sprinkle with cheese.

1 Serving: Calories 340 (Calories from Fat 70); Total Fat 7g (Saturated Fat 2g; Trans Fat 0g); Cholesterol 80mg; Sodium 930mg; Total Carbohydrate 48g (Dietary Fiber 4g; Sugars 2g); Protein 21g • **% Daily Value:** Vitamin A 50%; Vitamin C 35%; Calcium 15%; Iron 25% • **Exchanges:** 3 Starch, 1 Vegetable, 1 1/2 Lean Meat • **Carbohydrate Choices:** 3

WHY IT WORKS: **THE FACTS ON ORZO** It may look, and sometimes even taste, like rice, but orzo is actually pasta. Adding to the confusion is the fact that the word *orzo* is Italian for barley. But there is no need to be confused on how to cook it. Orzo is best cooked like rice, in a small amount of water. To further improve flavor, cook orzo like the Greeks do: sautéing it in oil or butter before boiling. As with rice, this seals the pasta and helps individual grains remain separate after cooking.

Shrimp Pilaf Florentine

New Orleans Best Gumbo

PREP TIME: 1 HOUR • START TO FINISH: 3 HOURS 10 MINUTES · 15 SERVINGS

6 cups water

1 package (1 lb) chicken gizzards, chopped

2 tablespoons seasoned salt

1 tablespoon onion powder

1 tablespoon garlic powder

2 teaspoons parsley flakes

1 teaspoon dried thyme leaves

1 teaspoon black pepper

1 teaspoon paprika

Dash of ground red pepper (cayenne)

1 large green bell pepper, chopped (1 1/2 cups)

1 large onion, chopped (1 cup)

5 cloves garlic, finely chopped

2 lb uncooked turkey or beef sausage links, cut into 1-inch slices

2 lb uncooked medium shrimp, thawed if frozen

1/2 cup vegetable oil

1 cup all-purpose flour

4 cups hot water

1 bag (1 lb) frozen chopped okra

1 package (6 oz) frozen ready-to-serve crabmeat, thawed and drained

1 can (8 oz) regular or smoked oysters, drained

Hot cooked rice, if desired

1. In 8-quart pot, heat 6 cups water to boiling. Add gizzards (this will be good!), seasoned salt, onion powder, garlic powder, parsley, thyme, black pepper, paprika, ground red pepper, bell pepper, onion and garlic. Heat to boiling; reduce heat. Simmer uncovered 1 hour, stirring occasionally. Stir in sausage. Cover and simmer 1 hour, stirring occasionally.

2. Meanwhile, peel shrimp, leaving tails on. Using a small, pointed knife or shrimp deveiner, make a shallow cut along the center back of each shrimp, and wash out vein.

3. In heavy 2-quart saucepan, heat oil over high heat. Stir in flour; reduce heat to medium. Cook 15 to 20 minutes, stirring constantly, until mixture is dark brown (be careful not to burn or gumbo will taste bitter); remove from heat.

4. Stir flour mixture into gizzard mixture until blended. Add 4 cups hot water, 1 cup at a time, stirring constantly. Stir in okra, crabmeat, shrimp and oysters. Heat to boiling; reduce heat to low. Simmer uncovered 5 to 10 minutes or until shrimp are pink and firm. Serve over rice if desired.

1 Serving: Calories 310 (Calories from Fat 150); Total Fat 17g (Saturated Fat 3.5g; Trans Fat 0g); Cholesterol 150mg; Sodium 1100mg; Total Carbohydrate 14g (Dietary Fiber 2g; Sugars 3g); Protein 27g • **% Daily Value:** Vitamin A 10%; Vitamin C 15%; Calcium 8%; Iron 25% • **Exchanges:** 1 Starch, 3 Medium-Fat Meat • **Carbohydrate Choices:** 1

WHY IT WORKS:

ALL ABOUT OKRA Hold on to your gumbo: Okra is a fruit! Botanically, a fruit is the part of a plant that contains the seeds. That makes eggplant, tomatoes and even green beans, fruit. Okra is unique in that when heated, it releases carbohydrate to form a sticky, gelatinous compound. Although undesirable when fried, this compound is what traditionally makes gumbo "gumbo." (The word comes from the African word for okra: *ngombo*.) Once cut and simmered, okra thickens gumbo and gives it the correct texture and flavor (a little like asparagus).

Pan-Seared Tilapia
WITH LEMON-BUTTER SAUCE

PREP TIME: 30 MINUTES • START TO FINISH: 30 MINUTES   4 SERVINGS

Sauce

1/2 cup dry white wine or
     chicken broth
1/4 cup fresh lemon juice
3 tablespoons finely chopped shallots
3/4 cup whipping (heavy) cream
1 teaspoon grated lemon peel
1/4 cup cold firm butter, cut into
     4 pieces
1/4 teaspoon salt
1/8 teaspoon white pepper

Tilapia

4 skinless tilapia fillets or other
     medium-firm fish fillets
     (6 oz each)
1/4 teaspoon salt
1 tablespoon vegetable oil
1/4 cup chopped toasted hazelnuts
     (filberts) or almonds

1. In 2-quart saucepan, heat wine, lemon juice and shallots to boiling over medium-high heat. Boil uncovered 4 minutes, stirring occasionally, until liquid is reduced by half.

2. Add whipping cream to pan and heat to boiling, stirring occasionally. Boil uncovered 6 minutes, stirring occasionally, until sauce is thickened and reduced to about 1/2 cup. Remove from heat and add lemon peel. Beat in butter, 1 piece at a time, with wire whisk, adding the next piece only after the first has been completely beaten in and melted. When all of the butter has been beaten in, add 1/4 teaspoon salt and the white pepper. Cover to keep warm.

3. Sprinkle fish with 1/4 teaspoon salt; set aside.

4. In 12-inch skillet (preferably nonstick), heat oil over medium-high heat until shimmering and hot. Add fish and cook 3 minutes. Flip and cook 3 minutes longer or until edges begin to brown and fish flakes easily with fork.

5. To serve, spoon sauce over fish and sprinkle with nuts.

1 Serving: Calories 460 (Calories from Fat 310); Total Fat 35g (Saturated Fat 16g; Trans Fat 1g); Cholesterol 160mg; Sodium 510mg; Total Carbohydrate 4g (Dietary Fiber 1g; Sugars 3g); Protein 31g • **% Daily Value:** Vitamin A 20%; Vitamin C 6%; Calcium 8%; Iron 6% • **Exchanges:** 4 1/2 Medium-Fat Meat, 2 1/2 Fat • **Carbohydrate Choices:** 0

WHY IT WORKS: **OIL AND WATER** Alaskan oil slicks and vinaigrettes are examples of a general rule of nature: Oil and water do not mix. So how do we explain mayonnaise and the sauce for this dish? Both are full of oil and butter, yet they stay creamy and smooth. Both sauces (mayonnaise is technically a sauce) contain emulsifiers, which are attracted to both oil and water. When present in a sauce, emulsifiers act as a bridge between oil and water, preventing them from separating.

Braised Salmon
WITH SOY-GINGER SAUCE

PREP TIME: 10 MINUTES • START TO FINISH: 25 MINUTES

4 SERVINGS

Salmon

2 tablespoons olive oil

4 salmon steaks, about 3/4 inch thick
  (2 lb)

Sauce

1/4 cup plus 2 tablespoons soy sauce

1/4 cup mirin (sweet rice wine) or
  apple juice

2 tablespoons lime juice

2 tablespoons water

1 tablespoon honey

1 tablespoon grated gingerroot

1. In 10-inch skillet (preferably nonstick), heat oil over medium-high heat until shimmering and hot. Add salmon and cook 3 minutes or until brown on one side. Flip and brown other side, about 3 minutes longer.

2. In small bowl, mix all sauce ingredients. Add mixture to skillet. Reduce heat to medium-low.

3. Cover and cook 8 to 12 minutes or until salmon flakes easily with fork. Place salmon on serving plates and drizzle with sauce.

1 Serving: Calories 370 (Calories from Fat 160); Total Fat 18g (Saturated Fat 4g; Trans Fat 0g); Cholesterol 125mg; Sodium 1480mg; Total Carbohydrate 9g (Dietary Fiber 0g; Sugars 7g); Protein 42g • **% Daily Value:** Vitamin A 4%; Vitamin C 4%; Calcium 2%; Iron 10% • **Exchanges:** 1/2 Other Carbohydrate, 6 Lean Meat • **Carbohydrate Choices:** 1/2

WHY IT WORKS:

FLAKY FISH Would you ever confuse a salmon steak with a porterhouse or pork chop? While vastly different in color and flavor, the texture alone sets fish apart from other meats. This difference has much to do with where the animals live and how they use their muscles. Land animals, like chickens and pigs, spend most of their time moving fairly slowly. Their muscles are grouped in long, thin bundles; when cooked, you need a knife to cut through the muscle. Fish, on the other hand, need quick movement in the water in order to swim. Their muscles are short and round; when cooked, their muscles separate and become flaky.

Braised Salmon with Soy-Ginger Sauce

Finishing the Plate

TEMPTING SIDES

Tuscan Bread Salad

PREP TIME: 20 MINUTES • START TO FINISH: 1 HOUR 20 MINUTES   6 SERVINGS

Salad

4 cups pieces (1 inch) day-old Italian
    or other firm-textured bread
    (not fluffy)
2 medium very ripe tomatoes,
    cut into bite-size pieces (2 cups)
2 cloves garlic, finely chopped
1 medium green bell pepper,
    coarsely chopped (1 cup)
1/3 cup chopped fresh basil leaves
2 tablespoons chopped fresh parsley

Dressing

1/3 cup extra-virgin or regular olive oil
2 tablespoons red wine vinegar
1/2 teaspoon salt
1/8 teaspoon pepper

1. In large glass or plastic bowl, mix bread, tomatoes, garlic, bell pepper, basil and parsley.

2. In tightly covered container, shake remaining ingredients. Pour over bread mixture; toss gently until bread is evenly coated.

3. Cover and refrigerate at least 1 hour until bread is softened and flavors are blended but no longer than 8 hours. Toss before serving.

1 Serving: Calories 190 (Calories from Fat 120); Total Fat 13g (Saturated Fat 2g; Trans Fat 0g); Cholesterol 0mg; Sodium 340mg; Total Carbohydrate 16g (Dietary Fiber 2g; Sugars 1g); Protein 3g • **% Daily Value:** Vitamin A 15%; Vitamin C 25%; Calcium 2%; Iron 6% • **Exchanges:** 1 Starch, 2 Fat • **Carbohydrate Choices:** 1

WHY IT WORKS: CHOOSING THE RIGHT OLIVE OIL

Extra-virgin olive oil is like fine wine in its incredible depth of flavor and the enjoyment it can bring to a meal. And as with wine, there are many grades of olive oil. After being washed, olives are ground to a paste with a large stone. This paste is then pressed to extract the oil. The first pressing of the oil is called "extra-virgin" and is distinguished from other olive oils by its low level of acidity (less than 1%). Oil made from the remaining olive paste is called "virgin" oil and has more free acid (although it is not acidic in taste). The final type is just called "olive oil" and refers to chemically extracted oil.

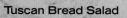
Tuscan Bread Salad

Gorgonzola and Toasted Walnut Salad

PREP TIME: 25 MINUTES • START TO FINISH: 25 MINUTES   6 SERVINGS

Dressing

2/3 cup coarsely chopped walnuts

1/3 cup olive oil

2 tablespoons lemon juice

1 clove garlic

1/8 teaspoon salt

Dash of pepper

Salad

8 cups ready-to-eat mixed salad
greens (about 10 oz)

1/2 cup crumbled Gorgonzola or
Roquefort cheese (2 oz)

1/2 cup 1/2-inch pieces fresh chives

1. To toast walnuts, cook in ungreased heavy skillet over medium-low heat 5 to 7 minutes, stirring frequently until browning begins, then stirring constantly until fragrant and golden brown. Remove walnuts from skillet and spread on plate to cool slightly.

2. In blender or food processor, place 1/3 cup toasted walnuts and remaining dressing ingredients. Cover and blend on high speed about 1 minute or until smooth.

3. In large bowl, toss remaining 1/3 cup toasted walnuts and salad ingredients. Pour dressing over salad mixture; toss gently until salad is evenly coated.

1 Serving: Calories 250 (Calories from Fat 210); Total Fat 23g (Saturated Fat 4g; Trans Fat 0g); Cholesterol 10mg; Sodium 240mg; Total Carbohydrate 5g (Dietary Fiber 3g; Sugars 2g); Protein 5g • **% Daily Value:** Vitamin A 50%; Vitamin C 30%; Calcium 10%; Iron 8% • **Exchanges:** 1 Vegetable, 1/2 Medium-Fat Meat, 4 Fat • **Carbohydrate Choices:** 1/2

WHY IT WORKS:

IT'S IN THE BAG Just like animals, vegetables breathe. If you lock a head of lettuce in your crisper drawer in a plastic bag you will find that it soon turns brown and limp. Moisture from the lettuce's "breath" helped speed the growth of bacteria. The bags of pre-cut lettuce you purchase from the grocery store are made up of a special material that regulates the amount of carbon dioxide, oxygen and other gases that come in and go out of the bag, extending the shelf life. To get more life out of your own lettuce, wrap separated leaves in paper towels and place in a plastic bag. Then squeeze as much air as possible from the bag before refrigerating.

Tangy Horseradish Coleslaw

1 head green cabbage (about 2 lb)

2 cups mayonnaise or salad dressing

2 tablespoons prepared horseradish

2 tablespoons cider vinegar

1 tablespoon Dijon mustard

1 tablespoon sugar (omit if using
   salad dressing)

1 teaspoon salt

1/2 teaspoon celery seed

1/2 teaspoon freshly ground pepper

1 clove garlic, finely chopped

3 medium carrots, shredded
   (1 1/4 cups)

1. Use sharp knife to cut cabbage head into quarters and remove core. Place 1 quarter, flat side down, on cutting board. Slice cabbage thinly with knife. Cut slices several times to make smaller pieces. Repeat with remaining quarters. You will need about 10 cups shredded cabbage.

2. In large bowl, mix mayonnaise, horseradish, vinegar, mustard, sugar, salt, celery seed, pepper and garlic. Add carrots and cabbage. Stir well to combine. Serve immediately or refrigerate up to 3 hours.

1 Serving: Calories 230 (Calories from Fat 200); Total Fat 22g (Saturated Fat 3.5g; Trans Fat 0g); Cholesterol 15mg; Sodium 350mg; Total Carbohydrate 6g (Dietary Fiber 2g; Sugars 4g); Protein 1g • **% Daily Value:** Vitamin A 45%; Vitamin C 35%; Calcium 4%; Iron 4% • **Exchanges:** 1 Vegetable, 4 1/2 Fat • **Carbohydrate Choices:** 1/2

WHY IT WORKS: **CONDIMENT WITH KICK** Typically horseradish is available whole, as a large root, or as prepared horseradish. To make prepared horseradish, the root is peeled and ground, crushing its cells and starting the chemical reaction that produces its infamous sinus-clearing chemicals. Vinegar is then added to the horseradish paste; the faster the vinegar is added, the less hot the horseradish will be because vinegar calms and stabilizes the chemical reaction. As horseradish sits, the pungent chemicals break down and lose their punch. Therefore, it is best to use refrigerated prepared horseradish within four to six months.

Roasted Sweet Potato Salad

4 medium sweet potatoes
   (about 1 1/2 lb), peeled and
   cut into 1 1/4-inch cubes
2 tablespoons butter, melted
1/2 teaspoon salt
2 tablespoons olive oil
2 tablespoons raspberry jelly or
   seedless jam
1 teaspoon packed brown sugar
2 tablespoons lemon juice
1/4 teaspoon ground cinnamon
Dash of crushed red pepper

1. Adjust oven rack to middle position. Heat oven to 400°F.

2. In large bowl, toss sweet potato cubes with butter and salt.

3. Spread sweet potatoes on cookie sheet and roast 20 minutes. Use pan-cake turner to turn potatoes over. Roast 10 to 15 minutes longer or until evenly browned and cooked through but not mushy. Remove from oven and transfer to large bowl.

4. Meanwhile, in 1-quart saucepan, heat oil, jam, brown sugar, lemon juice, cinnamon and red pepper to boiling, stirring until jam melts. Pour dressing over hot sweet potatoes and toss gently to coat. Cool slightly and serve warm.

1 Serving: Calories 180 (Calories from Fat 80); Total Fat 8g (Saturated Fat 2.5g; Trans Fat 0g); Cholesterol 10mg; Sodium 230mg; Total Carbohydrate 24g (Dietary Fiber 2g; Sugars 15g); Protein 1g • **% Daily Value:** Vitamin A 230%; Vitamin C 15%; Calcium 2%; Iron 2% • **Exchanges:** 1 1/2 Other Carbohydrate, 1 Vegetable, 1 1/2 Fat • **Carbohydrate Choices:** 1 1/2

WHY IT WORKS: **CONCENTRATED FLAVOR OF JELLY** For strong flavor, many chefs rely on the power of reduction. As stock, wine or fruit juice boils, the chemicals responsible for flavor are concentrated and sometimes altered to result in a very strong sauce. Most people don't keep reduced stock or wine in their pantry, yet they do have jelly. Jellies, jams and preserves all begin with fruit juice that is boiled until it achieves a thick, syrupy consistency. Good-quality jellies and preserves deliver a sweet, concentrated dose of fruit with no work.

Roasted Sweet Potato Salad

Make-Ahead Potato Bread Dough

PREP TIME: 30 MINUTES • **START TO FINISH:** 8 HOURS 30 MINUTES · 2 LOAVES (16 SLICES EACH)

1 package regular active dry yeast
    (2 1/4 teaspoons)
1 1/2 cups warm water
    (105°F to 115°F)
1 cup lukewarm unseasoned
    mashed potatoes
2/3 cup sugar
2/3 cup butter, softened
1 1/2 teaspoons salt
2 eggs
7 to 7 1/2 cups all-purpose flour

1. In large bowl, dissolve yeast in warm water. (If you've just cooked the potatoes, use 1 1/2 cups of warm potato water.) Stir in potatoes, sugar, butter, salt, eggs and 3 cups of the flour. Beat with electric mixer on low speed until smooth. Beat on medium speed 1 minute, scraping bowl frequently. Stir in enough remaining flour to make dough easy to handle.

2. Place dough on lightly floured surface; gently roll in flour to coat. Knead about 5 minutes or until dough is smooth and springy. Grease large bowl with shortening or spray with cooking spray. Place dough in bowl, turning dough to grease all sides. Cover bowl tightly with plastic wrap and refrigerate at least 8 hours but no longer than 5 days.

3. Gently push fist into dough to deflate. Divide dough into 2 equal pieces for loaves or 4 equal pieces for rolls. Shape and bake as directed below.

Bread Loaves: Grease bottom and sides of 9 × 5-inch loaf pan with shortening or cooking spray. On lightly floured surface, roll half of dough into 18 × 9-inch rectangle. Roll up dough, beginning at 9-inch side. Press with thumbs to seal after each turn. Pinch edge of dough into roll to seal. Pinch each end of roll to seal. Fold ends under loaf. Place loaf, seam side down, in pan. Brush with softened butter. Cover and let rise in warm place about 2 hours or until dough has doubled in size. (Dough is ready if indentation remains when touched.) Heat oven to 375°F. Place pan on low oven rack so top of pan is in center of oven. Bake 30 to 35 minutes or until loaf is deep golden brown and sounds hollow when tapped. Remove from pan to wire rack. Brush with softened butter; cool. Makes 1 loaf (16 slices).

Cloverleaf Rolls: Grease bottoms and sides of 8 to 10 regular-size muffin cups with shortening or cooking spray. Shape one-fourth of dough into 2-inch balls. Place 1 ball in each muffin cup. With kitchen scissors, snip each ball completely in half, then into fourths. Brush with softened butter. Cover and let rise in warm place about 1 hour or until dough has doubled in size. Heat oven to 400°F. Bake 15 to 20 minutes. Makes 8 to 10 rolls.

1 Slice: Calories 160 (Calories from Fat 45); Total Fat 5g (Saturated Fat 2g; Trans Fat 0g); Cholesterol 25mg; Sodium 150mg; Total Carbohydrate 26g (Dietary Fiber 0g; Sugars 4g); Protein 3g • **% Daily Value:** Vitamin A 4%; Vitamin C 0%; Calcium 0%; Iron 8% • **Exchanges:** 2 Starch • **Carbohydrate Choices:** 2

WHY IT WORKS: **RISING WITH POTATOES** Adding mashed potatoes to yeast dough may seem unusual, but it does more than add flavor. Cooked potatoes are made up of mostly starch. This starch readily converts to sugar in the dough, which is hungrily eaten by the yeast. With this "jump start," the yeast alters the flavor of the bread. In addition, the extra potato starch in the bread holds moisture longer than bread made without potatoes. Bread made with mashed potatoes, then, lasts longer before going stale.

Roasted Rosemary Red Potatoes

2 tablespoons olive oil

12 small red potatoes (about 1 1/2 lb)

2 medium green onions, sliced
    (2 tablespoons)

2 tablespoons chopped fresh or
    2 teaspoons dried rosemary
    leaves, crushed

1. Heat oven to 350°F.

2. In ungreased 8- or 9-inch square pan or 13 × 9-inch pan, drizzle oil over potatoes; turn potatoes so all sides are coated. Sprinkle with green onions and rosemary; stir.

3. Roast uncovered about 1 hour 15 minutes, stirring occasionally, until potatoes are tender when pierced with fork.

1 serving: Calories 330 (Calories from Fat 60); Total Fat 7g (Saturated Fat 1g; Trans Fat 0g); Cholesterol 0mg; Sodium 30mg; Total Carbohydrate 59g (Dietary Fiber 7g; Sugars 4g); Protein 7g • **% Daily Value:** Vitamin A 2%; Vitamin C 25%; Calcium 4%; Iron 20% • **Exchanges:** 3 1/2 Starch, 1 Vegetable, 1 Fat • **Carbohydrate Choices:** 4

WHY IT WORKS: **ONE POTATO, TWO POTATO** Cousin to tobacco and eggplant, potatoes are grown throughout the world in over a hundred varieties. Botanically, potatoes are considered stems that store energy in the form of starch. Some potatoes have more starch than others and tend to more tightly pack it away. These potatoes—called waxy—hold together when cooked. (Red potatoes are an example.) Other potatoes contain less starch and cook up fluffy or mealy because the starch is less compact (Russets, for example). When roasting, go for a waxy potato because it will hold together in the oven.

Potato Pancakes

1 tablet (500 mg) Vitamin C
2 cups cold water
4 medium Idaho or russet baking
    potatoes (1 1/2 lb), peeled
4 eggs, beaten
1 small onion, finely chopped
    (1/4 cup), if desired
1/4 cup all-purpose flour
1 teaspoon salt
1/4 cup vegetable oil

1. In medium bowl, crush 500 mg Vitamin C tablet. Add about 2 cups cold water; stir until tablet is dissolved. Shred potatoes, adding to bowl as you go. Drain potatoes; measure 4 cups and pat dry.

2. In large bowl, mix potatoes, eggs, onion if desired, flour and salt.

3. In 12-inch skillet, heat 2 tablespoons of the oil over medium heat. For each pancake, pour about 1/4 cup batter into skillet. Flatten each with spatula into pancake about 4 inches in diameter.

4. Cook pancakes about 2 minutes on each side or until golden brown. (To keep cooked pancakes warm while cooking remaining pancakes, place in a single layer on a cookie sheet and cover with foil. Place in 200°F oven up to 10 minutes.)

5. Repeat with remaining batter; as batter stands, liquid and potatoes will separate, so stir to mix as necessary. Add remaining oil as needed to prevent sticking.

1 Pancake: Calories 80 (Calories from Fat 45); Total Fat 5g (Saturated Fat 1g; Trans Fat 0g); Cholesterol 55mg; Sodium 160mg; Total Carbohydrate 8g (Dietary Fiber 0g; Sugars 0g); Protein 2g • **% Daily Value:** Vitamin A 0%; Vitamin C 2%; Calcium 0%; Iron 0% • **Exchanges:** 1/2 Starch, 1 Fat • **Carbohydrate Choices:** 1/2

WHY IT WORKS: POTATOES NEED THEIR VITAMINS, TOO!

When potatoes, apples and bananas are cut, chemicals contained in the plants' cells are released. One of these chemicals, an enzyme known as PPO, reacts with oxygen in the air to turn the flesh of fruits and vegetables brown. (Interestingly, a component similar to PPO causes age spots on human skin.) Although this reaction cannot be stopped completely (other than by cooking) it can be slowed. Salt and acids slow PPO down, so soaking your cut potato or apples in salt water or lemon juice will delay browning. Because both of these additions have their own flavor, a better technique is to use ascorbic acid (Vitamin C). Other than a bit of tartness, it lacks flavor of its own. Simply dissolve a 500-milligram tablet in the soaking water.

Whipped Maple Sweet Potatoes

PREP TIME: 15 MINUTES • **START TO FINISH:** 1 HOUR 30 MINUTES

6 SERVINGS

8 medium red garnet sweet potatoes
(about 3 lb)
2 tablespoons real maple syrup
2 tablespoons butter, softened
1/2 teaspoon salt
Dash of nutmeg
Additional real maple syrup, if desired

1. Heat oven to 350°F.

2. Pierce sweet potatoes with fork. Place potatoes in 13 × 9-inch pan. Cover with foil and bake about 1 hour 15 minutes or until potatoes can be easily pierced with a knife. Cool until easy to handle. (Be careful! When sweet potatoes cook, they exude a sticky syrup that can burn if it gets on your skin.) Remove skins.

3. In large bowl, beat potatoes with electric mixer on medium speed until no lumps remain. Add 2 tablespoons syrup, the butter, salt and nutmeg. Continue beating until potatoes are light and fluffy. Drizzle with additional syrup if desired.

1 Serving: Calories 200 (Calories from Fat 35); Total Fat 4g (Saturated Fat 2g; Trans Fat 0g); Cholesterol 10mg; Sodium 240mg; Total Carbohydrate 38g (Dietary Fiber 4g; Sugars 24g); Protein 2g • **% Daily Value:** Vitamin A 410%; Vitamin C 30%; Calcium 4%; Iron 4% • **Exchanges:** 1 Starch, 1 1/2 Other Carbohydrate, 1 Fat • **Carbohydrate Choices:** 2 1/2

WHY IT WORKS: **IT'S NOT A YAM** First things first: Sweet potatoes are not yams! They are often referred to and labeled as yams because of their resemblance to the African root of the same name. However, sweet potatoes are completely different in flavor and texture. Sweet potatoes are unusual in the amount of sugar they contain—upwards of 5%. This amount increases during cooking as the starch turns to sugar. The sweet potato's color is due to the same pigment that colors carrots and squash. For best texture and flavor, do not store sweet potatoes in the refrigerator or they will become bitter.

Garden Ratatouille

PREP TIME: 25 MINUTES • START TO FINISH: 25 MINUTES   8 SERVINGS

3 cups 1/2-inch cubes eggplant (1 lb)

1 small zucchini, cut into
     1/4-inch slices (1 cup)

1 small onion, sliced

1/2 medium green bell pepper,
     cut into strips

2 cloves garlic, finely chopped

2 tablespoons chopped fresh parsley

1 tablespoon chopped fresh or
     1/2 teaspoon dried basil leaves

2 tablespoons water

1/2 teaspoon salt

1/4 teaspoon pepper

2 medium very ripe tomatoes, cut
     into eighths

Olive oil if desired

1. In 10-inch skillet, cook all ingredients except tomatoes over medium heat about 10 minutes, stirring occasionally, until vegetables are tender; remove from heat.

2. Stir in tomatoes. (For added flavor, drizzle with about 2 tablespoons olive oil, if desired.) Cover and let stand 2 to 3 minutes until tomatoes are warm.

1 Serving: Calories 25 (Calories from Fat 0); Total Fat 0g (Saturated Fat 0g; Trans Fat 0g); Cholesterol 0mg; Sodium 150mg; Total Carbohydrate 5g (Dietary Fiber 2g; Sugars 2g); Protein 0g • **% Daily Value:** Vitamin A 10%; Vitamin C 15%; Calcium 0%; Iron 2% • **Exchanges:** 1 Vegetable • **Carbohydrate Choices:** 1/2

WHY IT WORKS: **EGGPLANT FACT AND FICTION** Eggplant has spent much of its history being shunned by one part of the world and celebrated by another. This unfair treatment has to do with family history: Eggplant is related to the deadly nightshade. Of course eggplants are not poisonous, but many people are afraid to eat or cook them. Never cooked eggplant? It is important to understand its structure. An eggplant is—for lack of a better term—a sponge. Looking closely at a cut piece, you see thousands of tiny holes. These holes absorb an amazing amount of oil, causing fried eggplant to become heavy and greasy. To help prevent this, cut the eggplant into pieces and then salt it. The salt draws out any bitter juices and collapses some of the holes. Fry salted eggplant quickly over high heat to seal the outside. Because the eggplant isn't fried in this recipe, there is no need to salt it first.

Garden Ratatouille

Down-Home Mashed Potatoes

PREP TIME: 10 MINUTES • START TO FINISH: 40 MINUTES   4 TO 6 SERVINGS

6 medium round red or white
potatoes (2 lb)
1/3 to 1/2 cup milk, half-and-half or
whipping (heavy) cream
1/4 cup butter, softened
1/2 teaspoon salt
Dash of pepper
Chopped fresh parsley or chives,
if desired

1. In 2-quart saucepan, place potatoes and enough water just to cover potatoes. Heat to boiling; reduce heat. Cover and simmer 20 to 30 minutes or until potatoes are tender; drain. Shake pan with potatoes over low heat to dry (this will help mashed potatoes be fluffier).

2. Mash potatoes in pan with potato masher until no lumps remain. Add milk in small amounts, mashing after each addition (amount of milk needed to make potatoes smooth and fluffy depends on kind of potatoes used).

3. Add butter, salt and pepper. Mash vigorously until potatoes are light and fluffy. If desired, sprinkle with small pieces of butter or sprinkle with paprika, parsley or chives.

1 Serving: Calories 270 (Calories from Fat 110); Total Fat 12g (Saturated Fat 6g; Trans Fat 0.5g); Cholesterol 30mg; Sodium 390mg; Total Carbohydrate 38g (Dietary Fiber 4g; Sugars 2g); Protein 4g • **% Daily Value:** Vitamin A 10%; Vitamin C 10%; Calcium 4%; Iron 4% • **Exchanges:** 2 1/2 Starch, 2 Fat • **Carbohydrate Choices:** 2 1/2

WHY IT WORKS:

THE SPIRIT OF SPUDS There are three types of potatoes: floury (also known as starchy), waxy and all-purpose. Floury potatoes are highest in starch, waxy are lowest and all-purpose land in the middle. Floury potatoes—such as Russet—are best for making mashed potatoes. Because of their high starch content and low water content, floury potatoes absorb butter and cream well, yet still remain light and fluffy. Store all potatoes in a cool dry place with good ventilation. Keep them out of the refrigerator as cold storage causes their starch to turn to sugar, making them very sweet. Remove potatoes from their plastic bag once home from the grocery store. The high humidity of the bag will cause them to sweat and mold.

Lemon-Glazed Spring Asparagus

PREP TIME: 20 MINUTES • **START TO FINISH:** 20 MINUTES

4 SERVINGS

1 1/2 lb fresh asparagus spears
1 tablespoon butter
1 tablespoon honey
1 teaspoon lemon juice
1/4 cup water
1 teaspoon cornstarch

1. Trim asparagus; cut spears diagonally in half. In 4-quart Dutch oven, heat 3 inches of water to boiling. Add asparagus; reduce heat. Cover and cook 3 to 5 minutes or until crisp-tender. (Make sure bottom portions are cooked through.) Drain; place in serving bowl.

2. Meanwhile, in 1-quart saucepan, heat butter, honey and lemon juice over medium-low heat, stirring frequently, until butter is melted.

3. In small bowl, mix 1/4 cup water and the cornstarch. Stir into lemon juice mixture. Cook over medium heat, stirring constantly, until bubbly and thickened. Pour glaze over asparagus. Serve immediately (lemon juice will cause asparagus to lose its color quickly).

1 **Serving:** Calories 50 (Calories from Fat 25); Total Fat 3g (Saturated Fat 1.5g; Trans Fat 0g); Cholesterol 10mg; Sodium 20mg; Total Carbohydrate 5g (Dietary Fiber 0g; Sugars 5g); Protein 0g • **% Daily Value:** Vitamin A 4%; Vitamin C 0%; Calcium 0%; Iron 0% • **Exchanges:** 1 Vegetable, 1/2 Fat • **Carbohydrate Choices:** 1/2

WHY IT WORKS: **PICKING A LEMON** Lemons are a fruit without a home. Botanists have never discovered their country of origin, although many guess it may be somewhere in India. Like other citrus fruits, lemons are picky about where they grow. Most are grown in this country, on the coasts, where the temperature fluctuates only a few degrees all growing season. Dramatic changes in temperature can radically alter the sugar-to-acid ratio of the fruit. Growers pick lemons based on their concentration of sugar (measured using the Brix scale). Unlike other fruits whose starch content turns to sugar after being picked, lemons never get any sweeter once picked.

Honey-Lemon Brussels Sprouts and Carrots

PREP TIME: 10 MINUTES • START TO FINISH: 25 MINUTES   8 SERVINGS (1/2 CUP EACH)

3 cups (16 to 20) Brussels sprouts
(12 oz)

2 cups water

2 1/2 cups ready-to-eat baby-cut
carrots (12 oz)

2 tablespoons butter

1 tablespoon honey

1 teaspoon grated lemon peel

1/4 teaspoon salt

1/8 teaspoon pepper

1. Trim Brussels sprouts. Cut small "X" in stem end, about 1/4 inch deep. If Brussels sprouts are very large, cut in half.

2. In 2-quart saucepan, heat water to boiling over medium-high heat. Add Brussels sprouts and carrots. Boil uncovered 6 to 8 minutes or until tender. Drain and return vegetables to saucepan.

3. Add remaining ingredients to vegetables; toss to coat. Spoon into serving bowl.

1 Serving: Calories 80 (Calories from Fat 30); Total Fat 3g (Saturated Fat 1.5g; Trans Fat 0g); Cholesterol 10mg; Sodium 115mg; Total Carbohydrate 10g (Dietary Fiber 3g; Sugars 5g); Protein 2g • **% Daily Value:** Vitamin A 160%; Vitamin C 20%; Calcium 2%; Iron 2% • **Exchanges:** 2 Vegetable, 1/2 Fat • **Carbohydrate Choices:** 1/2

WHY IT WORKS:

STOPPING THE STINK The longer you cook Brussels sprouts, or any member of the cabbage family, the more they smell. This is because heat activates a series of compounds that include hydrogen sulfide (better known as rotten egg smell) and mercaptans ("skunk"). Follow these tips to reduce the offending odors: Cook sprouts in enough water to cover; the extra water dilutes the chemicals. Also, heat the water to boiling before adding the vegetable. And do not cover the pan. Although you would think smells can be trapped, a closed area actually concentrates the reaction. Finally, cook the spouts as quickly as possible and remove them as soon as they are cooked through.

Honey-Lemon Brussels Sprouts and Carrots

Sautéed Cauliflower
WITH BROWNED BREAD CRUMBS

PREP TIME: 10 MINUTES • **START TO FINISH:** 25 MINUTES · 4 SERVINGS (3/4 CUP EACH)

1 teaspoon salt

1 medium head cauliflower
(about 2 lb), trimmed and
cut into florets

4 tablespoons butter

1 tablespoon Dijon mustard

2 cups soft bread crumbs
(about 3 slices bread)

2 tablespoons olive oil

1. In 10-inch skillet, heat 1 inch water to boiling. Stir in salt. Add cauliflower and return to boiling. Boil uncovered 3 minutes or until almost tender. Drain cauliflower in colander and immediately rinse under cold water to stop cooking. Set cauliflower aside.

2. In same skillet, melt 3 tablespoons of the butter over medium heat. Stir mustard into butter and add bread crumbs. Cook 8 to 10 minutes, stirring frequently, until crumbs are golden brown. Remove crumbs to plate.

3. In same skillet, melt remaining tablespoon butter and the oil over medium-high heat. Stir in cauliflower and cook about 5 minutes, stirring occasionally, until lightly browned and cooked through. Sprinkle crumbs over top.

1 Serving: Calories 420 (Calories from Fat 200); Total Fat 22g (Saturated Fat 7g; Trans Fat 0.5g); Cholesterol 30mg; Sodium 1270mg; Total Carbohydrate 47g (Dietary Fiber 5g; Sugars 7g); Protein 10g • **% Daily Value:** Vitamin A 10%; Vitamin C 60%; Calcium 15%; Iron 20% • **Exchanges:** 2 1/2 Starch, 1/2 Other Carbohydrate, 1 Vegetable, 4 Fat • **Carbohydrate Choices:** 3

WHY IT WORKS: BEST PRACTICES FOR BREAD CRUMBS

One of the best ways to season a food is to remove its natural liquid and replace it with a more flavorful one. The same concept holds for bread crumbs. Bread can best absorb butter and spices when dried. In a pinch, bread can be cut into slices and placed in a warm oven to dry. However, this method toasts the bread without removing most of the liquid. A better way is to slice the bread and let it sit, uncovered, overnight. This drying method allows the starch to release its water (heating causes starch to hold more water).

Sesame Green Beans

PREP TIME: 15 MINUTES • **START TO FINISH:** 15 MINUTES   6 SERVINGS

1 1/2 lb fresh green beans
1 tablespoon sesame seed
2 tablespoons rice vinegar or
    white wine vinegar
2 tablespoons soy sauce
2 teaspoons sugar
1 teaspoon crushed red pepper

1. In 2 1/2-quart saucepan, place beans in 1 inch of water. Heat to boiling. Boil uncovered 6 to 8 minutes or until beans are crisp-tender (they shouldn't be "squeaky" when you bite into one). Drain beans in strainer.

2. Meanwhile, in ungreased 10-inch heavy skillet, cook sesame seed over medium heat about 2 minutes, stirring frequently until browning begins, then stirring constantly until golden brown. Remove from heat. Stir in vinegar, soy sauce, sugar and red pepper. Cook 1 to 2 minutes longer or until mixture is hot. Drain beans in strainer.

3. In large bowl, gently toss beans and sesame mixture with fork until beans are evenly coated.

1 **Serving:** Calories 50 (Calories from Fat 10); Total Fat 1g (Saturated Fat 0g; Trans Fat 0g); Cholesterol 0mg; Sodium 310mg; Total Carbohydrate 9g (Dietary Fiber 3g; Sugars 4g); Protein 2g • **% Daily Value:** Vitamin A 15%; Vitamin C 4%; Calcium 4%; Iron 6% • **Exchanges:** 2 Vegetable • **Carbohydrate Choices:** 1/2

WHY IT WORKS: **A TOAST TO SEEDS** Strangely enough, this recipe could be called "Seeds with Seeds." Green beans are nothing more than the seeds of the bean plant. Many nuts and seeds (including sesame seed), because of their high oil content, benefit greatly from toasting to bring out their flavor. Heat causes the essential oils in the center of seeds to volatilize (escape into the air) and the outside of the seed to brown. Toasting can be done in the oven or on the stovetop. Care must be taken not to burn the seeds, as the resulting bitter flavor will be so strong you will have to discard even the unburnt seeds.

RECIPE R_x: OVERBROWNING Sesame seeds have a distinct flavor and aroma, especially when toasted (they actually contain sulfur chemicals similar to those found in roasted coffee beans). As a prime component of this recipe, make sure you start with fresh

seeds. At 50% oil by weight, sesame seeds can turn rancid quickly. When toasted, they can rapidly go from pleasantly nutty to bitter and burnt. The best method for determining if the toasted seeds are done is by smell. As the seeds go from pale beige to light brown, waft your hand over the pan. As soon as you smell something like a cross between peanut butter and roasted coffee, remove the pan from heat.

Green Beans with Browned Butter

PREP TIME: 25 MINUTES • **START TO FINISH:** 25 MINUTES   6 SERVINGS (1/2 CUP EACH)

3/4 lb fresh green beans, cut in half

2 tablespoons butter (do not use margarine or vegetable oil spreads)

2 tablespoons chopped pecans

1 teaspoon grated lemon peel

1. In 2-quart saucepan, place beans in 1 inch of water. Heat to boiling. Boil uncovered 6 to 8 minutes or until crisp-tender (they shouldn't be "squeaky" when you bite into one); drain. Keep warm.

2. Meanwhile, in 1-quart saucepan, melt butter over low heat. Be careful not to let butter burn or it will taste bitter. Stir in pecans. Heat, stirring constantly, until butter is golden brown. (If bottom of saucepan is dark, it may be difficult to see the difference between brown butter and burnt butter. Try spooning a little of the butter onto a white plate to see the color more clearly.) Immediately remove from heat. Pour butter mixture over beans; toss to coat. Sprinkle with lemon peel.

1 Serving: Calories 70 (Calories from Fat 50); Total Fat 6g (Saturated Fat 2g; Trans Fat 0g); Cholesterol 10mg; Sodium 30mg; Total Carbohydrate 3g (Dietary Fiber 2g; Sugars 1g); Protein 0g • **% Daily Value:** Vitamin A 8%; Vitamin C 2%; Calcium 2%; Iron 2% • **Exchanges:** 1 Vegetable, 1 Fat • **Carbohydrate Choices:** 0

WHY IT WORKS: **THE BEAUTY OF BROWNED BUTTER** Butter is approximately 80% milk fat, 18% water and 2% milk solids. When cooking with butter you will notice that when melted, it separates into a clear yellow layer (the fat) and a white layer (the milk solids). In India, butter is often melted and the fat separated from the solids. This butter—called clarified butter—can be kept without refrigeration. (Butter goes rancid because of the milk solids, not because of the fat.) If the milk solids are not separated from the fat, but instead allowed to brown, they develop a wonderful nutty flavor and aroma that complements vegetables and meats.

Green Beans with Browned Butter

Sesame-Garlic Broccoli

PREP TIME: 20 MINUTES • **START TO FINISH:** 20 MINUTES

4 SERVINGS (1/2 CUP EACH)

2 cups broccoli florets (3/4 lb)
1/4 cup chicken broth
2 tablespoons rice wine or
   chicken broth
1 teaspoon cornstarch
1 teaspoon packed brown sugar
1 tablespoon sesame seed
3 tablespoons vegetable oil
1/4 teaspoon dark sesame oil,
   if desired
1 tablespoon finely chopped garlic
2 teaspoons grated gingerroot

1. In 10-inch skillet, heat 1 inch water to boiling. Add broccoli and boil uncovered 3 to 5 minutes or until just tender. Drain broccoli in colander and immediately rinse under cold water to stop cooking. Set broccoli aside.

2. In small bowl, mix broth, rice wine, cornstarch and brown sugar until smooth.

3. Sprinkle sesame seed evenly over bottom of same skillet. Heat over medium-low heat 5 to 7 minutes, stirring frequently, until browning begins. Then stir constantly until seeds are golden brown. Immediately remove seeds from skillet; set aside.

4. In same skillet, heat vegetable oil and sesame oil if desired over medium heat until oils shimmer. Add broccoli and cook about 1 minute, stirring frequently. Clear center of skillet and add garlic and gingerroot. Stir into broccoli and cook 1 minute longer; do not let garlic burn.

5. Stir cornstarch mixture again to dissolve any lumps and add to skillet. Heat mixture to boiling, stirring constantly. Cook and stir 1 minute longer. Remove from heat and sprinkle with sesame seed.

1 **Serving:** Calories 130 (Calories from Fat 110); Total Fat 12g (Saturated Fat 1.5g; Trans Fat 0g); Cholesterol 0mg; Sodium 105mg; Total Carbohydrate 5g (Dietary Fiber 2g; Sugars 1g); Protein 2g • **% Daily Value:** Vitamin A 10%; Vitamin C 30%; Calcium 2%; Iron 4% • **Exchanges:** 1 Vegetable, 2 1/2 Fat • **Carbohydrate Choices:** 1/2

WHY IT WORKS: **IT'S NOT EASY BEING GREEN** Cooking broccoli can be tricky. Cook it right and it is crisp and green. Overcook it and you end up with a limp, olive drab floret. Your best safeguard against this is understanding why broccoli is green in the first place. Broccoli, and all green plants, contains a pigment called chlorophyll. In the living plant, chlorophyll is protected because its job is to turn sunlight into food. When heated, chlorophyll loses this protection and is exposed to its enemy: acid. Lemon juice, vinegar and even broccoli's natural acidity can turn chlorophyll's lovely green to brown. To keep chlorophyll and acid far apart, follow these rules: Cook broccoli quickly (no more than 8 minutes), keep the pot uncovered (that would concentrate the acid) and add acid just before serving.

Sesame-Garlic Broccoli

Orange-Glazed Baby Carrots with Cumin

PREP TIME: 20 MINUTES • **START TO FINISH:** 20 MINUTES

4 SERVINGS (1/2 CUP EACH)

1 bag (1 lb) ready-to-eat
   baby-cut carrots
1/2 cup orange juice
3 tablespoons butter
2 tablespoons sugar
1/2 teaspoon salt
1/2 teaspoon ground cumin
   or cinnamon
2 tablespoons chopped fresh
   parsley leaves

1. In 10-inch skillet, heat all ingredients except parsley to boiling over medium heat. Reduce heat, cover and simmer 7 to 9 minutes or until carrots are barely cooked through.

2. Uncover skillet and stir carrots. Simmer about 2 minutes longer or until liquid is reduced to about 1 tablespoon and carrots have a glazed appearance. Remove from heat and sprinkle with parsley.

1 Serving: Calories 170 (Calories from Fat 80); Total Fat 9g (Saturated Fat 4.5g; Trans Fat 0.5g); Cholesterol 25mg; Sodium 390mg; Total Carbohydrate 21g (Dietary Fiber 3g; Sugars 15g); Protein 2g • **% Daily Value:** Vitamin A 420%; Vitamin C 20%; Calcium 4%; Iron 4% • **Exchanges:** 1 Other Carbohydrate, 1 Vegetable, 2 Fat • **Carbohydrate Choices:** 1 1/2

WHY IT WORKS:

SLOW COOKED Carrots are a member of a large family of vegetables and herbs (parsley, coriander, fennel and dill, just to name a few). Rich in vitamin A and beta-carotene, carrots have been used for their medicinal properties for centuries. One of the great pleasures of cooking with carrots is their promised sweetness. Young, baby carrots are especially sweet, a characteristic that can be enhanced by slowly cooking them to convert their starch into sugar. A pinch of salt also intensifies their natural flavor.

Grilled Corn with Chile-Lime Spread

1/2 cup butter, softened

1/2 teaspoon grated lime peel

3 tablespoons lime juice

1 to 2 teaspoons ground red chiles
   or chili powder

8 ears corn with husk

1. Heat coals or gas grill for medium heat. (Check the temperature of the coals by placing your hand, palm side down, near but not touching the cooking grill rack. If you can keep your hand there for 2 seconds [one-thousand one, one-thousand two], the temperature is high; 3 seconds is medium-high; 4 seconds is medium; 5 seconds is low.)

2. In small bowl, mix all ingredients except corn.

3. Remove large outer husks from each ear of corn; gently pull back inner husks and remove silk. Spread each ear of corn with about 2 teaspoons butter mixture; reserve remaining butter mixture. Pull husks up over ears; tie with fine wire to secure.

4. Grill corn uncovered 10 to 15 minutes, turning frequently, until tender. Let stand 5 minutes. Serve corn with remaining butter mixture.

1 Serving: Calories 230 (Calories from Fat 120); Total Fat 13g (Saturated Fat 6g; Trans Fat 0.5g); Cholesterol 30mg; Sodium 100mg; Total Carbohydrate 26g (Dietary Fiber 4g; Sugars 3g); Protein 4g • **% Daily Value:** Vitamin A 15%; Vitamin C 6%; Calcium 0%; Iron 4% • **Exchanges:** 1 1/2 Starch, 1 Vegetable, 2 Fat • **Carbohydrate Choices:** 2

WHY IT WORKS:

STAYING SWEET Corn, or maize as its called by the rest of the world, originated in America. One of our largest field crops, most corn ends up as feed and corn syrup. Corn grown for human consumption is called sweet corn. Both field corn and sweet corn produce sugar as they grow. After it is picked, field corn quickly turns its sugar into starch. Sweet corn, however, maintains its sugar level throughout shipping, storage and cooking. When cooking corn, the goal is to just heat it through; overcooking results in tough corn.

Green Rice

WITH TOASTED PUMPKIN SEEDS

PREP TIME: 20 MINUTES • **START TO FINISH:** 40 MINUTES   10 SERVINGS (1/2 CUP EACH)

Pumpkin Seeds

1/3 cup raw unsalted hulled pumpkin
    seeds (pepitas), pine nuts or
    slivered almonds
1 tablespoon olive oil

Rice

1/2 cup tightly packed fresh cilantro
    (stems and leaves)
1/2 cup tightly packed fresh parsley
    (stems and leaves)
1 medium green bell pepper,
    coarsely chopped (1 cup)
1 small onion, chopped (1/3 cup)
2 cloves garlic, finely chopped
1 jalapeño chile, seeded
1 1/2 teaspoons salt
1/4 teaspoon ground cumin
2 3/4 cups water
3 tablespoons olive oil
1 1/2 cups uncooked regular
    long-grain rice

1. In 8-inch skillet, heat pumpkin seeds and 1 tablespoon oil over medium heat about 3 minutes, stirring occasionally, until seeds are lightly toasted. (Watch carefully—they can burn quickly.) Use slotted spoon to remove pumpkin seeds from pan and cool on paper towel–lined plate.

2. In food processor or blender, puree cilantro, parsley, bell pepper, onion, garlic, chile, salt, cumin and water until smooth; set aside.

3. In 3-quart saucepan, heat 3 tablespoons oil over medium heat until hot. Add rice and cook 3 minutes, stirring occasionally, until slightly translucent around edges. Add pureed liquid and heat to boiling. Reduce heat to low; cover and simmer 20 minutes or until all liquid is absorbed. Fluff with fork and stir in pumpkin seeds. Serve hot.

1 Serving: Calories 210 (Calories from Fat 80); Total Fat 9g (Saturated Fat 1.5g; Trans Fat 0g); Cholesterol 0mg; Sodium 360mg; Total Carbohydrate 27g (Dietary Fiber 1g; Sugars 0g); Protein 5g • **% Daily Value:** Vitamin A 8%; Vitamin C 15%; Calcium 2%; Iron 15% • **Exchanges:** 1 1/2 Starch, 1 Vegetable, 1 1/2 Fat • **Carbohydrate Choices:** 2

WHY IT WORKS: SEPARATE RICE IS NICE

All rice begins its life surrounded by a thin coating called bran. When milled, this outer layer is removed to expose the raw grain. To improve appearance, most rice in the United States is polished using a series of wire brushes or spinning drums. Although this process results in a beautiful, stark white grain, it also causes a thin layer of rice starch to accumulate on the surface. When rice is cooked, this outer starch layer mixes with water and causes the grains of rice to stick together. If you'd rather your rice grains were separate and fluffy, you have several options. You can wash the rice to remove residual starch, but this takes time. The best technique is to first cook the rice in hot oil. Coating every grain, the oil forms a nonstick coating, resulting in fluffy rice every time.

Green Rice with Toasted Pumpkin Seeds

Slow Cooker Sweet Maple Baked Beans

PREP TIME: 10 MINUTES • START TO FINISH: 10 HOURS 30 MINUTES   8 SERVINGS (1/2 CUP EACH)

2 cups dried navy beans (8 oz), sorted and rinsed

10 cups water

3/4 cup water

1 medium onion, chopped (1/2 cup)

3/4 cup real maple syrup

3 tablespoons packed brown sugar

2 teaspoons ground mustard

1 teaspoon salt

1/2 teaspoon ground ginger

1. In 6-quart Dutch oven, heat beans and 10 cups water to boiling; reduce heat. Cover and simmer 2 hours; drain. (You are just precooking the beans; they don't have to be soft.)

2. In 3 1/2- to 4-quart slow cooker, mix beans and remaining ingredients.

3. Cover and cook on Low heat setting 8 to 10 hours or until beans are very tender and most of the liquid has been absorbed.

1 Serving: Calories 200 (Calories from Fat 5); Total Fat 0.5g (Saturated Fat 0g; Trans Fat 0g); Cholesterol 0mg; Sodium 300mg; Total Carbohydrate 44g (Dietary Fiber 4g; Sugars 26g); Protein 6g • **% Daily Value:** Vitamin A 0%; Vitamin C 0%; Calcium 8%; Iron 10% • **Exchanges:** 1 Starch, 1 1/2 Other Carbohydrate, 1 Vegetable • **Carbohydrate Choices:** 3

WHY IT WORKS:

DON'T KNOW BEANS? Although a can of beans is good in a pinch, cooked dried beans deliver the best flavor and texture. The goal when cooking dried beans is twofold: hydrating and cooking the starch. If your beans are old, the first part can be much harder than it sounds. The best practice is to cook beans in plain water. Acid and some minerals can actually strengthen the cell wall of the bean, preventing water from entering. Add tomato sauce and molasses near the end of cooking time. The high acid of the tomato and the minerals in molasses will guarantee your beans will never cook through.

Lemon-Parmesan Risotto

4 cups chicken broth

1 cup water

1/2 teaspoon salt

2 tablespoons butter

1 tablespoon olive oil

2 cups uncooked Arborio rice

2/3 cup dry white wine or
    chicken broth

1/2 cup grated Parmesan cheese

1 tablespoon finely shredded
    lemon peel

1 tablespoon fresh lemon juice

2 tablespoons finely chopped fresh
    parsley leaves

1. In 2-quart saucepan, heat broth, water and salt to a simmer over medium-high heat. Reduce heat to low to keep broth warm.

2. In 4- to 5-quart Dutch oven, heat butter and oil over medium heat until butter stops sizzling. Stir in rice until coated and heat, stirring constantly, until kernels are slightly translucent around edges. Add wine and heat 3 minutes longer, stirring constantly, until rice absorbs liquid.

3. Reduce heat to medium-low and stir well. Add 1 cup broth (a 1/2-cup ladle works well for adding the broth) to rice so there is just enough to barely cover the rice. Continue cooking and stirring about 5 minutes or until rice has absorbed most of the broth. Add another 1 cup broth and cook about 5 minutes longer, stirring constantly, until broth is almost absorbed. Repeat twice, adding 1 cup broth each time and cooking until broth is almost absorbed and rice is al dente (firm to the bite) and creamy. Stir in cheese, lemon peel and lemon juice. Remove from heat and sprinkle with parsley.

1 Serving: Calories 270 (Calories from Fat 70); Total Fat 8g (Saturated Fat 3g; Trans Fat 0g); Cholesterol 15mg; Sodium 800mg; Total Carbohydrate 41g (Dietary Fiber 0g; Sugars 0g); Protein 9g • **% Daily Value:** Vitamin A 4%; Vitamin C 2%; Calcium 10%; Iron 10% • **Exchanges:** 2 1/2 Starch, 1 1/2 Fat • **Carbohydrate Choices:** 3

WHY IT WORKS: THROUGH THICK AND THIN

Think of risotto as savory rice pudding. Rice pudding achieves its texture as the rice cooks and releases starch to thicken the surrounding milk. Unlike rice pudding, risotto is characterized by slightly firm rice. Because the rice does not cook through, there is not enough time for the starch to thicken the broth. Several techniques are used to solve this problem. Short-grain rice (usually Italian Arborio or Carnaroli) is used for its greater amount of surface starch. And the rice is constantly stirred as it cooks in broth. The friction of each grain hitting its neighbor pushes more starch into the surrounding liquid. For that reason, broth is added a little at a time; if it was added all at once, you would lose the friction and the creamy consistency.

RECIPE R$_x$: MUSHY VS. CREAMY Risotto is not something that most of us eat on a daily basis. It is cooked very differently than regular rice and spotting the right finished texture can be tricky. The final consistency you are looking for is creamy but not runny or

mushy. The Italians (who invented risotto) say that the right texture is *all'onda,* which roughly translates as "with waves." This means that when you stir the finished dish it should still be thin enough to create a small wave in the pot. In the end, though, it is your pot of risotto. Find the texture you like and enjoy.

Grandma's Macaroni and Cheese

PREP TIME: 25 MINUTES • **START TO FINISH:** 50 MINUTES   4 SERVINGS

1 1/2 teaspoons salt, if desired
2 cups uncooked elbow macaroni
    (7 oz)
1/4 cup butter
1/4 cup all-purpose flour
1/2 teaspoon salt
1/4 teaspoon pepper
1/4 teaspoon ground mustard
1/4 teaspoon Worcestershire sauce
2 cups milk
2 cups shredded sharp Cheddar
    cheese (8 oz)

1. Heat oven to 350°F.

2. Fill 5-quart Dutch oven with 3 quarts water; heat to boiling over high heat. When water is boiling, add 1 1/2 teaspoons salt if desired. When water returns to boil, add macaroni. Stir immediately to make sure it doesn't stick to itself or pan. Boil macaroni 8 to 10 minutes or until cooked through but still slightly firm. Drain in colander. There is no need to shake off excess moisture.

3. Meanwhile, in 3-quart saucepan, melt butter over low heat. Stir in flour, 1/2 teaspoon salt, the pepper, mustard and Worcestershire sauce. Cook over low heat, stirring constantly, until mixture is smooth and bubbly; remove from heat. Stir in milk. Heat to boiling, stirring constantly. Boil and stir 1 minute; remove from heat. Stir in cheese until melted.

4. Drain macaroni. Gently stir macaroni into cheese sauce. Pour into ungreased 2-quart casserole.

5. Bake uncovered 20 to 25 minutes or until bubbly.

1 Serving: Calories 610 (Calories from Fat 300); Total Fat 34g (Saturated Fat 19g; Trans Fat 1g); Cholesterol 100mg; Sodium 790mg; Total Carbohydrate 51g (Dietary Fiber 3g; Sugars 8g); Protein 26g • **% Daily Value:** Vitamin A 25%; Vitamin C 0%; Calcium 45%; Iron 15% • **Exchanges:** 3 Starch, 1/2 Other Carbohydrate, 2 1/2 High-Fat Meat, 2 Fat • **Carbohydrate Choices:** 3 1/2

WHY IT WORKS: **PASTA PRIMER** Contrary to popular belief, Marco Polo did not bring pasta back from his trip to Asia. New archeological evidence suggests that pasta was invented independently in both Asia and Italy. Both regions had the same idea! In its simplest form, pasta is flour mixed with water to create dough that is cut and boiled. Wheat flour is most commonly used, as wheat dough holds its shape best due to its high protein (gluten) content. If the dough is dried immediately after cutting, durum wheat semolina is the preferred flour. Unlike regular flour, semolina is almost entirely protein. Less water must be added to form a dough (starch absorbs most of the water in regular dough) and less time is needed for drying.

Grandma's Macaroni and Cheese

Hearty Polenta with Swiss Cheese

1 cup yellow cornmeal, preferably stone-ground

1/2 cup cold water

3 cups boiling water

1 teaspoon salt

1 tablespoon butter

1 1/2 cups shredded Swiss or Gruyère cheese (6 oz)

1. In 2-quart saucepan, mix cornmeal and 1/2 cup cold water. Stir in 3 cups boiling water and the salt. Cook over medium heat, stirring constantly, until mixture thickens and boils; reduce heat to low. (When making polenta, or any other thick pudding, the mixture tends to bubble and plop, which can lead to burns.)

2. Cover and simmer 10 minutes, stirring occasionally until very thick; remove from heat. Stir until smooth. Stir in butter and 1 cup of the cheese.

3. Sprinkle each serving with remaining cheese.

1 Serving: Calories 210 (Calories from Fat 90); Total Fat 10g (Saturated Fat 6g; Trans Fat 0g); Cholesterol 30mg; Sodium 480mg; Total Carbohydrate 19g (Dietary Fiber 0g; Sugars 0g); Protein 10g • **% Daily Value:** Vitamin A 8%; Vitamin C 0%; Calcium 30%; Iron 6% • **Exchanges:** 1 1/2 Starch, 1 High-Fat Meat • **Carbohydrate Choices:** 1

WHY IT WORKS: **GOURMET GRUEL** Polenta is the Italian version of American cornmeal mush. Made from ground, dried corn, polenta refers to both the cornmeal itself and the finished dish. Typically, dried corn for polenta is ground coarser than its American cousin, which means the dish usually takes longer to cook. Most families in Italy have their own technique for making polenta, but a common method is to heat a liquid (stock, water, milk or a mixture) to a simmer in a large pan. A handful of polenta is then held above the pot and slowly drizzled in by letting it slip between the fingers. Constant stirring is necessary to prevent lumps from forming. An easier method, as described in this recipe, is to first hydrate the polenta in cold water. Hydrating causes the starch in the corn to swell, making it less likely to form lumps.

Curried Pineapple Chutney

PREP TIME: 30 MINUTES • **START TO FINISH:** 3 HOURS 45 MINUTES   24 SERVINGS (1/4 CUP EACH)

1 medium pineapple (3 lb) or 1 1/2 lb
    purchased fresh pineapple chunks
3 medium purple or red plums
    (about 1 lb) or 1 can (16 oz) whole
    pitted plums, drained
1 medium onion, chopped (1/2 cup)
1 jalapeño chile, seeded and
    finely chopped
1 tablespoon finely chopped
    gingerroot
1 clove garlic, finely chopped
2/3 cup cider vinegar
1/2 cup water
1 1/3 cups packed light brown sugar
1 teaspoon ground cinnamon
1 teaspoon curry powder
1/2 teaspoon salt
1/8 teaspoon ground red pepper
    (cayenne)
2 teaspoons grated orange peel
1 cup dried cranberries or cherries

1. Peel and core pineapple. Cut pineapple into 1-inch chunks to make 5 cups. (If using purchased pineapple chunks, cut large pieces into 1-inch chunks.) Cut plums in half and remove pits; cut each half into 3 pieces. (If using canned plums, cut each into 6 pieces.)

2. In 4- to 5-quart Dutch oven, heat onion, chile, gingerroot, garlic, vinegar and water to boiling over high heat. Reduce heat to medium and simmer 5 minutes.

3. Stir in brown sugar, cinnamon, curry powder, salt, red pepper and orange peel to combine. Add pineapple, plums and dried cranberries. Increase heat to high and heat to boiling. Reduce heat to medium-low and simmer 30 to 45 minutes, stirring occasionally, until fruit is soft and dried cranberries have hydrated. Remove from heat and pour into bowl. Cool at room temperature 30 minutes.

4. Cover and refrigerate at least 2 hours until chilled. Chutney can be refrigerated up to 10 days.

1 Serving: Calories 90 (Calories from Fat 0); Total Fat 0g (Saturated Fat 0g; Trans Fat 0g); Cholesterol 0mg; Sodium 55mg; Total Carbohydrate 21g (Dietary Fiber 1g; Sugars 19g); Protein 0g • **% Daily Value:** Vitamin A 0%; Vitamin C 4%; Calcium 0%; Iron 2% • **Exchanges:** 1/2 Fruit, 1 Other Carbohydrate • **Carbohydrate Choices:** 1 1/2

WHY IT WORKS:

PERFECT PICKLING Before refrigerators, food could not be stored more than a few days without bacteria or mold causing it to go bad. To get around this, several preservation methods were used. One of the most common was pickling. In its simplest form, pickling involves immersing cooked or blanched foods in a vinegar solution. The low pH (high acidity) of vinegar stops any unwanted growth. To flavor the pickles (which could include vegetables, nuts and even meat), spices, herbs and sugar were often added to the vinegar. Even though refrigerators are now available, people have grown to enjoy the sharp, refreshing taste of pickles.

Sweet Somethings

EASY BUT

SATISFYING DESSERTS

Tres Leches Cake

PREP TIME: 30 MINUTES • START TO FINISH: 4 HOURS 15 MINUTES   15 SERVINGS

Cake

2 1/4 cups all-purpose flour
1 1/2 cups sugar
1/2 cup butter, softened
1 1/4 cups milk
3 1/2 teaspoons baking powder
1 teaspoon salt
1 teaspoon vanilla
3 eggs

Tres Leches Mixture

1 cup whipping (heavy) cream
1 cup whole milk
1 can (14 oz) sweetened condensed
    milk (not evaporated)
1/3 cup rum or 1 tablespoon rum
    extract plus enough water to
    measure 1/3 cup

Topping

1 cup whipping (heavy) cream
2 tablespoons rum or 1 teaspoon
    rum extract
1/2 teaspoon vanilla
1/2 cup chopped pecans, toasted

1. Heat oven to 350°F. Grease bottom only of 13 × 9-inch pan with shortening.

2. In large bowl, beat all cake ingredients with electric mixer on low speed 30 seconds, scraping bowl constantly. Beat on high speed 3 minutes, scraping bowl occasionally. Pour into pan.

3. Bake 35 to 40 minutes or until toothpick inserted in center comes out clean or until cake springs back when touched lightly in center. Let stand 5 minutes.

4. Pierce top of hot cake every 1/2 inch with long-tined fork, wiping fork occasionally to reduce sticking.

5. In large bowl, stir 1 cup whipping cream, the whole milk, condensed milk and 1/3 cup rum until well mixed. Carefully pour milk mixture evenly over top of cake. Cover and refrigerate about 3 hours or until chilled and most of milk mixture has been absorbed into cake.

6. In chilled large bowl, beat 1 cup whipping cream, 2 tablespoons rum and 1/2 teaspoon vanilla with electric mixer on high speed until soft peaks form. Frost cake with whipped cream mixture. Sprinkle with pecans. Store covered in refrigerator.

1 Serving: Calories 450 (Calories from Fat 210); Total Fat 23g (Saturated Fat 12g; Trans Fat 0.5g); Cholesterol 105mg; Sodium 390mg; Total Carbohydrate 52g (Dietary Fiber 0g; Sugars 37g); Protein 8g • **% Daily Value:** Vitamin A 15%; Vitamin C 0%; Calcium 20%; Iron 8% • **Exchanges:** 1 Starch, 2 Other Carbohydrate, 1/2 Low-Fat Milk, 4 Fat • **Carbohydrate Choices:** 3 1/2

WHY IT WORKS: **THE CONDENSED VERSION** To extend shelf life, almost all canned goods are heated to stop harmful bacteria from growing. Sweetened condensed milk is an exception. This thick dairy product receives only a mild heat treatment. The reason? Unlike canned soup or canned peas, sweetened condensed milk is protected by sugar. Sweetened condensed milk starts out as regular milk. Then, up to half of its water is evaporated by placing the milk in a vacuum chamber. Finally, up to 45% sugar is added to the milk. At this high sugar concentration, very few bacteria can live; the sugar takes all of their water. The resulting sweet milk is then placed into cans and is ready to use.

Tres Leches Cake

Moist Chocolate-Mint Layer Cake

PREP TIME: 45 MINUTES • START TO FINISH: 2 HOURS 35 MINUTES   12 SERVINGS

Cake

3 cups cake flour or 2 2/3 cups
    all-purpose flour
2 teaspoons baking powder
1 teaspoon baking soda
3/4 teaspoon salt
1 1/4 cups unsweetened baking cocoa
1 1/2 cups hot strong coffee
1 cup butter, softened
1/3 cup vegetable oil
2 teaspoons vanilla
1 teaspoon peppermint extract
2 cups packed light brown sugar
3 eggs
2 egg yolks

Frosting

1/2 cup butter, softened
1 package (8 oz) cream cheese,
    softened
3 oz unsweetened baking chocolate,
    melted
2 tablespoons milk
1 teaspoon peppermint extract
1/2 teaspoon vanilla
3 1/2 cups powdered sugar

1. Adjust oven rack to middle position. Heat oven to 350°F. Grease two 9-inch round pans with shortening and dust with flour; set aside.

2. In medium bowl, beat flour, baking powder, baking soda and salt with wire whisk; set aside.

3. In another medium bowl, beat cocoa and hot coffee with wire whisk, making sure no lumps remain; set aside.

4. In large bowl, beat 1 cup butter and the oil with electric mixer on medium speed 5 minutes or until fluffy (7 minutes if using handheld mixer). Add 2 teaspoons vanilla and 1 teaspoon peppermint extract and beat 1 minute. Add brown sugar and beat 3 minutes longer, stopping halfway to scrape side of bowl. Add 2 of the eggs and beat 1 minute. Scrape side of bowl. Add remaining egg and the egg yolks and beat 2 minutes longer.

5. Add about 1 cup of the dry ingredients and 1/2 cup of the coffee mixture to butter mixture. Beat on low speed just until combined. Continue alternately adding dry ingredients and coffee mixture, beating after each addition to combine. When all ingredients have been added, scrape side of bowl. Divide batter evenly between pans.

6. Bake 35 to 40 minutes or until cake tester or toothpick inserted in center comes out clean or cake springs back when touched lightly in center. Cool on wire rack 10 minutes. Run knife or metal spatula between cake and edge of pan to loosen. Invert cakes onto wire rack and cool completely, about 1 hour.

7. In large bowl, beat 1/2 cup butter and the cream cheese with electric mixer on medium speed until soft. Mix in chocolate, milk, 1 teaspoon peppermint extract and 1/2 teaspoon vanilla. On low speed, add powdered sugar, 1 cup at a time, beating until smooth. When all of the powdered sugar has been added, beat 1 minute longer or until smooth.

8. Place 1 layer on serving plate or stemmed cake plate. Spread 2/3 cup frosting over layer to about 1/4 inch from edge. Top with second layer. Frost side and top with remaining frosting.

1 Serving: Calories 850 (Calories from Fat 390); Total Fat 43g (Saturated Fat 20g; Trans Fat 1.5g); Cholesterol 170mg; Sodium 580mg; Total Carbohydrate 106g (Dietary Fiber 5g; Sugars 70g); Protein 9g • **% Daily Value:** Vitamin A 25%; Vitamin C 0%; Calcium 15%; Iron 30% • **Exchanges:** 2 1/2 Starch, 4 1/2 Other Carbohydrate, 8 Fat • **Carbohydrate Choices:** 7

WHY IT WORKS: **BAKING BUILDING BLOCKS** Eggs, specifically egg yolks, are the cornerstone of baking. The yolks contain all of the egg's fat and fat-soluble vitamins (A, D, E and K). More importantly, the yolk is the storehouse for a wonderful substance called lecithin. Chemically, lecithin is defined as an emulsifier. Emulsifiers are the diplomats of the food world. Water and oil are not fond of one another, and lecithin serves to bring them together. This ability allows lecithin to make ice cream smoother, cakes more tender and dressings creamier. In this recipe, the extra yolks add fat, which keeps the cake moist, and the lecithin makes for a smooth crumb texture.

Individual Chocolate Lava Cakes
WITH CARAMEL SAUCE

PREP TIME: 30 MINUTES • START TO FINISH: 2 HOURS · 6 SERVINGS

Cakes

1 cup butter, melted
2 cups packed light brown sugar
4 eggs
1 egg yolk
1 tablespoon vanilla
3/4 cup all-purpose flour
1 cup unsweetened baking cocoa
1 1/2 teaspoons baking powder

Sauce

3/4 cup granulated sugar
1/3 cup light corn syrup
3 tablespoons water
1/2 cup whipping (heavy) cream
1/2 teaspoon vanilla

1. Butter six 8-ounce ramekins and dust with sugar; set aside.

2. In medium bowl, beat butter, brown sugar, eggs, egg yolk and 1 tablespoon vanilla with electric mixer on medium speed 2 minutes or until smooth. In another medium bowl, mix flour, cocoa and baking powder. Add to butter mixture and beat on low speed about 1 minute until smooth.

3. Divide batter equally among ramekins. Cover with plastic wrap and refrigerate 1 hour.

4. In 2-quart saucepan, heat granulated sugar, corn syrup and water to boiling over medium heat. Boil uncovered 15 minutes or until mixture turns deep golden brown. Add whipping cream and stir until smooth. Remove from heat and add 1/2 teaspoon vanilla. Cool to room temperature before serving, about 45 minutes.

5. Heat oven to 350°F. Place ramekins in two 13×9-inch pans or pan with low sides. Bake 25 to 30 minutes or until outside edges are firm and centers are still soft and creamy. Do not overbake.

6. Place ramekins on serving plates. Split center of each cake and pour about 2 tablespoons sauce inside each. Serve immediately.

1 Serving: Calories 960 (Calories from Fat 390); Total Fat 43g (Saturated Fat 22g; Trans Fat 2g); Cholesterol 280mg; Sodium 430mg; Total Carbohydrate 132g (Dietary Fiber 5g; Sugars 104g); Protein 10g • **% Daily Value:** Vitamin A 30%; Vitamin C 0%; Calcium 20%; Iron 25% • **Exchanges:** 2 Starch, 7 Other Carbohydrate, 1/2 High-Fat Meat, 7 1/2 Fat • **Carbohydrate Choices:** 9

WHY IT WORKS: **NUTS FOR COCOA** One of the purest forms of chocolate flavor you can buy is cocoa powder. It is literally the powder left after squeezing the cocoa butter out of the cocoa bean and it comes in two basic forms: natural and Dutch-process. Regular, or natural unsweetened cocoa, is the type you probably grew up with and your mother used to make brownies and cakes. Alkalized or Dutch-process cocoa is the same natural cocoa with a base (alkali) added. Dutch-process cocoa is washed with an alkaline solution, which gives it a smoother taste and a redder color. Both types of cocoa have pros and cons. Natural cocoa has more of the subtle flavors of the cocoa bean, but it can also taste a little too bitter. Dutch-process cocoa has a more rounded flavor and mixes more easily with liquid, but it is often hard to find in the grocery store. Because success in baking often relies on the amount of acidic ingredients you have versus the amount of base (alkaline) ingredients, substituting natural cocoa for Dutch-process in a recipe, and vice versa, is not recommended.

"All-the-Stops-Out" Chocolate Cake

PREP TIME: 1 HOUR 10 MINUTES • START TO FINISH: 4 HOURS
16 SERVINGS

Cake

2 cups strong coffee

2 cups butter

1 1/2 cups unsweetened baking
cocoa (preferably Dutch process)

4 cups all-purpose flour

2 cups granulated sugar

2 cups packed dark brown sugar

1 tablespoon baking soda

1 teaspoon salt

3 eggs

1 egg yolk

1 1/3 cups sour cream

2 teaspoons vanilla

Icing

32 oz semisweet or bittersweet
baking chocolate, chopped

1 quart (4 cups) whipping
(heavy) cream

2 tablespoons light corn syrup

2 teaspoons vanilla

Coating

40 thin chocolate wafer cookies,
finely crushed (about 1 3/4 cups)

1. Adjust oven racks to middle and bottom positions. Heat oven to 350°F. Spray three 9-inch round pans with cooking spray. Line bottom of pans with cooking parchment paper rounds; spray with cooking spray.

2. In 3-quart saucepan, heat coffee and butter over medium heat until butter melts and mixture just comes to a boil. Remove from heat and add cocoa. Beat with wire whisk until there are no lumps; set aside and cool 5 minutes.

3. In very large bowl, beat flour, granulated sugar, brown sugar, baking soda and salt with wire whisk. Pour coffee mixture over dry ingredients and stir just until no dry flour mixture is visible. In small bowl, beat eggs and egg yolk with wire whisk. Add to flour mixture, beating well. Stir in sour cream and 2 teaspoons vanilla until well mixed. Batter will be thin and watery.

4. Pour batter into pans. (Batter will nearly reach tops of pans.) Carefully place pans in oven, 2 on bottom rack and 1 on middle rack. Bake 45 to 50 minutes or until cake tester or toothpick inserted in center comes out clean and cake top is no longer wobbly. Cool on wire racks, about 10 minutes. Invert cake layers onto wire racks and remove parchment paper. Cool completely, about 1 hour. (Layers are easier to handle when cold, so you may want to wrap them in plastic wrap and refrigerate 8 to 12 hours before frosting.)

5. In large bowl, place chopped chocolate and set aside. In 4-quart saucepan, heat whipping cream and corn syrup to a simmer over medium heat. Remove from heat and add 2 teaspoons vanilla. Pour mixture over chocolate and cover bowl with plastic wrap; let stand 5 minutes. Remove plastic wrap and beat with wire whisk until chocolate is smooth. Cover bowl with plastic wrap and chill 30 minutes. Stir well and refrigerate 30 minutes longer. Continue to stir every 30 minutes until icing is spreadable, about 2 hours total.

6. Place about 2 tablespoons icing in center of serving plate or stemmed cake plate. (This will steady the cake as you ice it.) Place 1 layer on plate and spread approximately 1 1/2 cups icing to edge of layer. Top with another layer and spread 1 1/2 cups icing to edge. Top with last layer. Frost side and top with remaining icing. Smooth top and side of cake. Use hands to liberally press coating into side of cake. Repeat all around cake to cover side with coating, filling in any bare spots.

1 Serving: Calories 1160 (Calories from Fat 600); Total Fat 67g (Saturated Fat 37g; Trans Fat 2.5g); Cholesterol 195mg; Sodium 670mg; Total Carbohydrate 129g (Dietary Fiber 7g; Sugars 89g); Protein 11g • **% Daily Value:** Vitamin A 35%; Vitamin C 0%; Calcium 15%; Iron 30% • **Exchanges:** 2 1/2 Starch, 6 Other Carbohydrate, 13 Fat • **Carbohydrate Choices:** 8

"All-the-Stops-Out" Chocolate Cake

S'Mores Cheesecake

Crust

1 1/4 cups graham cracker crumbs
3 tablespoons granulated sugar
1/4 cup plus 2 tablespoons butter, melted

Cheesecake

3 packages (8 oz each) cream cheese, softened
1 cup packed light brown sugar
1/3 cup marshmallow creme
1 tablespoon vanilla
4 eggs
1/4 teaspoon ground cinnamon
1 cup milk chocolate chips (6 oz)

Topping

1 cup milk chocolate chips (6 oz)
1/4 cup whipping (heavy) cream

1. Heat oven to 425°F. Spray 10-inch springform pan with cooking spray.

2. In small bowl, mix all crust ingredients. Remove 1/2 cup mixture for topping; set aside. Press remaining mixture evenly into bottom of pan. Bake 5 minutes or until crust is just turning deep golden around edge.

3. In large bowl, beat cream cheese with electric mixer on medium speed, stopping to scrape side occasionally, until smooth. Add brown sugar, marshmallow creme and vanilla, and beat until smooth. Add eggs, 1 at a time, beating 1 minute after each addition. Use rubber spatula to stir in cinnamon. Sprinkle 1 cup chocolate chips over crust. Pour batter over chips.

4. Bake cheesecake 15 minutes; reduce oven temperature to 225°F. Bake 55 minutes longer or until cheesecake is set around edge and center is almost set but just slightly wiggly. (Do not insert knife to test doneness because hole could cause cheesecake to crack.) Turn off oven, open oven door slightly and allow cheesecake to cool to room temperature. Remove from oven, cover loosely with foil and refrigerate at least 3 hours.

5. In 1-quart saucepan, heat 1 cup chocolate chips and the whipping cream over low heat, stirring occasionally, until chocolate chips are melted. Spread over cheesecake and sprinkle with reserved 1/2 cup crumbs.

6. Cover with foil and refrigerate cheesecake 1 hour or up to 48 hours. Run metal spatula along side of cheesecake to loosen and remove side of pan before serving. Store any leftovers covered in refrigerator.

1 Serving: Calories 430 (Calories from Fat 260); Total Fat 29g (Saturated Fat 17g; Trans Fat 1g); Cholesterol 120mg; Sodium 230mg; Total Carbohydrate 36g (Dietary Fiber 0g; Sugars 32g); Protein 7g • **% Daily Value:** Vitamin A 20%; Vitamin C 0%; Calcium 10%; Iron 8% • **Exchanges:** 2 1/2 Other Carbohydrate, 1 High-Fat Meat, 4 Fat • **Carbohydrate Choices:** 2 1/2

WHY IT WORKS: **LOW AND SLOW** Making a cheesecake can be intimidating. When is it done? Why did it crack? Can it be frozen? To understand cheesecake you must first know that it is more of a custard than a cake. Eggs play a key role in its structure. The other ingredients are important of course, but the eggs determine doneness and whether it has a surface crack. Because eggs are easy to overcook, it is important to bake the cheesecake at a low temperature and possibly in a water bath. For the same reason, cheesecakes should not be baked until set (the residual heat will cook them through without overcooking and causing the dreaded crack). And finally, yes, cheesecakes freeze very well.

WHY IT WORKS: **REVVING UP CHOCOLATE** You can never have enough chocolate—in life or in a recipe! However, adding more chocolate to a recipe does not necessarily provide more chocolate flavor. The best way to increase chocolate flavor is to increase the other flavors present in chocolate. Chocolate contains subtle hints of coffee, vanilla, spice and even smoke. By adding elements of these flavors to your recipe, such as the coffee in this cake, you make it more "chocolaty." (To get a smoke flavor, one famous pastry maker has even served brownies with tobacco leaves—an ingredient that is definitely not recommended!)

"All-the-Stops-Out" Chocolate Cake

Harvest Apple Cupcakes

WITH CREAM CHEESE FROSTING

PREP TIME: 30 MINUTES • **START TO FINISH:** 2 HOURS

Cupcakes

1 1/2 cups granulated sugar

1 cup vegetable oil

3 eggs

2 cups all-purpose flour

2 teaspoons ground cinnamon

1 teaspoon baking soda

1 teaspoon vanilla

1/2 teaspoon salt

3 cups chopped tart apples

1 cup coarsely chopped nuts

Frosting

1 package (8 oz) cream cheese, softened

1/4 cup butter, softened

2 to 3 teaspoons milk

1 teaspoon vanilla

4 cups powdered sugar

1. Heat oven to 350°F. Line 24 regular-size muffin cups with paper baking cups.

2. In large bowl, beat granulated sugar, oil and eggs with electric mixer on low speed about 30 seconds or until blended. Add flour, cinnamon, baking soda, 1 teaspoon vanilla and the salt; beat on low speed 1 minute. Stir in apples and nuts. Divide batter evenly among muffin cups (about 1/2 cup per cupcake).

3. Bake 30 to 35 minutes or until toothpick inserted in center of cupcake comes out clean. Cool 10 minutes; remove cupcakes from pan to wire rack. Cool completely, about 30 minutes.

4. In medium bowl, beat cream cheese, butter, milk and 1 teaspoon vanilla with electric mixer on low speed until smooth. Gradually beat in powdered sugar, 1 cup at a time, on low speed until smooth and spreadable. Frost cupcakes with frosting. Store frosted cupcakes or any remaining frosting covered in refrigerator.

1 Cupcake: Calories 350 (Calories from Fat 160); Total Fat 18g (Saturated Fat 5g; Trans Fat 0g); Cholesterol 40mg; Sodium 150mg; Total Carbohydrate 44g (Dietary Fiber 1g; Sugars 34g); Protein 3g • **% Daily Value:** Vitamin A 6%; Vitamin C 0%; Calcium 2%; Iron 6% • **Exchanges:** 1 Starch, 2 Other Carbohydrate, 3 1/2 Fat • **Carbohydrate Choices:** 3

WHY IT WORKS:

TAKE THE CAKE! It is obvious that cupcakes are little versions of standard cakes. However, because of their miniscule stature and shorter bake time, cupcakes have their own baking challenges. As with standard cakes, the flour type used makes a huge difference in the end result. Cake or all-purpose flour (because of their low protein content) results in the best texture. Because cupcake batter is handled more, care must be taken not to overwork it; doing so activates the protein and causes small tunnels to form in the baked cakes. Also, the small size of cupcakes means they bake faster and dry out more easily. Begin checking for doneness early.

Lemon Swirl Cheesecake

PREP TIME: 25 MINUTES • START TO FINISH: 24 HOURS 55 MINUTES   10 SERVINGS

3/4 cup graham cracker crumbs

1 tablespoon sugar

2 tablespoons butter, melted

1 cup sugar

3 tablespoons cornstarch

1 cup water

1/3 cup lemon juice

2 egg yolks, beaten

2 packages (8 oz each) cream
    cheese, cubed and softened

2 teaspoons grated lemon peel

1/2 cup whipping (heavy) cream

1. Heat oven to 350°F. In small bowl, mix cracker crumbs and 1 tablespoon sugar. Stir in butter. Press evenly in bottom of 8×2-inch springform pan. Bake 9 to 11 minutes or until set. Cool completely.

2. Meanwhile, in 1 1/2-quart saucepan, mix 1 cup sugar and the cornstarch. Stir in water, lemon juice and egg yolks. Cook over medium heat, stirring constantly, until mixture thickens and boils. Boil 1 minute; remove from heat. Reserve 1/2 cup lemon mixture. Stir cream cheese and lemon peel into remaining 1 1/2 cups lemon mixture until smooth. Press plastic wrap on surfaces of each mixture (this helps prevent a "skin" forming on top). Refrigerate about 30 minutes or until cool.

3. In chilled small bowl, beat whipping cream with electric mixer on high speed until soft peaks form. Fold whipped cream into cream cheese mixture; pour over baked layer. Drop reserved lemon mixture by tablespoonfuls onto cheesecake. Cut through dollops of lemon mixture, using knife, to form swirls.

4. Refrigerate at least 24 hours or until set. Run metal spatula along side of cheesecake to loosen; remove side of pan. Refrigerate any remaining cheesecake.

1 Serving: Calories 350 (Calories from Fat 210); Total Fat 23g (Saturated Fat 14g; Trans Fat 1g); Cholesterol 110mg; Sodium 190mg; Total Carbohydrate 30g (Dietary Fiber 0g; Sugars 25g); Protein 5g • **% Daily Value:** Vitamin A 20%; Vitamin C 2%; Calcium 6%; Iron 4% • **Exchanges:** 1/2 Starch, 1 1/2 Other Carbohydrate, 1/2 High-Fat Meat, 3 1/2 Fat • **Carbohydrate Choices:** 2

WHY IT WORKS: **EGG ON YOUR FACE** As proteins (think little springs) are heated, their structure changes. Add a little heat and proteins start to unwind and connect with neighboring proteins. Add more heat and proteins start to recombine and solidify. You see this last step when you fry an egg. The egg white changes from liquid to solid in a process called coagulation. All proteins coagulate when heated, but the temperature at which they solidify changes depending on their surroundings. For example, in this recipe, egg yolks are cooked with sugar and lemon juice. Normally egg yolks coagulate between 149°F and 158°F. However, here the sugar interferes with the proteins when they try to recombine. The lemon juice's acidity changes the protein's structure, making it harder for the proteins to reconnect. Because of these added ingredients, egg yolks can be cooked at a higher temperature without turning into sweet scrambled eggs.

S'Mores Cheesecake

Crust

1 1/4 cups graham cracker crumbs
3 tablespoons granulated sugar
1/4 cup plus 2 tablespoons butter, melted

Cheesecake

3 packages (8 oz each) cream cheese, softened
1 cup packed light brown sugar
1/3 cup marshmallow creme
1 tablespoon vanilla
4 eggs
1/4 teaspoon ground cinnamon
1 cup milk chocolate chips (6 oz)

Topping

1 cup milk chocolate chips (6 oz)
1/4 cup whipping (heavy) cream

1. Heat oven to 425°F. Spray 10-inch springform pan with cooking spray.

2. In small bowl, mix all crust ingredients. Remove 1/2 cup mixture for topping; set aside. Press remaining mixture evenly into bottom of pan. Bake 5 minutes or until crust is just turning deep golden around edge.

3. In large bowl, beat cream cheese with electric mixer on medium speed, stopping to scrape side occasionally, until smooth. Add brown sugar, marshmallow creme and vanilla, and beat until smooth. Add eggs, 1 at a time, beating 1 minute after each addition. Use rubber spatula to stir in cinnamon. Sprinkle 1 cup chocolate chips over crust. Pour batter over chips.

4. Bake cheesecake 15 minutes; reduce oven temperature to 225°F. Bake 55 minutes longer or until cheesecake is set around edge and center is almost set but just slightly wiggly. (Do not insert knife to test doneness because hole could cause cheesecake to crack.) Turn off oven, open oven door slightly and allow cheesecake to cool to room temperature. Remove from oven, cover loosely with foil and refrigerate at least 3 hours.

5. In 1-quart saucepan, heat 1 cup chocolate chips and the whipping cream over low heat, stirring occasionally, until chocolate chips are melted. Spread over cheesecake and sprinkle with reserved 1/2 cup crumbs.

6. Cover with foil and refrigerate cheesecake 1 hour or up to 48 hours. Run metal spatula along side of cheesecake to loosen and remove side of pan before serving. Store any leftovers covered in refrigerator.

1 Serving: Calories 430 (Calories from Fat 260); Total Fat 29g (Saturated Fat 17g; Trans Fat 1g); Cholesterol 120mg; Sodium 230mg; Total Carbohydrate 36g (Dietary Fiber 0g; Sugars 32g); Protein 7g • **% Daily Value:** Vitamin A 20%; Vitamin C 0%; Calcium 10%; Iron 8% • **Exchanges:** 2 1/2 Other Carbohydrate, 1 High-Fat Meat, 4 Fat • **Carbohydrate Choices:** 2 1/2

WHY IT WORKS: **LOW AND SLOW** Making a cheesecake can be intimidating. When is it done? Why did it crack? Can it be frozen? To understand cheesecake you must first know that it is more of a custard than a cake. Eggs play a key role in its structure. The other ingredients are important of course, but the eggs determine doneness and whether it has a surface crack. Because eggs are easy to overcook, it is important to bake the cheesecake at a low temperature and possibly in a water bath. For the same reason, cheesecakes should not be baked until set (the residual heat will cook them through without overcooking and causing the dreaded crack). And finally, yes, cheesecakes freeze very well.

RECIPE Rx: TEARS OF JOY Did you take the baked cheesecake out of the refrigerator and see a big puddle of liquid on top? The worst-case scenario is that you overbaked the cake. Just like when you overcook scrambled eggs, the protein in your cake, if overcooked, will squeeze out its water. Or it could be that you refrigerated the cheesecake too soon after pulling it from the oven and the moisture condensed on the cake top. You will know which case you are in when you cut the cake. The overcooked cake will be dry and contain small holes. The other cake will just have a soggy top. If yours was overcooked, there's not much you can do but serve it with extra sauce and hope people don't notice. In the future, check your oven temperature and make sure it is correct.

S'Mores Cheesecake

Applescotch Pie

PREP TIME: 55 MINUTES • START TO FINISH: 2 HOURS 35 MINUTES   6 SERVINGS

Filling

5 cups thinly sliced peeled tart apples
    (about 5 medium)
1 cup packed brown sugar
1/4 cup water
1 tablespoon lemon juice
1/4 cup all-purpose flour
2 tablespoons granulated sugar
3/4 teaspoon salt
1 teaspoon vanilla
3 tablespoons butter

Crust

2 cups all-purpose flour
1 teaspoon salt
2/3 cup plus 2 tablespoons shortening
4 to 6 tablespoons cold water

1. In 2-quart saucepan, mix apples, brown sugar, water and lemon juice. Heat to boiling; reduce heat. Cover and simmer 7 to 8 minutes or just until apples are tender. In small bowl, mix 1/4 cup flour, the granulated sugar and 3/4 teaspoon salt; stir into apple mixture. Cook, stirring constantly, until mixture thickens and boils. Boil and stir 1 minute; remove from heat. Stir in vanilla and butter; cool.

2. Heat oven to 425°F.

3. In medium bowl, mix 2 cups flour and 1 teaspoon salt. Cut in shortening, using pastry blender (or pulling 2 table knives through ingredients in opposite directions), until particles are size of small peas. Sprinkle with cold water, 1 tablespoon at a time, tossing with fork until all flour is moistened and pastry almost leaves side of bowl (1 to 2 teaspoons more water can be added if necessary).

4. Gather pastry into a ball. Divide pastry in half; shape each half into flattened round surface. Wrap flattened rounds of pastry in plastic wrap and refrigerate about 45 minutes or until dough is firm and cold, yet pliable. This allows shortening to become slightly firm, which helps make pastry more flaky. If refrigerated longer, let pastry soften slightly before rolling.

5. Roll one round of pastry on lightly floured surface, using floured rolling pin, into circle 2 inches larger than upside-down 9-inch glass pie plate. Fold one pastry circle into fourths and place in pie plate. Unfold pastry and ease into plate, pressing firmly against bottom and side and being careful not to stretch pastry, which will cause it to shrink when baked.

6. Spoon apple mixture into pastry-lined pie plate. Trim overhanging edge of bottom pastry 1/2 inch from rim of pan. Roll other round of pastry. Fold top pastry into fourths and cut slits so steam can escape. Place pastry over filling and unfold. Trim overhanging edge of top pastry 1 inch from rim of pan. Fold and roll top edge under lower edge, pressing on rim to seal; flute. Cover edge with 2- to 3-inch strip of foil to prevent excessive browning; remove foil during last 15 minutes of baking.

7. Bake 40 to 45 minutes or until crust is golden brown. Cool on wire rack at least 2 hours.

WHY IT WORKS: **GETTING THE WATER OUT** A simple experiment: Cut up two apples and add them to separate saucepans. Add a few tablespoons of brown sugar to one, but leave the other plain. Cook both over low heat. Notice how the apple without brown sugar softens and falls apart faster. The brown sugar stops the apple from softening. Calcium and acid in the brown sugar strengthen the apple's cells, slowing their breakdown. This information helps whether you make applesauce (add the sugar after the apples cook down) or apple pie (add sugar early to help apples retain their form rather than turn to mush).

1 Serving: Calories 690 (Calories from Fat 300); Total Fat 33g (Saturated Fat 10g; Trans Fat 5g); Cholesterol 15mg; Sodium 740mg; Total Carbohydrate 92g (Dietary Fiber 3g; Sugars 52g); Protein 5g • **% Daily Value:** Vitamin A 6%; Vitamin C 4%; Calcium 4%; Iron 15% • **Exchanges:** 2 Starch, 1/2 Fruit, 3 1/2 Other Carbohydrate, 6 Fat • **Carbohydrate Choices:** 6

Decadent Chocolate Pie
WITH PRETZEL CRUST

PREP TIME: 20 MINUTES • **START TO FINISH:** 2 HOURS 15 MINUTES   12 SERVINGS

Crust

3 cups small pretzel twists (about 40)
1/2 cup butter, melted
1/4 cup granulated sugar

Filling

1 tablespoon butter
1 can (14 oz) sweetened condensed
    milk (not evaporated)
1 bag (12 oz) semisweet chocolate
    chips (2 cups)
1/2 cup chopped walnuts
1 teaspoon vanilla
Unsweetened whipped cream,
    if desired

1. Place a few pretzels at a time in resealable plastic food-storage bag; seal bag. Crush pretzels into fine crumbs with rolling pin. (You should have 1 1/4 cups of crumbs.) In medium bowl, mix the crumbs, 1/2 cup melted butter and the sugar. Press firmly and evenly against bottom and side of 9-inch pie plate. Cover and refrigerate about 30 minutes or until firm.

2. Heat oven to 350°F.

3. In 2-quart saucepan, melt 1 tablespoon butter over low heat. Stir in condensed milk and chocolate chips. Cook over low heat, stirring occasionally, until chocolate is melted. Stir in walnuts and vanilla. Spread in crust.

4. Bake about 25 minutes or until edge is set but chocolate appears moist in center. Cool in pan on wire rack 1 hour or until completely cooled. To serve, top each slice with whipped cream if desired.

1 Serving: Calories 410 (Calories from Fat 210); Total Fat 23g (Saturated Fat 12g; Trans Fat 0.5g); Cholesterol 35mg; Sodium 210mg; Total Carbohydrate 46g (Dietary Fiber 2g; Sugars 38g); Protein 5g • **% Daily Value:** Vitamin A 8%; Vitamin C 0%; Calcium 10%; Iron 8% • **Exchanges:** 1/2 Starch, 2 Other Carbohydrate, 1/2 Low-Fat Milk, 4 Fat • **Carbohydrate Choices:** 3

WHY IT WORKS: **SALT OF THE EARTH** Salt plays a key role in cooking and baking. Although it's well understood that savory dishes need salt to taste good, it may be surprising to learn that sweet dishes need salt too. Salt enhances the sweetness of many foods. Taste an apple slice. Now sprinkle a small amount of salt on a different slice and taste. Sweeter? Salt can do the same thing to a cake or pie. In this recipe, the salt in the pretzel crust enhances the flavor of the chocolate filling.

Banana-Coconut Cream Pie
WITH BUTTERMILK CRUST

PREP TIME: 1 HOUR 15 MINUTES • **START TO FINISH:** 4 HOURS 45 MINUTES   8 SERVINGS

Crust

3/4 cup all-purpose flour
1/2 cup cake flour
1 tablespoon powdered sugar
1/2 teaspoon salt
1/4 cup firm butter, cut into 8 pieces
1/4 cup cold shortening, cut into
   8 pieces
3 to 4 tablespoons buttermilk

Filling

1 1/3 cups sweetened shredded
   coconut
1 1/2 cups half-and-half
1 cup milk
1/2 cup canned cream of coconut
   (not coconut milk)
1/2 cup granulated sugar
8 egg yolks
1/4 cup cornstarch
2 tablespoons butter
2 teaspoons vanilla
2 ripe bananas, peeled and cut into
   1/2-inch pieces

1. In large bowl, beat all-purpose and cake flours, powdered sugar and salt with wire whisk. Cut 1/4 cup butter and the shortening into dry ingredients using pastry cutter or your fingertips until mixture looks like tiny pebbles. Not all butter and shortening pieces have to be same size.

2. Sprinkle buttermilk, 1 tablespoon at a time, over dry ingredients and mix until all flour is moistened and dough almost leaves side of bowl. Continue to stir until dough comes together. Knead a few times with your hands just to bring it together. Pat dough into a round and wrap in plastic wrap. Refrigerate dough at least 1 hour.

3. Adjust oven rack to middle position. Heat oven to 375°F.

4. Spread coconut evenly on ungreased cookie sheet. Toast coconut in oven 8 minutes, stirring occasionally, until golden brown. Pour coconut on plate to cool completely.

5. Place chilled dough on lightly floured surface. Roll dough into large circle about 1/8 inch thick and 2 inches larger than upside-down 9-inch pie plate. Place dough in 9-inch glass pie plate. Trim off any excess dough, leaving 1/2-inch overhang. Flute edge of crust. Line dough with piece of buttered foil, buttered side down. Shape foil so all crust is covered with foil. (Foil keeps crust from overbrowning.)

6. Bake crust 10 to 12 minutes or until set. Remove foil and bake 10 minutes longer or until dough is lightly browned. Cool to room temperature.

7. In 3-quart saucepan, heat 1/2 cup of the toasted coconut, the half-and-half, milk, cream of coconut and granulated sugar to a simmer over medium heat, stirring occasionally (do not boil or mixture may curdle).

8. Meanwhile, in medium bowl, beat egg yolks and cornstarch with wire whisk. When milk mixture simmers, use ladle to scoop 1 cup into yolk mixture, beating constantly with wire whisk. Repeat with another cup of milk mixture. Pour egg yolk mixture into simmering cream. Cook 3 to 4 minutes, stirring constantly with rubber spatula, until mixture simmers and thickens. Once thickened, cook 2 minutes longer, stirring constantly.

9. Remove custard from heat and stir in 2 tablespoons butter and the vanilla. Cool 10 minutes. Pour half of the custard into cooled pie crust. Sprinkle bananas over custard and top with remaining custard. Smooth top of custard and cover directly with plastic wrap to prevent a tough layer from forming. Refrigerate until filling is cold, at least 2 hours but no more than 24 hours. Before serving, sprinkle with remaining toasted coconut. Store covered in refrigerator.

1 Serving: Calories 580 (Calories from Fat 330); Total Fat 37g (Saturated Fat 21g; Trans Fat 2g); Cholesterol 255mg; Sodium 290mg; Total Carbohydrate 52g (Dietary Fiber 2g; Sugars 28g); Protein 9g • **% Daily Value:** Vitamin A 20%; Vitamin C 4%; Calcium 10%; Iron 15% • **Exchanges:** 1 Starch, 2 Other Carbohydrate, 1/2 Milk, 6 1/2 Fat • **Carbohydrate Choices:** 3 1/2

Banana-Coconut Cream Pie with Buttermilk Crust

Triple-Berry Pot Pies

PREP TIME: 25 MINUTES • START TO FINISH: 45 MINUTES   8 SERVINGS

Pastry

2 sheets frozen puff pastry
    (from 17.3-oz package), thawed
1 egg
2 teaspoons milk
3 tablespoons granulated sugar

Fruit

1 1/2 cups fresh blackberries
4 cups fresh raspberries
4 cups fresh blueberries
3/4 cup water
3 tablespoons cornstarch
1/4 cup plus 1 tablespoon cold water
3/4 cup granulated sugar
3 tablespoons packed brown sugar
1 tablespoon finely shredded
    lemon peel
3 tablespoons fresh lemon juice
1/8 teaspoon salt
1/8 teaspoon freshly grated nutmeg

1. Adjust oven rack to lower position. Heat oven to 425°F. Line large cookie sheet with cooking parchment paper; set aside.

2. On lightly floured surface, carefully unfold 1 sheet of puff pastry. Use fork to prick dough about every 2 inches. Use sharp knife or pizza cutter to cut out 4 circles, about 4 1/2 inches each. Place circles on cookie sheet. Repeat with remaining sheet of puff pastry.

3. In small bowl, beat egg and milk together. Lightly brush pastry rounds with egg mixture and sprinkle with 3 tablespoons sugar. Bake 15 minutes or until golden and puffed. Remove from cookie sheet and place on wire rack.

4. In 3-quart saucepan, mix blackberries, 1 cup of the raspberries, 1 cup of the blueberries and 3/4 cup water. Cover and heat to boiling over medium heat. When berries are boiling, remove lid and heat 3 minutes, stirring constantly, until a few berries burst.

5. In small bowl, mix cornstarch and cold water. Stir cornstarch mixture, 3/4 cup granulated sugar, the brown sugar, lemon peel, lemon juice, salt and nutmeg into saucepan. Heat to boiling, stirring constantly. Cook 2 minutes or until mixture thickens. Remove from heat and stir in remaining berries.

6. Divide berry mixture evenly among eight 8- or 9-ounce ramekins or eight 10-ounce custard cups. Top each with warm puff pastry round and serve immediately. (To serve later, spoon berry mixture into ramekins or custard cups. Cover and refrigerate up to 3 days. Before serving, bake pastry rounds as directed above. Reduce oven temperature to 350°F. Uncover ramekins and place on cookie sheet. Bake 15 minutes or until hot. Top each with warm puff pastry round.)

1 Serving: Calories 520 (Calories from Fat 190); Total Fat 21g (Saturated Fat 7g; Trans Fat 2g); Cholesterol 90mg; Sodium 180mg; Total Carbohydrate 76g (Dietary Fiber 8g; Sugars 43g); Protein 6g • **% Daily Value:** Vitamin A 4%; Vitamin C 25%; Calcium 4%; Iron 20% • **Exchanges:** 2 Starch, 1 Fruit, 2 Other Carbohydrate, 4 Fat • **Carbohydrate Choices:** 5

WHY IT WORKS: **NEW TO NUTMEG?** Most often associated with eggnog and old-fashioned cookies, nutmeg is a spice that deserves more attention. Native to New Guinea, nutmeg is the seed of a tree fruit currently grown throughout Indonesia and the Caribbean. Dark brown to black in color, nutmeg grows encased in a bright red web known more commonly as mace. Although both mace and nutmeg have similar flavors, nutmeg has a stronger citrus characteristic. For this reason, nutmeg is very good in any dessert or dish in which you would add lemon or orange zest. This includes berry pies, like this recipe, as well as white sauces, barbecued meats, and cakes. Care must be taken because both nutmeg and mace can turn bitter if cooked too long. Both spices are best if added right before serving.

Apple Pie Sandwich Cookies

PREP TIME: 50 MINUTES • **START TO FINISH:** 1 HOUR 40 MINUTES   22 SANDWICH COOKIES

Cookies

3/4 cup butter, softened
1 cup packed brown sugar
1/4 cup light corn syrup
1 egg
2 1/4 cups all-purpose flour
2 teaspoons baking soda
1 teaspoon ground cinnamon
1/4 teaspoon ground ginger
Dash of salt
1/2 cup granulated sugar

Filling

1 teaspoon butter
1 medium apple, peeled and finely
   chopped (1 cup)
1 tablespoon packed brown sugar
1/4 teaspoon ground cinnamon
1 cup mascarpone cheese or
   1 package (8 oz) cream cheese,
   softened

1. Heat oven to 350°F. Spray 2 large cookie sheets with cooking spray; set aside.

2. In large bowl, beat 3/4 cup butter and 1 cup brown sugar with electric mixer on medium speed 3 minutes or until well blended. Scrape side of bowl. Add corn syrup and egg. Beat 2 minutes or until blended.

3. In medium bowl, beat flour, baking soda, 1 teaspoon cinnamon, the ginger and salt with wire whisk. Add dry ingredients to butter mixture and beat on low speed just until dry ingredients are incorporated.

4. Place granulated sugar on plate. Shape 1 level measuring tablespoon dough into 1-inch ball and roll in sugar. Place on cookie sheet. Press dough with palm of hand until just flattened and about 2 inches in diameter. Repeat with remaining dough, making an additional 43 balls, and place them about 1 1/2 inches apart on cookie sheets.

5. Bake about 15 minutes or until golden. Cool on cookie sheet 1 to 2 minutes before removing to wire rack. Cool completely.

6. Meanwhile, in 8-inch skillet, heat 1 teaspoon butter over medium-low heat until melted. Add apple, 1 tablespoon brown sugar and 1/4 teaspoon cinnamon. Cook 5 to 7 minutes, stirring frequently, until apple softens. Set aside to cool completely, about 15 minutes. In small bowl, mix cooled apple mixture and mascarpone.

7. Spread 1 level tablespoon filling over bottom of 1 cookie. Top with second cookie. Repeat with remaining filling and cookies. Store in refrigerator.

1 Sandwich Cookie: Calories 220 (Calories from Fat 90); Total Fat 10g (Saturated Fat 6g; Trans Fat 0g); Cholesterol 40mg; Sodium 210mg; Total Carbohydrate 29g (Dietary Fiber 0g; Sugars 17g); Protein 2g • **% Daily Value:** Vitamin A 8%; Vitamin C 0%; Calcium 2%; Iron 6% • **Exchanges:** 1 Starch, 1 Other Carbohydrate, 2 Fat • **Carbohydrate Choices:** 2

WHY IT WORKS:

THE WAY THE COOKIE CRUMBLES Cookies taste great the day they are made; maintaining their taste and texture for another day is often a challenge. Sometimes after storing, crisp cookies become soft and chewy, and chewy cookies get hard. The culprit behind this texture change is water. Many ingredients in your kitchen love to absorb water. Even when baked into a cookie, these ingredients continue to absorb water from the air or from other cookies. There are ways around this. Store completely cooled cookies in an airtight container (if warm, condensation builds and is reabsorbed by the cookie) and separate soft and crisp cookies (the water from the chewy cookies will move to the crisp, drying the soft cookies and softening the crisp ones). In this recipe you are filling a crisp cookie with a wet filling. No matter how hard you try, some of that water will move from the filling to the cookie. So plan on serving them as soon as possible after filling.

Blueberry-Peach Cobbler

WITH WALNUT BISCUIT TOPPING

Fruit

8 medium fresh peaches (about 2 lb)
   or 2 bags (16 oz each) frozen
   sliced peaches, thawed
1 cup fresh blueberries
1/4 cup packed brown sugar
1 tablespoon cornstarch
1 tablespoon lemon juice
1/4 teaspoon ground cinnamon
Dash of salt

Biscuit Topping

2/3 cup all-purpose flour
2 tablespoons granulated sugar
1/2 teaspoon baking soda
1/2 teaspoon baking powder
1/8 teaspoon salt
1/8 teaspoon ground nutmeg
3 tablespoons cold butter,
   cut into pieces
1/4 cup plus 2 tablespoons buttermilk

Walnut Topping

2/3 cup chopped walnuts
1/4 cup packed brown sugar
1/4 teaspoon ground cinnamon

1. Heat oven to 400°F.

2. (If using frozen peaches, skip step 2.) In 4-quart Dutch oven, heat 2 quarts water to boiling. Add fresh peaches and allow them to bob in water 30 seconds. Use slotted spoon or strainer to remove peaches and immediately plunge into bowl of ice water to cool. Remove skins from peaches. Cut peaches in half and twist to separate halves. Remove and discard pits. Cut each peach half into 3 wedges. You should have 4 cups peaches.

3. In medium bowl, mix all fruit ingredients together. Let stand 10 minutes to allow sugar to pull juices from peaches. Transfer to 8-inch square (2-quart) glass baking dish and bake uncovered 10 minutes or until fruit is bubbling. Remove from oven and stir. Bake 10 to 12 minutes longer or until bubbly around edges. Fruit must be hot in the middle so biscuit topping bakes completely.

4. Meanwhile, in large bowl, mix flour, granulated sugar, baking soda, baking powder, salt and nutmeg with wire whisk. Scatter cold butter over dry ingredients and use your fingertips or pastry blender to incorporate. If using your fingers, submerge chunks of butter below surface of dry ingredients and pinch butter together. Do this with all of the butter until mixture has small, pebble-like pieces of butter throughout. Don't worry if butter pieces differ in size; some should be large and some small.

5. Pour about 3 tablespoons of the buttermilk over dry ingredients; slowly stir mixture with rubber spatula. (At first it will look like not enough liquid to make a dough; as you stir it will look like too much.) Stir until dry flour mixture is no longer visible and dough is moist but not sticky. If dough is too dry, add more buttermilk, 1 teaspoon at a time, stirring after each addition.

6. Place dough on lightly floured surface and knead 3 times to form a ball of dough. Use your fingers to pat dough, or roll to 1/4-inch thickness. Use 2 1/4-inch biscuit or cookie cutter to cut dough into 9 circles. If necessary, gather up any scrap dough, re-roll and cut.

7. In small bowl, mix all walnut topping ingredients; set aside.

8. Remove fruit from oven and stir. Place biscuits on top and brush with remaining 2 tablespoons buttermilk. Sprinkle with walnut topping.

9. Return baking dish to oven and bake 18 to 20 minutes or until biscuits are deep golden brown and center biscuit is baked completely. (Carefully lift center biscuit with metal spatula or knife to check that there is no raw biscuit dough.) Remove from oven and cool slightly on wire rack. Serve warm.

1 Serving: Calories 370 (Calories from Fat 130); Total Fat 15g (Saturated Fat 4g; Trans Fat 0g); Cholesterol 15mg; Sodium 310mg; Total Carbohydrate 55g (Dietary Fiber 6g; Sugars 36g); Protein 5g • **% Daily Value:** Vitamin A 10%; Vitamin C 10%; Calcium 8%; Iron 10% • **Exchanges:** 2 Starch, 1 Fruit, 1/2 Other Carbohydrate, 3 Fat • **Carbohydrate Choices:** 3 1/2

Blueberry-Peach Cobbler with Walnut Biscuit Topping

Swedish Gingersnaps

PREP TIME: 55 MINUTES • START TO FINISH: 1 HOUR 55 MINUTES   ABOUT 4 DOZEN COOKIES

1 cup packed brown sugar
3/4 cup shortening
1/4 cup molasses
1 egg
2 1/4 cups all-purpose flour
2 teaspoons baking soda
1 teaspoon ground ginger
1 teaspoon ground cinnamon
1/2 teaspoon ground cloves
1/4 teaspoon salt
Granulated sugar

1. In large bowl, beat brown sugar, shortening, molasses and egg with electric mixer on medium speed, or mix with spoon. Stir in remaining ingredients except granulated sugar. Cover and refrigerate at least 1 hour.

2. Heat oven to 375°F. Spray cookie sheet with cooking spray.

3. Shape dough by rounded teaspoonfuls into balls; dip tops into granulated sugar. Place balls, sugared sides up, about 3 inches apart on cookie sheet.

4. Bake 8 to 10 minutes or just until set. Remove from cookie sheet to wire rack. (Cookies left on cookie sheet too long will be difficult to remove and may break. To remedy this, put cookie sheet back in the oven 1 or 2 minutes. Once warmed, the cookies should slide off the sheet easily.)

1 Cookie: Calories 80 (Calories from Fat 30); Total Fat 3.5g (Saturated Fat 1g; Trans Fat 0.5g); Cholesterol 0mg; Sodium 70mg; Total Carbohydrate 12g (Dietary Fiber 0g; Sugars 7g); Protein 0g • **% Daily Value:** Vitamin A 0%; Vitamin C 0%; Calcium 0%; Iron 2% • **Exchanges:** 1/2 Other Carbohydrate, 1 Fat • **Carbohydrate Choices:** 1

WHY IT WORKS: **KEEPING THE CHEW** Although you may add dry sugar to a cookie recipe, the heat of baking causes the sugar to melt. Cookies are chewy or crisp depending on whether the sugar stays hard (making a crisp cookie) or melted (chewy). The deciding factor for the state of the sugar is water; the more water a cookie retains, the softer it will be. Brown sugar, corn syrup, honey and molasses attract water (why brown sugar gets clumpy). When you add these ingredients to your cookies, they keep water inside and the cookie chewy.

186 *Betty Crocker* WHY IT WORKS

Chocolate-Caramel Shortbread Bars

PREP TIME: 25 MINUTES • START TO FINISH: 1 HOUR 50 MINUTES   4 DOZEN BARS

Shortbread

2 cups all-purpose flour

1/4 cup sugar

3/4 cup butter, softened

2 oz semisweet baking chocolate, melted and cooled

Filling

1/2 cup butter

1/4 cup sugar

2 tablespoons corn syrup

1 can (14 oz) sweetened condensed milk (not evaporated)

Topping

1 oz semisweet baking chocolate, melted and cooled

1. Heat oven to 350°F.

2. In medium bowl, mix flour and 1/4 cup sugar. Stir in butter and 2 ounces chocolate until mixture forms a soft dough. Press in bottom of ungreased 13 × 9-inch pan.

3. Bake 20 to 25 minutes or until set. Cool completely.

4. In heavy 1 1/2-quart saucepan, mix all filling ingredients. Heat to boiling over medium heat, stirring constantly, until butter is melted. Continue boiling, stirring frequently, to 245°F on candy thermometer or until small amount of mixture dropped into cup of very cold water forms a firm ball that holds its shape until pressed.

5. Spread hot filling over cooled shortbread; cool. Drizzle with 1 ounce chocolate. Let stand at least 1 hour or until chocolate is set. For bars, cut into 8 rows by 6 rows.

1 Bar: Calories 110 (Calories from Fat 50); Total Fat 6g (Saturated Fat 3g; Trans Fat 0g); Cholesterol 15mg; Sodium 45mg; Total Carbohydrate 12g (Dietary Fiber 0g; Sugars 8g); Protein 1g • **% Daily Value:** Vitamin A 4%; Vitamin C 0%; Calcium 2%; Iron 0% • **Exchanges:** 1/2 Starch, 1/2 Other Carbohydrate, 1 Fat • **Carbohydrate Choices:** 1

WHY IT WORKS: **BUTTER YOU UP** A common first step in baking is "creaming" butter and sugar, meaning beating them until smooth and creamy. This process incorporates air into the butter and the finished baked good. Add softened butter directly to the flour, and a whole new baked texture is achieved. Try baking one batch of these shortbread cookies by creaming the butter and sugar together first before adding to the flour, and then another batch as indicated in the recipe. The creamed version will be lighter (have more air) and be flakier, whereas the version as written will be denser and more tender (the soft butter better coats the flour, making it tender). Try this in your favorite cookie recipe; you may be surprised at the results!

Caramel Cream Puffs

WITH CHOCOLATE–PEANUT BUTTER SAUCE

Whipped Cream

1/2 cup granulated sugar

2 tablespoons water

2 cups whipping (heavy) cream

1 teaspoon vanilla

Cream Puffs

3/4 cup water

6 tablespoons butter

2 teaspoons granulated sugar

1/8 teaspoon salt

3/4 cup all-purpose flour

2 eggs

1 egg white

Sauce

3 tablespoons packed dark
    brown sugar

1 tablespoon butter

1 tablespoon light corn syrup

1/2 cup whipping (heavy) cream

2 oz bittersweet baking chocolate,
    chopped

1 oz unsweetened baking chocolate,
    chopped

2 tablespoons creamy peanut butter

1 Serving: Calories 550 (Calories from Fat 370); Total Fat 41g (Saturated Fat 23g; Trans Fat 1.5g); Cholesterol 165mg; Sodium 180mg; Total Carbohydrate 38g (Dietary Fiber 2g; Sugars 26g); Protein 7g • **% Daily Value:** Vitamin A 25%; Vitamin C 0%; Calcium 8%; Iron 8% • **Exchanges:** 1/2 Starch, 2 Other Carbohydrate, 1 High-Fat Meat, 6 1/2 Fat • **Carbohydrate Choices:** 2 1/2

1. In 3-quart saucepan, mix 1/2 cup granulated sugar and 2 tablespoons water with wooden spoon. Heat over medium-high heat 5 to 7 minutes, without stirring, until sugar turns dark golden brown and just begins to smoke. (Do not allow to burn.)

2. Immediately add 2 cups whipping cream, stirring constantly with wooden spoon. (Be careful—mixture will bubble furiously and be very hot.) Reduce heat to low. Stir constantly until any lumps of sugar melt. When mixture is smooth, remove from heat and add vanilla. Pour into large bowl. Cover and refrigerate at least 2 hours or until cold.

3. Adjust oven rack to lowest position. Heat oven to 400°F. Line cookie sheet with cooking parchment paper if desired.

4. In heavy 3-quart saucepan, heat 3/4 cup water, 6 tablespoons butter, 2 teaspoons granulated sugar and the salt to boiling over medium heat. Quickly stir in flour. Mixture will form a sticky paste. Cook about 1 minute, stirring vigorously, until mixture is stiff and smooth and forms a ball. Remove from heat.

5. Add 1 of the eggs and stir vigorously with spoon until smooth (it will look like the egg will not blend in, but keep stirring and it will). Once egg is blended, add remaining egg and the egg white. Stir vigorously until dough is smooth and thick.

6. Spoon about 3 tablespoons dough into a mound on parchment-lined or ungreased cookie sheet. The mound should be about 2 inches wide and 1 1/2 inches high (you can also use pastry bag to pipe dough into mounds). Repeat with remaining dough, making 8 equal mounds placed at least 2 inches apart. If the mounds have peaks, wet your fingertips and smooth them down.

7. Bake dough 35 to 40 minutes or until puffs are very crisp and dark golden brown. Cool puffs on wire rack, about 30 minutes.

8. Meanwhile, in 2-quart saucepan, heat brown sugar, 1 tablespoon butter and the corn syrup over medium heat, stirring constantly, until brown sugar melts and mixture bubbles. Add 1/2 cup whipping cream and stir until brown sugar dissolves and cream simmers. Remove from heat and stir in bittersweet and unsweetened chocolates until smooth. Stir in peanut butter.

9. Beat cold cream mixture with electric mixer on high speed until stiff peaks form.

10. Use serrated knife to cut each cream puff in half horizontally. Divide whipped cream evenly among puffs and replace tops. Place cream puffs on serving plates and spoon sauce over tops.

Caramel Cream Puffs with Chocolate–Peanut Butter Sauce

Pistachio Biscotti

PREP TIME: 25 MINUTES • START TO FINISH: 1 HOUR 55 MINUTES   ABOUT 3 DOZEN BISCOTTI

2/3 cup sugar

1/2 cup vegetable oil

2 teaspoons vanilla

2 eggs

2 1/2 cups all-purpose flour

1 teaspoon baking powder

1/4 teaspoon baking soda

1/4 teaspoon salt

1/2 cup coarsely chopped
    pistachio nuts

1/2 cup semisweet chocolate chips

1 teaspoon shortening

1. Heat oven to 350°F.

2. In large bowl, beat sugar, oil, vanilla and eggs with spoon. Stir in flour, baking powder, baking soda, salt and nuts.

3. Place dough on lightly floured surface. Knead 15 times until smooth. Divide dough in half. Shape each half of dough into 10 × 3-inch rectangle on ungreased cookie sheet. (If dough is sticky, spray your hands with cooking spray before shaping.)

4. Bake 25 to 30 minutes or until toothpick inserted in center comes out clean. Cool on cookie sheet 15 minutes. Remove rectangles to cutting board. Cut each rectangle crosswise into 1/2-inch slices. Place slices, cut sides down, on cookie sheet.

5. Bake about 15 minutes, turning cookies once, until crisp and light brown. Immediately remove from cookie sheet to wire rack. Cool completely, about 30 minutes.

6. In small microwavable bowl, microwave chocolate chips and shortening uncovered on High 30 to 60 seconds; stir until smooth. Place cookies, cut-side up, on waxed paper. Drizzle chocolate over biscotti. Let stand until chocolate is set.

1 Biscotti: Calories 100 (Calories from Fat 45); Total Fat 5g (Saturated Fat 1g; Trans Fat 0g); Cholesterol 10mg; Sodium 45mg; Total Carbohydrate 12g (Dietary Fiber 0g; Sugars 5g); Protein 2g • **% Daily Value:** Vitamin A 0%; Vitamin C 0%; Calcium 0%; Iron 4% • **Exchanges:** 1/2 Starch, 1/2 Other Carbohydrate, 1 Fat • **Carbohydrate Choices:** 1

WHY IT WORKS:

HOLDING YOUR TEMPER Chocolate is made of fat, water, sugar and protein. If handled correctly, the fat and water stay suspended in the chocolate and do not separate. When using chocolate as a coating, as in this recipe, shortening is often added to prevent the chocolate from separating. Although much simpler than tempering chocolate (the technique used to make chocolate candy), melting chocolate can still be problematic. If you overheat the chocolate in the microwave it will burn. Be sure to stir the chocolate regularly (sometimes chocolate chips maintain their shape well past their melting temperature). Even if they still look solid they may be ready to burn.

Pistachio Biscotti

Peach Cobbler Ice Cream

PREP TIME: 55 MINUTES • START TO FINISH: 11 HOURS 25 MINUTES   12 SERVINGS (1/2 CUP EACH)

Ice Cream

1 1/3 cups whipping (heavy) cream

1 cup milk (preferably whole)

Dash of salt

1/2 cup granulated sugar

1 vanilla bean, split lengthwise in half, or 1 teaspoon vanilla

1/3 cup granulated sugar

7 egg yolks

3 medium fresh peaches (about 3/4 lb) or 1 bag (16 oz) frozen sliced peaches

1 tablespoon lemon juice

1/2 cup granulated sugar

2 tablespoons vodka (preferably peach vodka), if desired

Topping

1/2 cup quick-cooking oats

1/3 cup all-purpose flour

1/4 cup chopped walnuts

1/4 cup packed dark brown sugar

1/4 cup firm butter, cut into 16 pieces

1 teaspoon ground cinnamon

1/4 teaspoon ground nutmeg

1. In 3-quart saucepan, heat whipping cream, milk, 1/2 cup granulated sugar, salt and vanilla bean (if you are using 1 teaspoon vanilla, do not add here) uncovered to a gentle simmer over medium heat. Simmer about 15 minutes, stirring occasionally. Remove from heat. Cover and let stand 20 minutes. (This standing time will infuse the cream with vanilla flavor; skip it if not using vanilla bean.) Remove and discard vanilla bean.

2. In medium bowl, beat 1/3 cup granulated sugar and egg yolks with wire whisk 3 minutes or until yolks lighten to lemon yellow. Ladle about 1 cup warm cream mixture into egg yolks and beat with wire whisk to combine. Repeat with another cup of cream mixture. Add yolk mixture to remaining cream mixture in saucepan.

3. Stir constantly with rubber spatula, making sure to scrape the bottom of pan. Heat over medium heat 10 to 15 minutes or until mixture thickens slightly and coats back of metal spoon. (Do not boil or overheat mixture because eggs will curdle.) Pour into medium bowl, using a strainer if there are any lumps. (If using 1 teaspoon vanilla instead of vanilla bean, add it now.) Cover with plastic wrap, pushing wrap onto custard surface to prevent film from forming. Cool at room temperature 15 minutes. Refrigerate at least 8 hours but no more than 24 hours. Place ice-cream maker bowl in freezer.

4. (If using frozen peaches, skip step 4.) In 4-quart Dutch oven, heat 2 quarts water to boiling. Add fresh peaches and allow them to bob in water 30 seconds. Use slotted spoon or strainer to remove peaches and immediately plunge into bowl of ice water to cool. Remove skins from peaches. Cut peaches in half and twist to separate halves. Remove and discard pits. Cut each peach half into 4 pieces.

5. In bowl of food processor, pulse peaches, lemon juice and 1/2 cup granulated sugar until peaches are roughly chopped but not pureed (you are aiming for a chunky peach sauce). Stir in vodka if using. You should have about 2 cups chopped peaches. Refrigerate chopped peaches until cold, at least 1 hour.

6. Place large bowl in freezer at least 1 hour before churning ice cream. Strain the chilled peaches and collect any accumulated juices in a medium bowl. Combine the peach liquid with the cold ice cream custard mixture and stir well. Refrigerate drained peaches until needed. Freeze custard in ice-cream maker following manufacturer's directions until thick (like soft-serve ice cream). Scrape ice cream from ice-cream maker into the cold bowl. Quickly add chopped peaches; gently stir until peaches are evenly distributed.

7. Smooth top of ice cream flat and cover directly with plastic wrap. Cover top of bowl with more plastic wrap and then with foil. Freeze ice cream 8 hours or overnight.

8. Heat oven to 350°F. Line 15 × 10 × 1-inch pan with cooking parchment paper; set aside.

1 Serving: Calories 330 (Calories from Fat 170); Total Fat 19g (Saturated Fat 10g; Trans Fat 0.5g); Cholesterol 170mg; Sodium 65mg; Total Carbohydrate 37g (Dietary Fiber 1g; Sugars 31g); Protein 4g • **% Daily Value:** Vitamin A 15%; Vitamin C 0%; Calcium 6%; Iron 4% • **Exchanges:** 1/2 Starch, 2 Other Carbohydrate, 4 Fat • **Carbohydrate Choices:** 2 1/2

9. In bowl of food processor, pulse all topping ingredients 8 times or until nuts and butter are well mixed and crumbly.

10. Spread crumbs evenly on parchment in pan. Bake 8 minutes and then stir well. Bake 8 minutes longer or until crumbs are golden and crunchy. Do not let crumbs burn. There should be some large crumbs and some small; break up some of the larger chunks if necessary. Cool pan completely on wire rack.

11. Before serving, remove ice cream from freezer and place in refrigerator about 30 minutes to soften. To serve, scoop ice cream into serving bowls and sprinkle with topping. Ice cream can be stored tightly covered up to 1 week.

WHY IT WORKS: **ADDING ALCOHOL** Since its invention thousands of years ago, ice cream has been a food best enjoyed within minutes of being made. This is due not only to its wonderful flavor, but also its poor keeping qualities. Stored too long, ice cream becomes gritty. This can be avoided with a few tricks. Although it may not be diet-friendly, use cream with the highest fat level possible and all of the sugar called for in the recipe. Ice crystals are formed by water (which lower-fat milks have in excess) and too little sugar (sugar adds to the creamy texture by lowering the freezing temperature during mixing). Adding alcohol, as this recipe does, also lessens the chance of gritty ice cream and prevents the ice cream from becoming rock hard.

Peach Cobbler Ice Cream

Watermelon-Lime Sorbet with Asti Spumante

PREP TIME: 35 MINUTES • START TO FINISH: 3 HOURS 35 MINUTES   6 SERVINGS

1 whole watermelon (5 lb)

1 1/2 cups sugar

2 teaspoons finely shredded
    lime peel

2 tablespoons fresh lime juice

1 tablespoon vodka, if desired

1 1/2 cups Asti Spumante,
    champagne or sparkling
    grape juice

1. Remove rind from watermelon. Cut melon into 1-inch cubes to make 6 cups.

2. In bowl of food processor, puree watermelon, sugar, lime peel, lime juice and vodka if desired for 2 minutes or until smooth. Pour mixture into large bowl. Cover and refrigerate 1 hour. Place ice-cream maker bowl in freezer.

3. Freeze watermelon mixture in ice-cream maker following manufacturer's directions for sorbet. Spoon sorbet into medium bowl. Cover and freeze 2 hours or until firm.

4. To serve, scoop sorbet into 6 wine glasses. Pour 1/4 cup Asti Spumante over each and serve immediately.

1 Serving: Calories 300 (Calories from Fat 10); Total Fat 1g (Saturated Fat 0g; Trans Fat 0g); Cholesterol 0mg; Sodium 10mg; Total Carbohydrate 72g (Dietary Fiber 0g; Sugars 66g); Protein 1g • **% Daily Value:** Vitamin A 25%; Vitamin C 35%; Calcium 2%; Iron 2% • **Exchanges:** 1 Fruit, 4 Other Carbohydrate • **Carbohydrate Choices:** 5

WHY IT WORKS:

SORBET SECRETS When water freezes, it forms big ice crystals. The goal when making sorbet is to get these crystals as small as possible (0.0008 inch is ideal; at this width your tongue no longer feels them as individual crystals). To achieve this tiny size you have to do two things: churn the mixture as it freezes and add lots of sugar. Churning breaks up any large crystals (freezing fast also helps because the faster you freeze something, the smaller the crystals form). Adding sugar lowers the temperature at which water freezes. Ideally, you add enough sugar to sorbet so that part of it never freezes. You want to end up with something that is part liquid, part solid. Not adding sugar to sorbet results in an unscoopable block.

"Restaurant-Style" Crème Brûlée

PREP TIME: 20 MINUTES • START TO FINISH: 7 HOURS   4 SERVINGS

6 egg yolks
2 cups whipping (heavy) cream
1/3 cup sugar
1 teaspoon vanilla
Boiling water
8 teaspoons sugar

1. Heat oven to 350°F.

2. In small bowl, slightly beat egg yolks with wire whisk. In large bowl, stir whipping cream, 1/3 cup sugar and the vanilla until well mixed. Add egg yolks to cream mixture; beat with wire whisk until evenly colored and well blended.

3. In 13 × 9-inch pan, place four 6-ounce ceramic ramekins. (Do not use glass custard cups or glass pie plates; they cannot withstand the heat from the kitchen torch or broiler and may break.) Pour cream mixture evenly into ramekins.

4. Carefully place pan with ramekins in oven. Pour enough boiling water into pan, being careful not to splash water into ramekins, until water covers two-thirds of the height of the ramekins.

5. Bake 30 to 40 minutes or until tops are light golden brown and sides are set (centers will be jiggly).

6. Carefully transfer ramekins to wire rack, using tongs or grasping tops of ramekins with pot holder. Cool 2 hours or until room temperature. Cover tightly with plastic wrap and refrigerate until chilled, at least 4 hours but no longer than 48 hours.

7. Uncover ramekins; gently blot any condensation on custards with paper towel. Sprinkle 2 teaspoons sugar over each custard. Holding kitchen torch 3 to 4 inches from custard, caramelize sugar on each custard by heating with torch about 2 minutes, moving flame continuously over sugar in circular motion, until sugar is melted and light golden brown. (To caramelize sugar in the broiler, place ramekins in 15 × 10 × 1-inch pan or on cookie sheet with sides. Broil with tops 4 to 6 inches from heat 5 to 6 minutes or until sugar is melted and forms a glaze.) Serve immediately, or refrigerate up to 8 hours before serving.

1 Serving: Calories 540 (Calories from Fat 400); Total Fat 45g (Saturated Fat 25g; Trans Fat 1g); Cholesterol 450mg; Sodium 50mg; Total Carbohydrate 29g (Dietary Fiber 0g; Sugars 29g); Protein 7g • **% Daily Value:** Vitamin A 35%; Vitamin C 0%; Calcium 10%; Iron 6% • **Exchanges:** 2 Other Carbohydrate, 1 High-Fat Meat, 7 Fat • **Carbohydrate Choices:** 2

WHY IT WORKS:

BROWNING SUGAR Most of the sugar in the United States comes from one of two sources: sugar beets or sugar cane. After processing and extraction, the sugars—no matter their source—are identical. When sugar is heated, as it is in this recipe, it loses water. The more water it loses the more concentrated the sugar becomes. When approximately 350°F, the actual structure of sugar breaks down and forms new compounds (this explains why caramel has a different flavor than normal sugar syrup). Some of these new compounds are brown in color, giving caramel its golden hue.

Cashew Brittle

PREP TIME: 55 MINUTES • **START TO FINISH:** 1 HOUR 55 MINUTES · ABOUT 6 DOZEN CANDIES

1 1/2 teaspoons baking soda
1 teaspoon water
1 teaspoon vanilla
1 1/2 cups sugar
1 cup water
1 cup light corn syrup
3 tablespoons butter
1 lb cashews or unsalted raw
    Spanish peanuts (3 cups)

1. Heat oven to 200°F. Grease two large cookie sheets with butter; keep warm in oven. (This allows the candy to spread to 1/4-inch thickness without it setting up.) Grease long metal spatula with butter; set aside.

2. In small bowl, mix baking soda, 1 teaspoon water and the vanilla; set aside.

3. In 3-quart saucepan, mix sugar, 1 cup water and the corn syrup. Cook over medium heat about 25 minutes, stirring occasionally, to 240°F on candy thermometer or until small amount of mixture dropped into cup of very cold water forms a soft ball that flattens when removed from water.

4. Stir butter and cashews into saucepan. Cook about 13 minutes, stirring constantly, to 300°F or until small amount of mixture dropped into cup of very cold water separates into hard, brittle threads. (Watch carefully so mixture does not burn.) Immediately remove from heat. Quickly stir in baking soda mixture until light and foamy.

5. Pour half of the candy mixture onto each cookie sheet and quickly spread about 1/4 inch thick with buttered spatula. Cool 1 hour or until completely cooled. Break into pieces. Store in airtight container at room temperature.

1 Serving: Calories 70 (Calories from Fat 30); Total Fat 3.5g (Saturated Fat 1g; Trans Fat 0g); Cholesterol 0mg; Sodium 35mg; Total Carbohydrate 10g (Dietary Fiber 0g; Sugars 6g); Protein 1g • **% Daily Value:** Vitamin A 0%; Vitamin C 0%; Calcium 0%; Iron 2% • **Exchanges:** 1/2 Other Carbohydrate, 1 Fat • **Carbohydrate Choices:** 1/2

WHY IT WORKS: **AH, SUGAR!** The more sugar a water mixture contains, the higher the temperature it has to be before it boils. This simple fact is the key to any type of candy making. In this recipe, sugar and water are combined and brought to a boil. As this mixture boils, water evaporates, making the sugar solution more concentrated. The higher the sugar concentration, the hotter a syrup must be before it will boil. Therefore, you can use a thermometer to gauge the amount of sugar in syrup. At 234°F to 240°F (the soft-ball stage), the syrup is about 85% sugar and just right for brittle, fudge and pralines. At 250°F (the hard-ball stage), the syrup contains 92% sugar and is used for making marshmallows and divinity. As you can see, being a candy maker means having an accurate thermometer.

RECIPE Rx: STICKY MESS? So there you are, standing in your kitchen on a nice summer day making this cashew brittle. Everything works just fine (although it takes a long time for the sugar to come up to temperature) until you cool the candy. Even after the

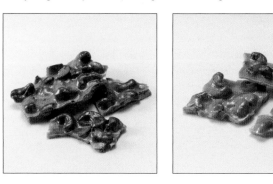

suggested hour of cooling, the candy is soft and tacky. Before blaming yourself or your thermometer, consider that the problem may be your timing. Making candy in the summer is usually not recommended. When the humidity is high, sugar syrup has a hard time boiling off its water because too much is already in the air. By the time sugar syrup finally gets to the brittle stage a lot of the water has boiled off. As soon as it starts to cool, though, water in the air is attracted back to the sugar. Hard candy doesn't stand a chance in high humidity, becoming sticky and gummy. Your best bet is to wait for a drier day.

Why It Works "At a Glance"

This section presents all of the *Why It Works* tips and Recipe Rx features in one place for easy reference. They're grouped into the following categories and presented in alphabetical order by title. Plus, the title of the recipe that each applies to is included.

- Add Some Flavor
- Baker's Secrets
- Choose a Food Group
- Kitchen Chemistry
- Know Your Ingredients
- Techniques

Add Some Flavor

Alcohol Enhances Flavor Food is made up of thousands of chemicals. (Chocolate alone contains over 2,000!) Some of these chemicals dissolve in water while others dissolve only in fat. When you chew a food, you taste only those substances that are dissolved. But many soups get most of their flavor from chemicals that need to be dissolved in fat. How to bring out a soup's flavors without adding extra fat to a recipe? Adding alcohol can help. Alcohol is unique in that it can act like water and fat. That's why a splash of wine or liquor at the end of cooking will heighten the flavor of dull soups or stews. *(Creamy Corn Chowder, page 48)*

The Beauty of Browned Butter Butter is approximately 80% milk fat, 18% water and 2% milk solids. When cooking with butter you will notice that when melted, it separates into a clear yellow layer (the fat) and a white layer (the milk solids). In India, butter is often melted and the fat separated from the solids. This butter—called clarified butter—can be kept without refrigeration. (Butter goes rancid because of the milk solids, not because of the fat.) If the milk solids are not separated from the fat, but instead allowed to brown, they develop a wonderful nutty flavor and aroma that complements vegetables and meats. *(Green Beans with Browned Butter, page 152)*

Coffee Perks When harvested, coffee beans (actually seeds taken from the coffee fruit called a coffee cherry) have very little flavor. Their seductive aroma and taste come after the beans have been fermented and roasted. Once brewed, coffee is useful in many aspects of cooking. It makes a great marinade and braising liquid because its natural acids tenderize meat (try adding a cup to your next pot roast before cooking). Coffee-tasting experts claim coffee contains hints of cinnamon, chocolate, wine, fruit and even caramel flavors. For this reason, coffee enhances and balances the flavor of a number of savory dishes, including this mole sauce. Try replacing some of the water with coffee the next time you make beef gravy, stew or soup. *(Coffee Chicken with Quick Mole Sauce, page 71)*

Concentrated Flavor of Jelly For strong flavor, many chefs rely on the power of reduction. As stock, wine or fruit juice boils, the chemicals responsible for flavor are concentrated and sometimes altered to result in a very strong sauce. Most people don't keep reduced stock or wine in their pantry, yet they do have jelly. Jellies, jams and preserves all begin with fruit juice that is boiled until it achieves a thick, syrupy consistency. Good-quality jellies and preserves deliver a sweet, concentrated dose of fruit with no work. *(Roasted Sweet Potato Salad, page 138)*

Condiment with Kick Typically horseradish is available whole, as a large root, or as prepared horseradish. To make prepared horseradish, the root is peeled and ground, crushing its cells and starting the chemical reaction that produces its infamous sinus-clearing chemicals. Vinegar is then added to the horseradish paste; the faster the vinegar is added, the less hot the horseradish will be because vinegar calms and stabilizes the chemical reaction. As horseradish sits, the pungent chemicals break down and lose their punch. Therefore, it is best to use refrigerated prepared horseradish within four to six months. *(Tangy Horseradish Coleslaw, page 137)*

Cutting the Grass At first, lemon grass doesn't even look edible. However, with a few easy steps it will be ready for this recipe. First, pick a stalk that is thick, heavy and not overly woody and has no brown discoloration. Make sure it has a delicate citrus perfume and the bulb is tightly bound together.

Next, use a knife or your fingernails to remove the thick outer leaves. You should see a tender white/yellow inner stalk. Slice this stalk into very thin circles and then use the side of your knife to lightly crush the slices. This releases the oils and the flavor from the stalk. The tough outer leaves can cleaned and added to Thai-inspired broths for a Thai accent; just remember to discard before eating. *(Thai Glazed Beef with Chile–Lemon Grass Sauce, page 120)*

Flavor Variations of Mushrooms Mushrooms are one of the most misunderstood foods in the produce section. First, many people call them a vegetable when they are really a fungus. (Fungi get energy from the plants they grow on rather than from the sun.) It is also assumed that all mushrooms taste like the common button mushroom; in reality, their flavors vary widely. Shiitake mushrooms are slightly smoky, morels are nutty and chanterelles taste distinctly like apricots. Adding mushrooms will also enhance the flavor of your dish, as these fungi are the natural source of the flavor enhancer MSG. *(Braised Chicken with Wild Mushrooms and Thyme, page 102)*

Flavorful Fish The culinary world is full of references to using fish in small amounts as a flavor enhancer. In Asia, as well as in ancient Greece and Rome, small fish are steeped in salt water to make a sauce (*nam pla* in Thailand, *nuoc mam* in Vietnam and *garum* in ancient Rome) used in hundreds of dishes. In the Mediterranean, anchovies are the fish of choice. To most Americans, anchovies are the overly fishy and salty pieces sometimes found on a pizza. However, these do not adequately represent the flavor of true anchovies. High-quality anchovies should smell like the sea, not like rotten fish. To experience the best, buy anchovies packed in salt. Rinse them well under water and, if you like, insert your thumb through the center to remove their small bone. Chopped finely, they add a great depth of flavor to many dishes. *(Tomato and Cannellini Bean Soup with Garlic and Basil, page 49)*

Frozen OJ to the Rescue More than 80% of the Florida orange crop goes into making frozen orange juice—about 30 pounds of juice per person per year! The cooking possibilities of frozen orange juice are often overlooked. Which is a shame, as the benefits of this freezer staple are immense. For one, frozen orange juice is concentrated, which means intense flavor. Also, it always has the same sweetness and acidity, unlike fresh oranges, where you gamble with flavor throughout the year. This is not to say that oranges are not useful in cooking— they are. Nothing can take the place of fresh orange juice in vinaigrettes and for finishing sauces. But when you need a reliable orange flavor for marinades, salad dressings and cooked sauces, look to the freezer. *(Grilled Citrus Chicken, page 70)*

The Heat Is On Mustard seed, which is ground to make the yellow ballpark condiment as well as the fancy brown variety, is a member of the cabbage family. Like its relatives broccoli

and Brussels sprouts, mustard can be quite potent if not prepared correctly. The offending ingredient responsible for its notorious smell—isothiocyanate—is activated by heat and water. This chemical is released when ground mustard is mixed with hot water or when cabbage is overcooked. Although pleasantly sharp in small amounts, mustard can be chokingly strong if too much is used. To avoid overpowering your guests, remember that once heated, ground mustard or crushed mustard seed gets hotter as it stands. *(Filet of Beef with Mustard-Herb Crust, page 119)*

The Heat Is On We've all experienced the invigorating rush of mouth-numbing heat that comes from eating Mexican and Thai food. But where does this heat that makes you sweat and burns your mouth come from? A chemical called capsaicin gives chile peppers their heat. Found mostly in the seeds and inner ribs of chiles, capsaicin levels vary depending on the type of chile. Scientists measure the capsaicin in chiles using Scoville units—the higher the number, the hotter the pepper. For example, sweet bell peppers have 0 Scoville units; jalapeños can have up to 10,000. (The poblano used in this recipe has a Scoville of 1,000.) The hottest of all peppers are habaneros, with levels of up to 300,000! *(Slow-Cooked Beef with Poblano-Lime Salsa, page 84)*

Heating Spices To best retain the flavor of spices and herbs, water is removed and spices and herbs are dried. This can be a problem as adding dried basil to a boiling soup or ground cinnamon to muffins may release only some of the herb's or spice's flavor. The secret to getting the most out of your spice cabinet? Preheat your herbs and whole spices by dry roasting or frying. Heating releases the trapped essential oils, allowing them to more easily flavor your dish. To experiment, try heating whole spices like cumin, peppercorn or cinnamon in a small skillet over medium-low heat. Within minutes you will smell the essential oils reawaken! Allow them to cool on a plate before grinding and adding to your dish. You will be surprised by the intensity of the flavor. *(Braised Chicken and Potatoes with Coconut-Curry Sauce, page 112)*

Herb How-To What is the difference between an herb and a spice? Herbs are generally leaves and come from subtropical or non-tropical plants (basil, rosemary or thyme, for example). Spices include just about everything else that is not a leaf: roots (ginger), flower buds (cloves), bark (cinnamon) and seeds (nutmeg). Spice preparation usually includes some form of grating or grinding. Herbs, especially fresh ones, need a lighter approach. Once the leaves of fresh herbs are damaged (crushed, sliced or torn) they begin to break down and release flavor. For this reason, add fresh herbs toward the end of cooking. *(Cuban Grilled Mojito Pork Tenderloins, page 114)*

The Life of Vinegar Vinegar is wine that went too far. Grape juice, with its high sugar content, is a favored home for friendly yeast. As the yeast eats the juice's sugar, alcohol is produced, turning the juice into wine. Usually the vintner, not wanting to lose money on a good bottle, stops the yeast either by either adding sulfites, heating the wine to kill the yeast, or separating the yeast out. However, if allowed to continue eating the wine's sugar, yeast will stop producing alcohol and produce acid instead. Voilà! Vinegar is born. Typical vinegars have around 4% to 5% acidity. *(Beef Tenderloin with Rosemary-Balsamic Reduction, page 123)*

Maple Match When pulled from a tree, maple sap is as thin as water and just about as flavorful. That may be why it takes about 40 gallons of maple sap to make one gallon of maple syrup! As maple sap boils down to make syrup, the water evaporates and the sugar concentrates. The longer it cooks, the more the sugar changes as it combines with other components of the sap and caramelizes. Real maple syrup is just a little thicker than water and is complex in flavor (slightly smoky, sometimes bitter and maybe even chocolaty). Used in sweet and savory cooking, maple is the perfect partner for matching and enhancing the slight sweetness of sautéed vegetables, the smokiness of grilled meat and the floral quality of fresh herbs. *(Maple-Thyme Roasted Chicken Breasts, page 74)*

New to Nutmeg? Most often associated with eggnog and old-fashioned cookies, nutmeg is a spice that deserves more attention. Native to New Guinea, nutmeg is the seed of a tree fruit currently grown throughout Indonesia and the Caribbean. Dark brown to black in color, nutmeg grows encased in a bright red web known more commonly as mace. Although both mace and nutmeg have similar flavors, nutmeg has a stronger citrus characteristic. For this reason, nutmeg is very good in any dessert or dish in which you would add lemon or orange zest. This includes berry pies, like this recipe, as well as white sauces, barbecued meats and cakes. Care must be taken because both nutmeg and mace can turn bitter if cooked too long. Both spices are best if added right before serving. *(Triple-Berry Pot Pies, page 182)*

Salt of the Earth Salt plays a key role in cooking and baking. Although it's well understood that savory dishes need salt to taste good, it may be surprising to learn that sweet dishes need salt too. Salt enhances the sweetness of many foods. Taste an apple slice. Now sprinkle a small amount of salt on a different slice and taste. Sweeter? Salt can do the same thing to a cake or pie. In this recipe, the salt in the pretzel crust enhances the flavor of the chocolate filling. *(Decadent Chocolate Pie with Pretzel Crust, page 179)*

Sesame Secrets Sesame seed—native to the Middle East—is probably best known in America for its use in Asian cooking. The seeds grow in pods that burst explosively when ripe (this

is thought to be the origin of the phrase "open sesame"). Uncooked, sesame seed has a nutty, slightly bitter flavor. When toasted, its nutty flavor intensifies greatly and is especially apparent in toasted sesame oil. Like all high-fat seeds and nuts, sesame is prone to rancidity. Buy sesame seed fresh (smell it first if you can). Tightly wrap and freeze any sesame seed not used within a week. *(Spicy Chicken with Broccoli, page 78)*

A Toast to Seeds Strangely enough, this recipe could be called "Seeds with Seeds." Green beans are nothing more than the seeds of the bean plant. Many nuts and seeds (including sesame seed), because of their high oil content, benefit greatly from toasting to bring out their flavor. Heat causes the essential oils in the center of seeds to volatilize (escape into the air) and the outside of the seed to brown. Toasting can be done in the oven or on the stovetop. Care must be taken to not burn the seeds, as the resulting bitter flavor will be so strong you will have to discard even the un-burnt seeds. *(Sesame Green Beans, page 151)*

Tomato Paste The Old World method of preserving the flavor of summer's bounty was to peel, grind and dry tomatoes in the warmth of the southern sun. Tomato paste is still a powerful ingredient in your kitchen pantry—just as it was in Italy centuries ago—if used correctly. Used in excess, it gives an overly sweet and fruity flavor to sauces and gravies. For best results, combine tomato paste with fresh or canned tomatoes. A small amount, about 1 tablespoon to a pot of spaghetti sauce, deepens the tomato flavor without overwhelming other ingredients. To increase the flavor even more, cook the paste along with the onions at the beginning of your recipe. *(Linguine with Caramelized Onions and Angry Tomato Sauce, page 92)*

Where's the Meat? Typically, vegetarian dishes contain starch (such as beans, potatoes or pasta) which often don't have much flavor. Starch, as with most carbohydrates, tends to dull the impact of certain flavors as it literally gets in the way of your taste buds. A solution is found in the classic cooking of vegetarian cuisines, such as Indian or Mexican. Use strong flavors to help build complexity. Another way to build complexity when making a vegetarian casserole is to roast the vegetables to enhance their sweetness and create a subtle smoky flavor. Or, consider a sharp or spicy condiment, like the horseradish sauce in this recipe. The powerful flavor of the condiment will be balanced by the mellowness of the bean burgers. *(California Black Bean Burgers with Horseradish Sauce, page 96)*

A Zest for Flavor You might be surprised to learn that the most flavorful part of a lemon is the part you normally throw away: the peel. The yellow part of the lemon peel (called the rind or the zest) contains lemon oil, a powerful concentrate of citrus. Including the zest of the lemon in your cooking adds a refreshing flavor without the acidity of lemon juice. Care must be taken when removing the zest so you don't remove the bitter white pith that lies just underneath. Although you can use a box grater, the best tool is called a Microplane® grater (similar to an old-fashioned wood rasp). It grates the zest evenly but avoids scraping the underlying pith. *(Apricot-Stuffed French Toast, page 32)*

Baker's Secrets

Baby Your Bread Yeast is alive and it is eating your dough! The yeast used to make your cinnamon rolls is actually a fungus related to the common button mushroom. When added to dough, yeast goes to work eating as much sugar as it can. In return, the yeast produces gas that makes your rolls rise. The more comfortable you make the yeast, the faster it will eat. Ideally yeast likes it warm, but not too warm (about 80°F). Too much sugar or spice (such as cinnamon) can slow down or even kill yeast. A good rule of thumb is to use no more than 1/4 teaspoon cinnamon per cup flour in the dough. Overly rich doughs, like those used for coffee cake, may need extra time to rise or extra yeast in the dough. *(Better-than-the-Mall Cinnamon Rolls, page 28)*

Bad Bread Rising So you used baking powder and baking soda but your bread still didn't rise? Before you throw the loaf away, let's figure out what happened. The most likely culprit is your baking soda or baking powder. Both of these leaveners go bad (one year is about their maximum life) and should be replaced often (don't use the baking soda deodorizing your fridge; it already has a job). To test baking soda for freshness: Add 1 1/2 teaspoons baking soda to a small bowl along with 1 tablespoon white vinegar. If the mixture fizzes, the baking soda is still good. If it doesn't, it's time to get a new box. For baking powder, place 1/2 teaspoon in a small bowl and add 1/4 cup hot water. The mixture should bubble dramatically. Discard the box if it doesn't. (By the way, don't throw away that loaf. Cut up the sunken creation and make it into dainty finger sandwiches with some cream cheese.) *(Banana-Chocolate Bread, page 20)*

Baking Building Blocks Eggs, specifically egg yolks, are the cornerstone of baking. The yolks contain all of the egg's fat and fat-soluble vitamins (A, D, E and K). More importantly, the yolk is the storehouse for a wonderful substance called lecithin. Chemically, lecithin is defined as an emulsifier. Emulsifiers are the diplomats of the food world. Water and oil are not fond of one another, and lecithin serves to bring them together. This ability allows lecithin to make ice cream smoother, cakes more tender and dressings creamier. In this recipe, the extra yolks add fat, which keeps the cake moist, and the lecithin makes for a smooth crumb texture. *(Moist Chocolate-Mint Layer Cake, page 170)*

Butter You Up A common first step in baking is "creaming" butter and sugar, meaning beating them until smooth and creamy. This process incorporates air into the butter and the finished baked good. Add softened butter directly to the flour, and a whole new baked texture is achieved. Try baking one batch of these shortbread cookies by creaming the butter and sugar together first before adding to the flour, and then another batch as indicated in the recipe. The creamed version will be lighter (have more air) and be flakier, whereas the version as written will be denser and more tender (the soft butter better coats the flour, making it tender). Try this in your favorite cookie recipe; you may be surprised at the results! *(Chocolate-Caramel Shortbread Bars, page 187)*

Buttered Up Despite its name, buttermilk is not full of butter. In fact, it is similar to 2% or skim milk in fat content. Traditional buttermilk is a fermented beverage made from the liquid that remained after butter was churned from fresh cream. Today, buttermilk is made by exposing milk to good bacteria (just like making yogurt), causing it to become acidic. Buttermilk's acid makes it a great baking ingredient. This acid tenderizes cakes and muffins by preventing the proteins in flour from binding and becoming stretchy like they do in bread. It also enhances flavor, just like a squirt of lemon brightens a soup. *(Dried Cherry–Lemon Scones, page 22)*

It's in the Water In its simplest form, all dough is made up of flour suspended in water. The amount of water determines if the mixture will be a dough or a batter. Water also determines the final texture of the baked good. The more water that remains after baking, the less crisp the baked product will be. By altering the water level, you can make the dough shatteringly crisp, flaky or anywhere in between. Crispness occurs when the water in the dough/batter leaves rapidly. You can speed this process up by slicing or rolling a dough paper-thin and baking at a high temperature (driving off the water). This recipe calls for an intermediate texture, so a moderate oven temperature is used and the dough is not cut too thin. *(Parmesan-Tomato Rounds, page 60)*

Keep Your Color Have you ever opened a delicious-looking blueberry muffin only to be greeted with streaks of green? What you've witnessed is a reaction between the blueberries and the baking soda. Blueberries get their color from a group of pigments called anthocyanins (literally "blue plant"). These are the same pigments that color apples, cherries and red cabbage. When exposed to a base, such as baking soda, the blueberries turn green. To avoid this colorful surprise, use only baking powder in your blueberry muffins. Because the amount of banana called for is so slight in this recipe, you do not need to use baking soda to ensure the muffins rise (see Banana-Chocolate Bread). *(Banana-Blueberry Muffins, page 21)*

Keeping the Chew Although you may add dry sugar to a cookie recipe, the heat of baking causes the sugar to melt. Cookies are chewy or crisp depending on whether the sugar stays hard (making a crisp cookie) or melted (chewy). The deciding factor for the state of the sugar is water; the more water a cookie retains, the softer it will be. Brown sugar, corn syrup, honey and molasses attract water (why brown sugar gets clumpy). When you add these ingredients to your cookies, they keep water inside and the cookie chewy. (*Swedish Gingersnaps, page 186*)

Low and Slow Making a cheesecake can be intimidating. When is it done? Why did it crack? Can it be frozen? To understand cheesecake you must first know that it is more of a custard than a cake. Eggs play a key role in its structure. The other ingredients are important of course, but the eggs determine doneness and whether it has a surface crack. Because eggs are easy to overcook, it is important to bake the cheesecake at a low temperature and possibly in a water bath. For the same reason, cheesecakes should be removed from the oven when they are not completely set (the residual heat will cook them through without overcooking and causing the dreaded crack). And finally, yes, cheesecakes freeze very well. (*S'Mores Cheesecake, page 176*)

Nuts for Cocoa One of the purest forms of chocolate flavor you can buy is cocoa powder. It is literally the powder left after squeezing the cocoa butter out of the cocoa bean and it comes in two basic forms: natural and Dutch-processed. Regular, or natural unsweetened cocoa, is the type you probably grew up with and your mother used to make brownies and cakes. Alkalized, or Dutch-processed cocoa, is the same natural cocoa with a base (alkali) added. Dutch-process cocoa is washed with an alkaline solution, which gives it a smoother taste and a redder color. Both types of cocoa have pros and cons. Natural cocoa has more of the subtle flavors of the cocoa bean, but it can also taste a little too bitter. Dutch-process cocoa has a more rounded flavor and mixes more easily with liquid, but it is often hard to find in the grocery store. Because success in baking often relies on the amount of acidic ingredients you have versus the amount of base (alkaline) ingredients, substituting natural cocoa for Dutch-processed in a recipe, and vice versa, is not recommended. (*Individual Chocolate Lava Cakes with Caramel Sauce, page 171*)

Revving Up Chocolate You can never have enough chocolate—in life or in a recipe! However, adding more chocolate to a recipe does not necessarily provide more chocolate flavor. The best way to increase chocolate flavor is to increase the other flavors present in chocolate. Chocolate contains subtle hints of coffee, vanilla, spice and even smoke. By adding elements of these flavors to your recipe, such as the coffee in this cake, you make it more "chocolaty." (To get a smoke flavor, one famous pastry maker has even served brownies with tobacco leaves—an ingredient that is definitely not recommended!) (*"All-the-Stops-Out" Chocolate Cake, page 172*)

Rising with Potatoes Adding mashed potatoes to yeast dough may seem unusual, but it does more than add flavor. Cooked potatoes are made up of mostly starch. This starch readily converts to sugar in the dough, which is hungrily eaten by the yeast. With this "jump start," the yeast alters the flavor of the bread. In addition, the extra potato starch in the bread holds moisture longer than bread made without potatoes. Bread made with mashed potatoes, then, lasts longer before going stale. (*Make-Ahead Potato Bread Dough, page 140*)

Take the Cake! It is obvious that cupcakes are little versions of standard cakes. However, because of their miniscule stature and shorter bake time, cupcakes have their own baking challenges. As with standard cakes, the flour type used makes a huge difference in the end result. Cake or all-purpose flour (because of low protein content) results in the best texture. Because cupcake batter is handled more, care must be taken not to overwork it; doing so activates the protein and causes small tunnels to form in the baked cakes. Also, the small size of cupcakes means they bake faster and dry out more easily. Begin checking for doneness early. (*Harvest Apple Cupcakes with Cream Cheese Frosting, page 174*)

Tears of Joy Did you take the baked cheesecake out of the refrigerator and see a big puddle of liquid on top? The worst-case scenario is that you overbaked the cake. Just like when you overcook scrambled eggs, the protein in your cake, if overcooked, will squeeze out its water. Or it could be that you refrigerated the cheesecake too soon after pulling it from the oven and the moisture condensed on the cake top. You will know which case you are in when you cut the cake. The overcooked cake will be dry and contain small holes. The other cake will just have a soggy top. If yours was overcooked, there's not much you can do but serve it with extra sauce and hope people don't notice. In the future, check your oven temperature and make sure it is correct. (*S'Mores Cheesecake, page 176*)

Tender vs. Flaky People are in two camps when it comes to pie crust preference: tender or flaky. It is difficult to have one crust with both characteristics. The same thing causes both of these attributes: fat. When you leave the fat (butter or shortening) in large pieces in the dough it will melt in the oven, creating many layers, giving a flaky effect. If you cut the fat into the dry ingredients until it is well distributed, it will melt and coat each grain of flour, making for a tender crust. To achieve the tender/flaky crust of people's dreams, leave big and little pieces of fat in your pie dough. (*Banana-Coconut Cream Pie with Buttermilk Crust, page 180*)

Top Banana In addition to providing flavor and moistness to banana bread, bananas actually have an effect on the bread rising. Like many fruits, bananas are acidic, and that means they react with baking soda to produce gas bubbles, which causes rising. But check your bananas. As bananas ripen they become sweeter and more flavorful, but they also lose their acidity. Banana bread recipes that contain only baking soda rely on the acid in the bananas to make the bread rise. The solution? Keep using ripened bananas, but use recipes that use both baking soda and baking powder to ensure a tall loaf. *(Banana-Chocolate Bread, page 20)*

The Way the Cookie Crumbles Cookies taste great the day they are made; maintaining their taste and texture for another day is often a challenge. Sometimes after storing, crisp cookies become soft and chewy, and chewy cookies get hard. The culprit behind this texture change is water. Many ingredients in your kitchen love to absorb water. Even when baked into a cookie, these ingredients continue to absorb water from the air or from other cookies. There are ways around this. Store completely cooled cookies in an airtight container (if warm, condensation builds and is reabsorbed by the cookie) and separate soft and crisp cookies (the water from the chewy cookies will move to the crisp, drying the soft cookies and softening the crisp ones). In this recipe you are filling a crisp cookie with a wet filling. No matter how hard you try, some of that water will move from the filling to the cookie. So plan on serving them as soon as possible after filling. *(Apple Pie Sandwich Cookies, page 183)*

Choose a Food Group

All about Okra Hold on to your gumbo: Okra is a fruit! Botanically, a fruit is the part of a plant that contains the seeds. That makes eggplant, tomatoes and even green beans, fruit. Okra is unique in that when heated, it releases carbohydrate to form a sticky, gelatinous compound. Although undesirable when fried, this compound is what traditionally makes gumbo "gumbo." (The word comes from the African word for okra: *ngombo*.) Once cut and simmered, okra thickens gumbo and gives it the correct texture and flavor (a little like asparagus). *(New Orleans Best Gumbo, page 128)*

Handle with Care Eggs, like meat, are made mostly of protein. Like towels, proteins can hold a lot of water. The more you heat eggs—or other high-protein foods—the more these proteins are wrung dry. With just a little heat, eggs turn out moist; with too much heat, the egg proteins are squeezed so tightly that they leave a puddle of liquid on your plate. The secret to moist scrambled eggs lies in gentle heat. By starting eggs cooking in liquid, you slowly raise their temperature without overheating. Pushing them off to the side of the pan when they are completed stops the cooking and saves your breakfast! *(Extra-Moist Scrambled Eggs with Chives, page 38)*

It's in the Bag Just like animals, vegetables breathe. If you lock a head of lettuce in your crisper drawer in a plastic bag you will find that it soon turns brown and limp. Moisture from the lettuce's "breath" helped speed the growth of bacteria. The bags of pre-cut lettuce you purchase from the grocery store are made up of a special material that regulates the amount of carbon dioxide, oxygen and other gases that come in and go out of the bag, extending the shelf life. To get more life out of your own lettuce, wrap separated leaves in paper towels and place in a plastic bag. Then squeeze as much air as possible from the bag before refrigerating. *(Gorgonzola and Toasted Walnut Salad, page 136)*

It's Not Easy Being Green Cooking broccoli can be tricky. Cook it right and it is crisp and green. Overcook it and you end up with a limp, olive drab floret. Your best safeguard against this is understanding why broccoli is green in the first place. Broccoli, and all green plants, contain a pigment called chlorophyll. In the living plant, chlorophyll is protected because its job is to turn sunlight into food. When heated, chlorophyll loses this protection and is exposed to its enemy: acid. Lemon juice, vinegar and even broccoli's natural acidity can turn chlorophyll's lovely green to brown. To keep chlorophyll and acid far apart, follow these rules: Cook broccoli quickly (no more than 8 minutes), keep the pot uncovered (that would concentrate the acid) and add acid just before serving. *(Sesame-Garlic Broccoli, page 154)*

It's Not a Yam First things first: Sweet potatoes are not yams! They are often referred to and labeled as yams because of their resemblance to the African root of the same name. However, sweet potatoes are completely different in flavor and texture. Sweet potatoes are unusual in the amount of sugar they contain—upwards of 5%. This amount increases during cooking as the starch turns to sugar. The sweet potato's color is due to the same pigment that colors carrots and squash. For best texture and flavor, do not store sweet potatoes in the refrigerator or they will become bitter. *(Whipped Maple Sweet Potatoes, page 143)*

Off-Centered Yolk You followed all the steps to cook a perfect egg only to discover, after peeling, that your yolk is positioned right on the edge or bottom of the white. Because deviled eggs are all about presentation (the special plate, garnish, etc.), this can really your mess up your plans. To prevent the yolk from moving off-center, simply store your raw eggs in the carton, on their side (overnight should do). The little strings that secure the yolk in the middle of the white will move it back to the center, and after boiling you will have perfect eggs to fill. (Deviled Eggs with a Kick, page 63)

One Potato, Two Potato Cousin to tobacco and eggplant, potatoes are grown throughout the world in over a hundred varieties. Botanically, potatoes are considered stems that store energy in the form of starch. Some potatoes have more starch than others and tend to more tightly pack it away. These potatoes—called waxy—hold together when cooked. (Red potatoes are an example.) Other potatoes contain less starch and cook up fluffy or mealy because the starch is less compact (Russets, for example). When roasting, go for a waxy potato because it will hold together in the oven. (Roasted Rosemary Red Potatoes, page 141)

Pairing Peanuts Believe it or not, peanuts are not really nuts at all! They're legumes (like beans). The peanut plant grows its nutlike seed underground encased in a papery brown skin. Only after the green leafy top withers and dies is the peanut ready to harvest. Rich in oil and vitamins, peanuts can be used in both sweet and savory cooking. Their flavor, without the sugar usually added in Western cooking, readily complements meat and poultry. In Africa, peanuts are known as groundnuts or nguba (where we get the synonym for peanuts—goobers) and are often included in stews. In Asian cooking the flavor of peanuts helps balance the heat of chilies. (Chicken Satay with Peanut Sauce, page 52)

Picking a Lemon Lemons are a fruit without a home. Botanists have never discovered their country of origin, although many guess it may be somewhere in India. Like other citrus fruits, lemons are picky about where they grow. Most are grown in this country, on the coasts, where the temperature fluctuates only a few degrees all growing season. Dramatic changes in temperature can radically alter the sugar-to-acid ratio of the fruit. Growers pick lemons based on their concentration of sugar (measured using the Brix scale). Unlike other fruits whose starch content turns to sugar after being picked, lemons never get any sweeter once picked. (Lemon-Glazed Spring Asparagus, page 147)

Potatoes Need Their Vitamins, Too! When potatoes, apples and bananas are cut, chemicals contained in the plants' cells are released. One of these chemicals, an enzyme known as PPO, reacts with oxygen in the air to turn the flesh of fruits and vegetables brown. (Interestingly, a component similar to PPO causes age spots on human skin.) Although this reaction cannot be stopped completely (other than by cooking) it can be slowed. Salt and acids slow PPO down, so soaking your cut potato or apples in salt water or lemon juice will delay browning. Because both of these additions have their own flavor, a better technique is to use ascorbic acid (Vitamin C). Other

than a bit of tartness, it lacks flavor of its own. Simply dissolve a 500-milligram tablet in the soaking water. (Potato Pancakes, page 142)

Slow Cooked Carrots are a member of a large family of vegetables and herbs (parsley, coriander, fennel and dill, just to name a few). Rich in vitamin A and beta-carotene, carrots have been used for their medicinal properties for centuries. One of the great pleasures of cooking with carrots is their promised sweetness. Young, baby carrots are especially sweet, a characteristic that can be enhanced by slowly cooking them to convert their starch into sugar. A pinch of salt also intensifies their natural flavor. (Orange-Glazed Baby Carrots with Cumin, page 156)

The Spirit of Spuds There are three types of potatoes: floury (also known as starchy), waxy and all-purpose. Floury potatoes are highest in starch, waxy are lowest and all-purpose land in the middle. Floury potatoes—such as Russet—are best for making mashed potatoes. Because of their high starch content and low water content, floury potatoes absorb butter and cream well, yet still remain light and fluffy. Store all potatoes in a cool dry place with good ventilation. Keep them out of the refrigerator as cold storage causes their starch to turn to sugar, making them very sweet. Remove potatoes from their plastic bag once home from the grocery store. The high humidity of the bag will cause them to sweat and mold. (Down-Home Mashed Potatoes, page 146)

Staying Sweet Corn, or maize as its called by the rest of the world, originated in America. One of our largest field crops, most corn ends up as feed and corn syrup. Corn grown for human consumption is called sweet corn. Both field corn and sweet corn produce sugar as they grow. After it is picked, field corn quickly turns its sugar into starch. Sweet corn, however, maintains its sugar level throughout shipping, storage and cooking. When cooking corn, the goal is to just heat it through; overcooking results in tough corn. (Grilled Corn with Chile-Lime Spread, page 157)

Stopping the Stink The longer you cook Brussels sprouts, or any member of the cabbage family, the more they smell. This is because heat activates a series of compounds that include hydrogen sulfide (better known as rotten egg smell) and mercaptans ("skunk"). Follow these tips to reduce the offending odors: Cook sprouts in enough water to cover; the extra water dilutes the chemicals. Also, heat the water to boiling before adding the vegetable. And do not cover the pan. Although you would think smells can be trapped, a closed area actually concentrates the reaction. Finally, cook the spouts as quickly as possible and remove them as soon as they are cooked through. (Honey-Lemon Brussels Sprouts and Carrots, page 148)

Kitchen Chemistry

Ah, Sugar! The more sugar a water mixture contains, the higher the temperature it has to be before it boils. This simple fact is the key to any type of candy making. In this recipe, sugar and water are combined and brought to a boil. As this mixture boils, water evaporates, making the sugar solution more concentrated. The higher the sugar concentration, the hotter a syrup must be before it will boil. Therefore, you can use a thermometer to gauge the amount of sugar in syrup. At 234°F to 240°F (the soft-ball stage), the syrup is about 85% sugar and just right for brittle, fudge and pralines. At 250°F (the hard-ball stage), the syrup contains 92% sugar and is used for making marshmallows and divinity. As you can see, being a candy maker means having an accurate thermometer. *(Cashew Brittle, page 196)*

Browning Sugar Most of the sugar in the United States comes from one of two sources: sugar beets or sugar cane. After processing and extraction, the sugars—no matter their source—are identical. When sugar is heated, as it is in this recipe, it loses water. The more water it loses, the more concentrated the sugar becomes. When approximately 350°F, the actual structure of sugar breaks down and forms new compounds (this explains why caramel has a different flavor than normal sugar syrup). Some of these new compounds are brown in color, giving caramel its golden hue. *("Restaurant-Style" Crème Brûlée, page 195)*

Dumpling Dough When mixed with water, flour is naturally sticky and elastic—a texture caused by a protein in wheat called gluten. All batters and doughs made from wheat flour benefit and suffer from the properties of gluten. In dumpling dough, the gluten helps hold the dough together when rolling and when submerged in the boiling water. The downside is that gluten sometimes makes the dough difficult to roll out. Because it is elastic, the gluten tends to snap the dough back after it is stretched. The secret is to allow the gluten to relax after mixing the dough and before rolling. After a short rest, the dough will roll out without fighting back. *(Pork Pot Stickers with Chipotle Honey Sauce, page 50)*

Egg on Your Face As proteins (think little springs) are heated, their structure changes. Add a little heat and proteins start to unwind and connect with neighboring proteins. Add more heat and proteins start to recombine and solidify. You see this last step when you fry an egg. The egg white changes from liquid to solid in a process called coagulation. All proteins coagulate when heated, but the temperature at which they solidify changes depending on their surroundings. For example, in this recipe, egg yolks are cooked with sugar and lemon juice. Normally egg yolks coagulate between 149°F and 158°F. However, here the sugar interferes with the proteins when they try to recombine. The lemon juice's acidity changes the protein's structure, making it harder for the proteins to reconnect. Because of these added ingredients, egg yolks can be cooked at a higher temperature without turning into sweet scrambled eggs. *(Lemon Swirl Cheesecake, page 175)*

Flour Power Flour is a good sauce thickener because it contains starch. However, the thickening power of flour's starch is released only when heated. Mixing flour with a little cold water results in a thick paste or dough. Mixing it with a lot of water and heating it to boiling gives you a smooth sauce. Why? When heated, starch (which usually looks like a little ball) breaks down into tiny pieces. These pieces now absorb great quantities of liquid and thicken your sauce. *(Thyme-Infused Chicken Breasts with Pomegranate Sauce, page 108)*

Getting to Know Roux Flour and water do not mix well. You can see this every time your gravy gets lumpy. This happens because flour would rather stick to itself than combine with water. To fix this situation, each grain of flour is surrounded with a nonstick coating, often a fat such as butter or oil. This mixture of flour and fat, called a roux, allows you to add liquid to flour without fear of lumps. Care must be taken when making and using a roux. The flour must be cooked either before or after adding the liquid to rid the flour of its raw taste. Although it adds a pleasant toasted flavor, browning a roux lessens the flour's thickening ability. *(Cheddar and Green Onion Biscuits with Sausage Gravy, page 37)*

Good Bacteria Over 3,000 years ago, yogurt was probably invented as a way to preserve fresh milk. Today, even with refrigerators, we enjoy the creamy, acidic taste of yogurt, and the process of making it hasn't changed much. Ingredients used are milk (fat-free [skim], 2% or whole) and bacteria. In the beginning, the bacteria might have been added by simply letting warm milk sit uncovered in hopes that the correct bacteria would come along. Today, the process is more controlled (and safer): Pure bacteria are added directly to milk. As the bacteria "eat" the sugar in the milk, it produces acid. And it's this acid that causes the milk to thicken into yogurt. *(Yogurt-Granola Parfaits with Berries, page 14)*

In the Thick of Things Corn, like all other grains, consists of starch, fat and protein. In modern industry, each part of the corn kernel is used: Fat goes into corn oil, protein is made into feed and starch is used to make high-intensity sweetener. Cornstarch is also used in home kitchens to thicken gravies and sauces. To maximize its thickening properties, keep a few things in mind. Always mix the cornstarch with a small amount of liquid or other dry ingredients before incorporating it into the larger amount of liquid. If added directly to the sauce, it may clump. Also, it is important that cornstarch mixtures are not cooked too long after thickening. Although it is important to heat the mixture to boiling, cooking out the raw starchy taste, overcooking can actually thin the starch. *(Blueberry-Peach Cobbler with Walnut Biscuit Topping, page 184)*

Just Add Water Some recipes for caramelized sugar have you start with dry sugar in a pan while others, such as this one, have you add a little water. Why? Surprisingly, in order for sugar to caramelize it must be heated until all of the water is evaporated off. Therefore it seems like a step in the wrong direct to add water. Actually, the small amount of water added in this recipe is really more for security than anything else. If we just heated the sugar itself it may heat unevenly, parts of it caramelizing before the rest even heated up. The water evens out the heat by making the sugar into a syrup. That doesn't mean that you can take your eye off of the pan. The process happens very fast, going from delicious caramel to bitter blackjack (the pastry name for burnt sugar), so watch carefully. *(Pan-Roasted Pork Chops with Apricot-Caramel Sauce, page 116)*

Keeping It Safe Grilling is one of the best ways to cook meat; the flavors are brighter and aromas are outstanding. However, anytime you are dealing with raw meat, care must be taken. All meat, no matter how fresh, clean or organic it is, naturally has bacteria on it. Once meat is cooked to the correct temperature (for cuts of beef at least 145°F), bacteria is destroyed and there is no more danger. The problem arises when surfaces (like cutting boards) and liquids (like marinades) come into contact with food that will not be heated to this safe temperature. In this recipe, make sure that you do not use the marinade from the meat as a sauce, because it probably contains bacteria. Also, wash all areas that come into contact with the raw meat. Understanding food safety is the best way not to get sick. *(Flank Steak with Chimichurri Sauce, page 124)*

Kitchen Chemistry Combining an acid and a base (alkaline) forms a gas. When you watch little holes form on top of your pancake as it cooks on the griddle, you're witnessing this reaction. One of the most important aspects of baking is achieving the right balance of acid and base in your recipe. Too much of either can ruin the taste and texture. When baking soda (the most common base in your pantry) is used with an acid (lemon juice, molasses, vinegar, etc.), gas is produced immediately. This works in recipes that contain an acidic ingredient, but what about those that don't, or that just have a tiny bit of acidity? Use some baking powder, which contains both acid and base. *(Banana Pancakes with Maple-Pecan Syrup, page 24)*

No Green Eggs Here Hard-cooked eggs become tough and tinged with green when exposed to heat for too long. The more egg proteins are heated, the more water they lose. After too much heat (usually anything more than 20 minutes), the eggs turn rubbery, and a sulfur compound and the iron in the yolk react to make an unsightly green ring. You can avoid these problems by cooking the eggs only as long as necessary and stopping the cooking by plunging the cooked eggs into ice water. To avoid the green color, use recently purchased eggs; they do not react as easily. *(Deviled Eggs with a Kick, page 63)*

No More Tears Cutting onions for French Onion Soup can cause a lot of tears. When cut, sulfur-containing chemicals in the onion combine, irritating your eyes and making you cry. Fresh, juicy onions contain the most potent of these chemicals. In nature, this reaction stops predators from nibbling away at the onion, but in the kitchen it can be annoying. Although not completely preventable, there are ways to lessen the problem. Chilling the onion about 30 minutes slows the reaction, and washing large chopped pieces rinses away the chemicals. Some people swear contact lenses are the answer. *(French Onion Soup, page 46)*

Oil and Water Alaskan oil slicks and vinaigrettes are examples of a general rule of nature: Oil and water do not mix. So how do we explain mayonnaise and the sauce for this dish? Both are full of oil and butter, yet they stay creamy and smooth. Both sauces (mayonnaise is technically a sauce) contain emulsifiers, which are attracted to both oil and water. When present in a sauce, emulsifiers act as a bridge between oil and water, preventing them from separating. *(Pan-Seared Tilapia with Lemon-Butter Sauce, page 129)*

Perfect Pickling Before refrigerators, food could not be stored more than a few days without bacteria or mold causing it to go bad. To get around this, several preservation methods were used. One of the most common was pickling. In its simplest form, pickling involves immersing cooked or blanched foods in a vinegar solution. The low pH (high acidity) of vinegar stops any unwanted growth. To flavor the pickles (which could include vegetables, nuts and even meat), spices, herbs and sugar were often added to the vinegar. Even though refrigerators are now available, people have grown to enjoy the sharp, refreshing taste of pickles. *(Curried Pineapple Chutney, page 165)*

Perfect Poaching Everyone knows that heat cooks an egg, but did you know vinegar does as well? Vinegar, as well as other acids like lemon juice, has the same effect on egg protein as does boiling water: It sets the white. This can be used to your advantage when poaching eggs. A small amount of vinegar (no more than a teaspoon per quart of water) stops the egg white from spreading before the heat of the poaching water has a chance to cook the egg. *(Classic Eggs Benedict, page 36)*

The Power of Egg Whites Egg whites are almost 100% protein. When beaten, as in a meringue, these proteins unwind and hold onto air (think of them as coiled springs). The resulting foam can then be used to make soufflés, angel food cakes and cookies. The same happens in this recipe, even though the egg whites are not beaten. As the cream puffs bake, the egg white proteins unwind and hold onto air. The heat of the oven causes water within the dough to turn to steam, lifting the dough as it boils. Just like an egg in a skillet, when enough heat is added, the egg white proteins solidify and trap air. The result is a light and airy cream puff, ready to be filled! *(Caramel Cream Puffs with Chocolate—Peanut Butter Sauce, page 188)*

Pre-cooked Potatoes The ideal hash brown is crispy on the outside and tender on the inside. When cooked over high heat, shredded raw potatoes brown nicely. But unless you spread them thinly in the pan, the outside will burn before the inside ever becomes soft. Because potatoes are mostly starch, high heat breaks down the starch on the outside of the hash brown into sugar, making for the golden color. The starch on the inside of the hash browns needs steam and time to cook through. The answer to the perfect hash brown is simple: Start with cooked potatoes. *(Cheesy Cheddar Hash Browns, page 40)*

Say Cheese! Everyone loves the taste of melted cheese, but making a cheese sauce can be time-consuming. And if overheated, cheese can separate. Processed cheese, made up of a combination of different types of natural cheese (usually an aged cheese for flavor and a young cheese for texture), was invented to make melting cheese foolproof. Processed cheese manufacturers can change the color, flavor and texture of their product by starting with different cheeses. These cheeses are melted and then mixed with emulsifying salts—chemicals that stop the cheese from separating. The result? Melted cheese with no fuss. *(Cheese Steak Sandwiches with Sautéed Onions and Peppers, page 79)*

Smooth Sailing Cheese is a complex mixture of fat and protein. When correctly melted, cheese stays smooth and creamy. When overcooked or overheated, the fat separates from the cheese and the protein clumps. Fortunately, there are several steps you can take to avoid these pitfalls when making fondue. First, bringing the cheese to room temperature before melting means you don't have to use high heat. Second, cutting the cheese into small pieces to speeds up the melting process. Third, adding a little starch to the fondue is a good idea too—it helps keep the fat from separating. Finally, adding some wine, with its acidity and minerals, lessens the stringiness of the cheese and helps keep the mixture smooth. *(Three-Cheese Fondue, page 56)*

Sorbet Secrets When water freezes, it forms big ice crystals. The goal when making sorbet is to get these crystals as small as possible (0.0008 inch is ideal; at this width your tongue no longer feels them as individual crystals). To achieve this tiny size you have to do two things: churn the mixture as it freezes and add lots of sugar. Churning breaks up any large crystals (freezing fast also helps because the faster you freeze something, the smaller the crystals form). Adding sugar lowers the

temperature at which water freezes. Ideally, you add enough sugar to sorbet so that part of it never freezes. You want to end up with something that is part liquid, part solid. Not adding sugar to sorbet results in an unscoopable block. *(Watermelon-Lime Sorbet with Asti Spumante, page 194)*

Know Your Ingredients

Add Instant Flour Some crepe recipes call for all-purpose flour and tell you to mix your batter and let it rest for hours to allow the flour to absorb the liquid. An easier and faster way is to use instant flour. In a process similar to the manufacture of instant milk, instant flour is made by combining low-protein flour with water before being dried. This pre-wetting process allows instant flour to absorb liquid very quickly without clumping. This guarantees thin delicious crepes every time! *(Spiced Crepes with Strawberry Filling, page 26)*

Blue Cheese Blue cheese owes its color to a familiar mold: penicillin. The three most common blues are Roquefort (from France), Gorgonzola (from Italy) and Stilton (from England). Until quite recently, the process of introducing mold to these cheeses was left to Mother Nature. (Blocks of Roquefort were actually held in ancient caves where the mold lived!) Today the mold spores are usually mixed with the milk or the curd during cheesemaking (the mold is not injected as sometimes thought). Enzymes in the mold that eat and digest milk fat are responsible for the unique flavor of blue cheese. Over time, the mold penetrates the cheese causing "veins" to form and the cheese to become crumbly. *(Caramelized Apple–Blue Cheese Spread, page 58)*

Busy Bees Honey begins its life in much the same way as maple syrup, as slightly sweet vegetable sap. But unlike maple syrup, whose sap is collected from trees, the sap of honey—called nectar—is collected from flowers. As the bee carries nectar from flowers to the hive, its body breaks down the nectar's complex sugars into simpler parts. At the hive, the nectar is stored in a very thin layer on the honeycomb to speed up evaporation of water, concentrating, or "ripening," the honey. By the time beekeepers remove the comb from the hive, honey can be over 80% sugar. *(Beef Tagine with Honey, Prunes and Almonds, page 125)*

Cheese and Fruit Combo Cheese begins its life as milk, but after being heated, salted and mixed with bacteria, the end results are quite different. Dramatic flavor changes are due in part to the breakdown of chemicals that made up the original milk. Some of the new chemicals formed as cheese ages are similar to chemicals naturally found in fruit. Successful flavor combinations are often the result of pairing similar flavors. For instance, a mild Cheddar cheese that hints of an apple's tart sweetness is complemented when served with a Granny Smith apple. A sharp Cheddar would better complement a sweet Golden Delicious apple, as in the recipe above. *(Cheddar-Apple Soup, page 44)*

Chipotle Chiles Of all of the peppers introduced to America in the last few decades, none has been as widely received as chipotle. Sweet, hot and smoky, chipotle complements everything from barbecue sauce to mayonnaise and has found its way into breads, biscuits and even stuffing recipes. Chipotle chiles are made by smoking jalapeño peppers (usually red jalapeños). The result is a leathery, brick-red chile that in Mexico is jokingly compared to a cigar butt in size and shape. Dried chipotles are not commonly found in American grocery stores. Instead they are usually mixed with a tomato-vinegar sauce called adobo and sold in small cans. When working with canned chipotle in adobo use caution and rubber gloves. One pepper is often more than enough to heat your whole dish; the remainder can be transferred to another container, covered and refrigerated. *(Chicken with Chipotle-Peach Glaze, page 106)*

Choosing the Right Olive Oil Extra-virgin olive oil is like fine wine in its incredible depth of flavor and the enjoyment it can bring to a meal. And as with wine, there are many grades of olive oil. After being washed, olives are ground to a paste with a large stone. This paste is then pressed to extract the oil. The first pressing of the oil is called "extra-virgin" and is distinguished from other olive oils by its low level of acidity (less than 1%). Oil made from the remaining olive paste is called "virgin" oil and has more free acid (although it is not acidic in taste). The final type is just called "olive oil" and refers to chemically extracted oil. *(Tuscan Bread Salad, page 134)*

Chuck It Hamburgers and meat loaf are best when juicy and flavorful. The secret to this combination is choosing the right cut of meat. For these dishes you don't need a tender cut, because the meat is ground. But you do need a flavorful cut. In addition, you need some fat (the juicy richness that we enjoy in these dishes comes from a balance of fat and protein). The cut meeting both criteria is chuck. From the upper shoulder of cattle, chuck is flavorful and has just enough fat to make your burger or meat loaf juicy but not greasy. *(Mini Mexican Meat Loaves with Chipotle Barbecue Sauce, page 88)*

The Condensed Version To extend shelf life, almost all canned goods are heated to stop harmful bacteria from growing. Sweetened condensed milk is an exception. This thick dairy product receives only a mild heat treatment. The reason? Unlike canned soup or canned peas, sweetened condensed milk is protected by sugar. Sweetened condensed milk starts out as regular milk. Then, up to half of its water is evaporated by placing the milk in a vacuum chamber. Finally, up to 45% sugar is added to the milk. At this high sugar concentration,

very few bacteria can live; the sugar takes all of their water. The resulting sweet milk is then placed into cans and is ready to use. *(Tres Leches Cake, page 168)*

Creating Couscous Although it may look like a seed or a grain, couscous is actually pasta. Unlike spaghetti or macaroni, couscous is not extruded or rolled out and cut into pieces. Instead, couscous is made by hand. Native to the North African countries of Morocco, Algeria and Tunisia, couscous is one of the world's first pastas. To make it, durum semolina flour (a harder, coarser wheat than used in regular wheat flour) is mixed with water and rolled between the palms of the hand. With time and a great deal of patience, small pellets of pasta are formed, steamed and finally dried. Traditionally, couscous is steamed in a large pot (called a couscousiere) above simmering stews called tagines. The boxed couscous available in stores is much easier to prepare because it has already been steamed and dried so it is ready to cook. *(Grilled Moroccan Spiced Chicken Breasts Stuffed with Couscous and Pine Nuts, page 105)*

The Dark Side of Chicken Every Thanksgiving you hear the debate: Some people like dark meat and others white. Other than their location (white meat on the breast; dark meat the thigh and leg), what makes one different from the other? The answer lies in how the bird uses the muscles in these locations. Muscles used for endurance exercise (running and walking, for example) need plenty of blood flow and fat, qualities that make the meat in these areas darker. Conversely, those muscles that see little work (like the breast) have less blood flow and fat, making them light in color. This also explains why dark and white meats cook differently. Dark meat, dense with extra bits of fat, takes longer to cook compared to white. *(Pulled Chicken Sandwiches with Root Beer Barbecue Sauce, page 68)*

Don't Know Beans? Although a can of beans is good in a pinch, cooked dried beans deliver the best flavor and texture. The goal when cooking dried beans is twofold: hydrating and cooking the starch. If your beans are old, the first part can be much harder than it sounds. The best practice is to cook beans in plain water. Acid and some minerals can actually strengthen the cell wall of the bean, preventing water from entering. Add tomato sauce and molasses near the end of cooking time. The high acid of the tomato and the minerals in molasses will guarantee your beans will never cook through. *(Slow Cooker Sweet Maple Baked Beans, page 160)*

Eggplant Fact and Fiction Eggplant has spent much of its history being shunned by one part of the world and celebrated by another. This unfair treatment has to do with family history: Eggplant is related to the deadly nightshade. Of course eggplants are not poisonous, but many people are afraid to eat or cook them. Never cooked eggplant? It is important to understand its structure. An eggplant is—for lack of a better term—a sponge. Looking closely at a cut piece, you see thousands of tiny holes. These holes absorb an amazing amount of oil, causing fried eggplant to become heavy and greasy. To help prevent this, cut the eggplant into pieces and then salt it. The salt draws out any bitter juices and collapses some of the holes. Fry salted eggplant quickly over high heat to seal the outside. Because the eggplant isn't fried in this recipe, there is no need to salt it first. (Garden Ratatouille, page 144)

The Facts on Orzo It may look, and sometimes even taste, like rice, but orzo is actually pasta. Adding to the confusion is the fact that the word "orzo" is Italian for barley. But there is no need to be confused on how to cook it. Orzo is best cooked like rice, in a small amount of water. To further improve flavor, cook orzo like the Greeks do: sautéing it in oil or butter before boiling. As with rice, this seals the pasta and helps individual grains remain separate after cooking. (Shrimp Pilaf Florentine, page 126)

Feeling Your Oats Oats are available in many forms, each requiring a slightly different preparation. Whole oats, or "groats," take the longest time to prepare—up to 2 hours. When cut into two or three pieces, the groats are called "Scotch oats" or "steel-cut oats" and need slightly less cooking (about an hour). Rolled oats—also called old-fashioned oats—are groats that have been steamed and pressed between heavy rollers. This process speeds up the cooking time 15 minutes. Instant oats are groats that have been pre-cooked and then dried, resulting in oats that can be cooked in minutes. (Baked Apple Oatmeal, page 18)

Flaky Fish Would you ever confuse a salmon steak with a porterhouse or pork chop? While vastly different in color and flavor, the texture alone sets fish apart from other meats. This difference has much to do with where the animals live and how they use their muscles. Land animals, like chickens and pigs, spend most of their time moving fairly slowly. Their muscles are grouped in long, thin bundles; when cooked, you need a knife to cut through the muscle. Fish, on the other hand, need quick movement in the water in order to swim. Their muscles are short and round; when cooked, their muscles separate and become flaky. (Braised Salmon with Soy-Ginger Sauce, page 130)

Got Milk? This ragu calls for the unusual step of adding half-and-half to the ground meat mixture. Cooking meat with dairy products (milk is common) is a very old technique used throughout the Middle East and medieval Europe. Cooking meat in milk does two things: First, because the meat is cooking in a liquid, and not oil, the temperature of the meat cannot rise above that of boiling milk (somewhere around 212°F). This means the meat will be moist but not brown. A second benefit is flavor. As milk heats, its flavors are radically changed

(compare the flavor of evaporated milk with fresh milk). These new flavors enhance the meat's flavor, making it even more rich and complex. (Parmesan Pasta with Beef Ragu, page 98)

Gourmet Gruel Polenta is the Italian version of American cornmeal mush. Made from ground, dried corn, polenta refers to both the cornmeal itself and the finished dish. Typically, dried corn for polenta is ground coarser than its American cousin, which means the dish usually takes longer to cook. Most families in Italy have their own technique for making polenta, but a common method is to heat a liquid (stock, water, milk or a mixture) to a simmer in a large pan. A handful of polenta is then held above the pot and slowly drizzled in by letting it slip between the fingers. Constant stirring is necessary to prevent lumps from forming. An easier method, as described in this recipe, is to first hydrate the polenta in cold water. Hydrating causes the starch in the corn to swell, making it less likely to form lumps. (Hearty Polenta with Swiss Cheese, page 164)

Great Garlic Just as with its cousin the onion, garlic is notorious for its strong odor and flavor when raw. The smell that we associate with garlic is caused by a chemical reaction between two sulfur compounds in the garlic bulb. When cooked, these chemicals break down and the natural sugars in the flesh caramelize. The resulting garlic is smooth, buttery and quite sweet. Overcooked garlic is bitter and will ruin a dish. For the best flavor, cook garlic over low heat. (Roasted-Garlic Hummus, page 57)

Heat and Meat You know the scene: You're seated at a Mexican restaurant. A waitress holding a sizzling fajita platter rushes by, filling your table with the delicious aroma of frying meat. Spices and herbs aside, this smell is quite different from that of beef stew. Why? It has everything to do with temperature and time. When meat is heated above 285°F, its proteins combine with natural sugars to produce the brown color and flavor we all know and love. (Boiling meat, because of its lower temperature, won't produce this color and flavor.) This browning process, called the Maillard reaction, happens best when your meat is dry. Make sure to pat the moisture off the surface before searing your steak (Beef Fajita Wraps with Pineapple Salsa, page 82)

Instant Noodles Saying that bread, cookie or pasta dough is "cooked" means that the starch in the flour has fully absorbed the water in the dough. Depending on the thickness of the dough, this process can take minutes (as with pasta) or almost an hour (as with bread). For traditional lasagna noodles, boiling causes the dough to absorb water and cook through. The no-boil lasagna noodles used in this recipe have been pre-treated with water; they do not need to be boiled before using. The heat of baking and the moisture from the sauce cook the noodles while the lasagna bakes. (Creamy Tomato Lasagna with Mascarpone Cheese, page 86)

Look to Lemon Grass Once a mysterious ingredient in Thai restaurants, lemon grass is now available in many supermarkets. Resembling a green reed, lemon grass is an ancient herb of Southeast Asia. If buying lemon grass, look for stalks with no brown discoloration. The outer leaves are often tough and should be removed before using the tender interior. Because of its fibrous qualities, lemon grass is often bruised instead of chopped before being used in recipes. Its flavor is reminiscent of citrus, bay leaves and pepper, and cuts through the more pungent ingredients of Thai cooking. As with lots of herbs, it's the oils in the lemongrass that hold all the flavor, so you may want to crush the stalk before you chop it in this recipe. *(Thai Glazed Beef with Chile–Lemon Grass Sauce, page 120)*

Mushy vs. Creamy Risotto is not something that most of us eat on a daily basis. It is cooked very differently than regular rice and spotting the right finished texture can be tricky. The final consistency you are looking for is creamy but not runny or mushy. The Italians (who invented risotto) say that the right texture is *all'onda,* which roughly translates as "with waves." This means that when you stir the finished dish it should still be thin enough to create a small wave in the pot. In the end, though, it is your pot of risotto. Find the texture you like and enjoy. *(Lemon-Parmesan Risotto, page 161)*

Panko The secret to extra crispy coating comes from Portugal via Japan. Panko (from the Portuguese root *pan* for bread and the Japanese *ko* for "son of" or "made from") is traditionally used in Japanese dishes. The starting place for panko and American bread crumbs is the same: a loaf of bread. However, American bread crumbs are baked, and panko is heated with microwaves or in a special oven. The result is a coarser crumb that produces a lighter and crunchier coating or topping. *(Almond-Crusted Shrimp, page 53)*

Pasta Primer Contrary to popular belief, Marco Polo did not bring pasta back from his trip to Asia. New archeological evidence suggests that pasta was invented independently in both Asia and Italy. Both nations regions had the same idea! In its simplest form, pasta is flour mixed with water to create dough that is cut and boiled. Wheat flour is most commonly used, as wheat dough holds its shape best due to its high protein (gluten) content. If the dough is dried immediately after cutting, durum wheat semolina is the preferred flour. Unlike regular flour, semolina is almost entirely protein. Less water must be added to form a dough (starch absorbs most of the water in regular dough) and less time is needed for drying. *(Grandma's Macaroni and Cheese, page 162)*

A Rainbow of Colors Just as plants owe their green color to chlorophyll, meat is red because of a pigment called myoglobin. Myoglobin is a sensitive chemical, readily changing color when exposed to light or air. For example, without air (before slaughter or when packaged in the airtight packages often found at warehouse clubs) myoglobin colors meat a dark purple. When exposed to oxygen, myoglobin changes meat to its characteristic cherry red. Too much oxygen, combined with the florescent lights in the grocery store, can make the meat turn brown. Although this brown is unattractive, it doesn't always mean the meat is spoiled—just handled improperly. The one color to watch out for is green; it signals bacteria growth and bad meat. *(Blue Cheese–Stuffed Pork Tenderloin, page 113)*

Slow and Steady with Cheese All cheese starts out looking like the curds and whey of cottage cheese. But with time, pressure and the help of friendly bacteria, we get the enormous variety of cheese available in your grocery store. All cheese is made up of fat and protein—two components that do not typically mix well. As it ages and loses moisture, cheese becomes concentrated in flavor. This means that the fat and protein in cheese also become concentrated. If they become too concentrated, it may lead to disaster as you try to melt cheese into sauces. Excess heat will change the protein's shape and melt the fat, leaving an oil slick on top of your sauce. To play it safe when using aged cheese like Gorgonzola, use a small amount near the end of cooking and do not heat it to boiling. To be extra safe, remove your sauce from the heat before adding the cheese. *(Penne with Caramelized Onion–Gorgonzola Cheese Sauce, page 99)*

Successful Steak Shopping Choosing a good steak is like choosing a good car. The package and price might be right, but there is no guarantee of what is inside. At least with a steak there are a few clues to perfection. When choosing a steak to grill, look for cuts with flavor and tenderness, such as fillet, tenderloin, top loin (New York Strip) or T-Bone. These steaks are from the short loin, or middle, of the steer's back. Because they get little exercise, they tend to be very tender. Next, look at the grade. The top three grades of beef are Prime, Choice and Select. Grades are given based on the amount of fat within the meat, not on the edges. This internal fat, called marbling, is important for flavor and cooking. Prime steaks (most of which are sold to restaurants) have a higher fat content than Choice or Select, so can withstand the heat of the grill without drying out. Finally, make sure the package is empty of liquid, which can indicate that the meat has been frozen. *(Texas T-Bones, page 122)*

Through Thick and Thin Think of risotto as savory rice pudding. Rice pudding achieves its texture as the rice cooks and releases starch to thicken the surrounding milk. Unlike rice pudding, risotto is characterized by slightly firm rice. Because the rice does not cook through, there is not enough time for the starch to thicken the broth. Several techniques are used to solve this problem. Short-grain rice (usually Italian Arborio or Carnaroli) is used for its greater amount of surface starch. And the rice is constantly stirred as it cooks in broth. The friction of each grain hitting its neighbor pushes more starch into the surrounding liquid. For that reason, broth is added a little at a time; if it was added all at once, you would lose the friction and the creamy consistency. *(Lemon-Parmesan Risotto, page 161)*

Techniques

Adding Alcohol Since its invention thousands of years ago, ice cream has been a food best enjoyed within minutes of being made. This is due not only to its wonderful flavor, but also its poor keeping qualities. Stored too long, ice cream becomes gritty and icy. This can be avoided with a few tricks. Although it may not be diet-friendly, use cream with the highest fat level possible and all of the sugar called for in the recipe. Ice crystals are formed by water (which lower-fat milks have in excess) and too little sugar (sugar adds to the creamy texture by lowering the freezing temperature during mixing). Adding alcohol, as this recipe does, also lessens the chance of gritty ice cream and prevents the ice cream from becoming rock hard because it lowers the freezing temperature. *(Peach Cobbler Ice Cream, page 192)*

Against the Grain Meat is a muscle, made up of fibers, that helps animals move. When cooked correctly, the connection between the fibers of the muscle loosen and we call the meat tender. In some muscles, such as flank or skirt steak, the fibers are glued together so tightly that no amount of cooking or marinating can soften them. For this reason, the meat has to be specially handled to make it tender. After cooking, allow the meat to rest a few minutes before slicing; this helps keep the meat juicy. Then look closely at the steak to identify the direction the strands of meat run. (The fibers of flank steak usually run the long way.) With a serrated knife, slice the meat thinly against the grain of the fibers—the short way. This will cut across each of the muscle fibers, making the meat tender. *(Chinese Barbecued Flank Steak, page 80)*

Best Practices for Bread Crumbs One of the best ways to season a food is to remove its natural liquid and replace it with a more flavorful one. The same concept holds for bread crumbs. Bread can best absorb butter and spices when dried. In a pinch, bread can be cut into slices and placed in a warm oven to dry. However, this method toasts the bread without removing most of the liquid. A better way is to slice the bread and let it sit, uncovered, overnight. This drying method allows the starch to release its water (heating causes starch to hold more water). *(Sautéed Cauliflower with Browned Bread Crumbs, page 150)*

Brining Soaking meat in salt water has been done for thousands of years to preserve meat. Salt pulls the water from meat and stops bacteria from making it go "bad." How then, can soaking meat in salted liquid make meat juicier? It's all in the timing. Soaking meat in a mild salt solution relaxes the protein in the meat. Water in the brine then has a chance to work its way between the proteins. This liquid becomes trapped inside the meat and serves as your insurance policy against drying out the meat during cooking. But caution is advised. Soaking meat for too long or in too strong a salt solution will dry your meat out. Stick with about 1 cup table salt for every 2 gallons liquid and do not leave meat in brine more than 12 hours unless the recipe directs you to do so. *(Oven-Fried Chicken with Sweet Onion—Mushroom Gravy, page 76)*

Broken Sauce If you returned to your hollandaise sauce after poaching your eggs only to find a pool of grainy butter floating on top, don't panic. What probably happened was that there was too much heat or butter for the emulsifier in the egg yolks to do their job right. The solution is to add another yolk to the mix and start again. In another 1-quart saucepan or a double boiler over low heat, combine 1 large egg yolk and 1 tablespoon of cold water and whisk well. Very slowly drizzle in the broken sauce, whisking constantly. The sauce should return to its unseparated self. Serve right away, or keep covered over low heat, whisking occasionally. *(Classic Eggs Benedict, page 36)*

Caramel: It's Not Just for Dessert Anymore Frying food in oil works well because oil can be heated hot enough (350°F) to brown meat, soften vegetables and even cause new flavors to form. Water, while great for some cooking, never gets hotter than its boiling point (212°F) and cannot develop the flavors that oil can. The boiling point of water, though, can be raised with the addition of sugar: The more sugar you add to water, the higher its boiling point. Add enough sugar and you can even heat water as hot as oil. At this temperature, sugar breaks down into caramel and turns golden brown. Vegetables, fruits and meats cooked in caramel soften, brown and acquire a deep flavor and mild sweetness. *(Pan-Roasted Pork Chops with Apricot-Caramel Sauce, page 116)*

Caramelizing Onions Browned onions are browned onions, right? Not necessarily. The onions in this recipe start to brown within about 15 minutes of cooking. However, the true flavor of this soup is developed when the onions are cooked down and really brown. French onion soup served in Paris is a rich and much sought-after meal. In many American restaurants, French onion soup is often looked down upon as too salty and lacking in flavor. The secret to getting the best flavor of this simple but elegant soup is browning, but not burning, the onions. So take your time and don't rush this step. *(Fench Onion Soup, page 46)*

Careful with the Custard Successful custard, such as the one in this pudding, should be creamy and smooth, with no pooling of water on the top or holes inside. The secret to this success rests firmly with the way you treat your eggs. As eggs cook in custard, their proteins unwind and spread out, trapping all of the milk and thickening the mixture. If this heating happens quickly, the egg proteins may recombine, and the trapped liquid will squeeze out, leaving you with a watery mess. To make sure this doesn't happen, cook custard at a low temperature and remove it from the oven when it is almost done (it will continue to cook on the counter). For extra insurance, you can add sugar to the custard to slow the cooking of the eggs. *(Apple Cinnamon–Raisin Bread Pudding, page 30)*

Cast Iron Cooking involves the transfer of heat. Yet some things transfer heat better than others. You can put your unprotected hand in a 350°F oven without fear of getting burned, but you can't touch the metal rack in that oven. Why? Metal holds and transfers heat better than air. But metals differ in their heat-efficiency. Iron—an excellent heat conductor—is ideal for cooking. But before you invest in cast iron, know that food will stick to a cast-iron pan unless you season it. A new cast-iron pan's surface is made of microscopic pits and bumps. By seasoning the pan (rubbing it with oil and baking it 1 hour at 300°F) you smooth out the surface, making it nonstick and rust proof. *(Yankee Corn Bread, page 62)*

Deep-Frying Science The secret to successfully deep-frying fritters lies in the temperature of the oil. During frying, the water inside the fritter batter quickly heats up, boils and turns to steam. You can actually see small bubbles rising from the surface of the fritters as they fry. The quick exit of water from the fritter stops the oil from entering and your fritters get crisp on the outside rather than soggy. But if the oil is too hot, the outside of the fritter will become too dark before the inside cooks. So make sure the temperature is just right—not too hot or not too cold. *(Corn Fritters with Pineapple-Jalapeñño Sauce, page 64)*

Getting the Water Out A simple experiment: Cut up two apples and add them to separate saucepans. Add a few tablespoons of brown sugar to one, but leave the other plain. Cook both over low heat. Notice how the apple without brown sugar softens and falls apart faster. The brown sugar stops the apple from softening. Calcium and acid in the brown sugar strengthen the apple's cells, slowing their breakdown. This information helps whether you make applesauce (add the sugar after the apples cook down) or apple pie (add sugar early to help apples retain their form rather than turn to mush). *(Applescotch Pie, page 78)*

Grilling Heat Grilling may be one of the most exciting activities of summer, but it can also be the most frustrating. The intense heat of the grill and its unpredictability (especially charcoal grills) can mean burning the outside of your food before the inside even gets warm. One of the best secrets to avoiding this problem is called "two-stage grilling." In a charcoal grill this means filling half of your grill with your normal amount of charcoal but placing only a single charcoal layer on the other half. Food can then be started on the hot side and moved to the less intense side to finish cooking. The same effect can be achieved by using the racks that some gas grills have on their lids. This method guarantees an even cook and a successful barbecue. *(Pineapple-Glazed Spicy Chicken Breasts, page 72)*

Hitting the Sauce Sauces are one of the cleverest inventions in the kitchen. Although many people think sauces are only for masking a poorly cooked dish, their true purpose is extending the flavor of your meat. When you fry meat and vegetables, especially when the pan is not nonstick, crispy bits of meat juices collect and glaze the bottom of the pan. This glaze, called the "fond" (French for bottom), contains concentrated meat flavor. To release the fond, deglaze the pan by adding liquid such as stock, wine or juice. This simple sauce can now be thickened, concentrated (by boiling) or enriched by adding butter. *(Lemon-Rosemary Roasted Chicken with White Wine Sauce, page 104)*

Holding Your Temper Chocolate is made of fat, water, sugar and protein. If handled correctly, the fat and water stay suspended in the chocolate and do not separate. When using chocolate as a coating, as in this recipe, shortening is often added to prevent the chocolate from separating. Although much simpler than tempering chocolate (the technique used to make chocolate candy), melting chocolate can still be problematic. If you overheat the chocolate in the microwave it will burn. Be sure to stir the chocolate regularly (sometimes chocolate chips maintain their shape well past their melting temperature). Even if they still look solid they may be ready to burn. *(Pistachio Biscotti, page 190)*

The Incredible Shrinking Steak You went to the butcher and bought a good-looking flank steak, just for this recipe. The problem is your finished steak is almost half the size it was when it was raw! No, this isn't a conspiracy by butchers to get you to buy more meat; it is a natural property of the meat. As meat is heated, the muscle fibers start to contract and pull. In meats where the fibers all run in one direction, such as flank steak, this effect can be quite dramatic. Although this can't be completely avoided, using gentle heat can minimize it. If the heat is really high not only will the meat burn more easily but also it will shrink faster. So cook as instructed and next time buy enough meat to compensate for the shrink. *(Chinese Barbecued Flank Steak, page 80)*

Jelling the Jelly If you enjoy the consistency of jams, jellies and preserves, you owe a debt of gratitude to a carbohydrate called pectin. Found mostly in the seeds and skins of fruits (especially apples), pectin traps and holds water so that your jelly is wobbly, not runny or clumpy. In order for this to happen, pectin needs the help of sugar and acid (usually lemon juice)—which "pull" the individual pieces of pectin as far away from one another as possible, allowing room for more water. This process requires a lot of sugar, so don't be tempted to cut back on the sugar in a recipe unless you want strawberry sauce instead of jam! *(Strawberry Freezer Jam, page 16)*

Keep It Clean   There are two ways to make American bacon. The current way is to quickly brine the belly of the pig in a salt/sugar solution. The second way, commonly used years ago, is to rub the belly with salt and spices, a slower but more flavorful process. Unfortunately, the former process leaves a large amount of liquid in the bacon. When this liquid escapes from the bacon as it cooks, it encounters the hot melted fat. The result is a lot of popping and a big mess. The solution? Bake your bacon in the oven instead of frying it on the stovetop. Because the heat is more evenly distributed in the oven, there's less mess. *(Maple-Glazed Peppered Bacon, page 41)*

The Melt Factor   Considering the wide variety of cheese available, it's amazing that they all start as milk. Although some cheeses are made from milk other than cow's, the main flavor differences between cheese varieties are due to the type of bacteria used and the way it is fermented or aged. Aging also affects how cheese cooks. In general, the drier a cheese, the better its melting characteristics. Fresh cheeses, like creamy fresh mozzarella, usually resist melting. The very best melting cheeses are hard cheeses (like Cheddar) and very hard cheeses (like Parmesan, if grated finely). To ensure a good melting texture and prevent separation, keep cooking temperatures low and cooking times brief. *(Apple, Cheddar and Sausage Sandwiches, page 34)*

Overbrowning   Sesame seeds have a distinct flavor and aroma, especially when toasted (they actually contain sulfur chemicals similar to those found in roasted coffee beans). As a prime component of this recipe, make sure you start with fresh seeds. At 50% oil by weight, sesame seeds can turn rancid quickly. When toasted, they can quickly go from pleasantly nutty to bitter and burnt. The best method for determining if the toasted seeds are done is by smell. As the seeds go from pale beige to light brown, waft your hand over the pan. As soon as you smell something like a cross between peanut butter and roasted coffee, remove the pan from heat. *(Sesame Green Beans, page 151)*

Puff Pastry   Question: How is puff pastry like a sandwich? Answer: Both are made from layers. Puff pastry has two separate parts: dough and fat (usually butter). The pastry is made by first rolling the dough into a thin sheet. Next, a sheet of cold butter about half the size of the dough is placed on top and the dough is folded over to create a sandwich. This sandwich is then re-rolled and re-folded numerous times, each time gaining layers of dough and butter. During baking, the butter melts and its water (butter is 20% water) turns to steam, pushing up each layer of dough as it rises. The result is a dramatic, flaky pastry. *(Blueberry Turnovers, page 17)*

The Right Oil for Frying   There has been much talk lately about health and flavor differences among oils, but oils also differ in frying behavior. As oil is exposed to the high heat of frying, it begins to break down. If heated to too high a temperature, oil quickly begins to smoke and break down; this temperature is called its "smoke point." Every time oil is heated, its smoke point is lowered. For example, a fresh pan of peanut oil may begin to smoke at 450°F, but after the oil is used two or three times, it may smoke at 375°F. Oil at its smoke point can be dangerous because it can catch fire. It may also give off-flavors to foods. Keep it safe by only using an oil a few times to deep-fry. Also choose oils that have a high smoke point when fresh. The best oils for deep-frying are soybean (vegetable), corn, sunflower, peanut and canola. *(Crispy Fish Tacos with Spicy Sweet-and-Sour Sauce, page 94)*

The Right Pan for the Job   Not all cooking equipment is created equal. When sautéing the pork chops for this recipe it is essential that your pan heats up evenly to efficiently conduct the range top's heat to the pork. Copper and aluminum—the best heat conductors—make poor pans as they react easily with food. Instead, use a pan made with stainless steel (a nonreactive metal) coating a copper or aluminum core. This makes a heavy pan that heats slowly, but maintains even heat on the pan bottom. *(Cashew-Breaded Pork Loin Chops with Spiced Peach Chutney, page 118)*

Sautéing Is Simple   Although it may sound like a fancy gourmet technique, sautéing is very simple to learn and extremely useful. The word *sauté* is a French term meaning "to jump." As the food cooks it is often stirred, shaken or flipped (jumped) to ensure even cooking. When sautéing, the pan is coated with a thin layer of oil and placed over fairly high heat. The main goal of sautéing is to quickly cook or brown; therefore, vegetables and meats are cut or pounded thin, like the turkey cutlets in this recipe. Choose to sauté when you have meats and vegetables that are naturally tender. The speed of the cooking process is too brief to soften tough or fibrous foods. *(Sautéed Turkey Cutlets with Asparagus and Red Bell Peppers, page 110)*

Saving Your Skin   One of the secrets of making the great ribs is removing the thin membrane located on the bony side of the slab. This membrane can stop the sauce from penetrating the meat and make your ribs less than "fall-off-the-bone" tender. Start by using a sharp knife to scrape the membrane loose from the top of the wide end of the slab. Once you have freed about 1 inch of it from the bone, use a wad of paper towels to grab hold of it and pull (it's too slippery to grab with bare hands). The membrane will probably not come off in one shot, but sometimes you get lucky. In the end, it is a simple trick for great ribs. *(Oven-Barbecued Baby Back Ribs with Vinegar-Molasses Sauce, page 90)*

Separate Rice Is Nice All rice begins its life surrounded by a thin coating called bran. When milled, this outer layer is removed to expose the raw grain. To improve appearance, most rice in the United States is polished using a series of wire brushes or spinning drums. Although this process results in a beautiful, stark white grain, it also causes a thin layer of rice starch to accumulate on the surface. When rice is cooked, this outer starch layer mixes with water and causes the grains of rice to stick together. If you'd rather your rice grains were separate and fluffy, you have several options. You can wash the rice to remove residual starch, but this takes time. The best technique is to first cook the rice in hot oil. Coating every grain, the oil forms a nonstick coating, resulting in fluffy rice every time. *(Green Rice with Toasted Pumpkin Seeds, page 158)*

Skip the Marinade Marinades, whether for shrimp, poultry or meat, are used more often for flavor than for tenderizing. Tough cuts of meat, such as flank steak, can become more tender if soaked in an acidic marinade, but too long of a dip will make the outside of the meat mushy. Shrimp are naturally tender, so an overly acidic marinade can actually start the shrimp ''cooking'' before you even put them in the pan! If you want to marinate shrimp prior to cooking, don't use an acid—save it for your serving sauce. *(Margarita Shrimp Cocktail, page 54)*

Stale Bread When bread dough begins to bake, water is evenly mixed within the dough. However, as the dough's starch cooks, the starch pulls the water to itself. This combination of water and starch forms the texture of bread. After baking, the water in the loaf moves again, this time away from the starch towards the crust. This process is called staling, and you can see it happen as the interior of the bread gets dry and the crust gets leathery. The good news is that stale (or day-old) bread is perfectly willing to absorb a new liquid, such as the custard in this casserole. *(Cheesy Apple-Bacon Strata, page 33)*

Stewing in Your Own Juices The toughest cuts of meat have the most flavor. If cooked incorrectly, though, no amount of flavor will compensate for a rubbery texture. The secret to flavorful and tender meat is time and temperature. Tough cuts of meat are full of collagen (a glue-like substance that holds meat together). If cooked for a long time at a low temperature,

collagen dissolves into gelatin, making for tender meat. However, cook at too high of a temperature for too long and the meat will re-toughen. So how do you create gelatin but keep the meat tender? A good rule: Never boil meat. If the liquid surrounding the meat in a stew, soup or oven braise boils, your meat will be chewy. Remember to keep it low and slow! *(Oven-Barbecued Baby Back Ribs with Vinegar-Molasses Sauce, page 90)*

Sticky Mess? So there you are, standing in your kitchen on a nice summer day making this cashew brittle. Everything worked just fine (although it took a long time for the sugar to come up to temperature) until you cool the candy. Even after the suggested hour of cooling, the candy is soft and tacky. Before you blame yourself or your thermometer, consider that the problem may be your timing. Making candy in the summer is usually not recommended. When the humidity is high, the sugar syrup has a hard time boiling off its water because there is too much already in the air. By the time sugar syrup finally gets to the brittle stage a lot of the water has been driven off. As soon as it starts to cool, though, the water in the air is attracted back to the sugar. Hard candy doesn't stand a chance in high humidity, becoming sticky and gummy. Your best bet is to wait for a drier day. *(Cashew Brittle, page 196)*

That's a Tender Meatball! A great meatball is more like a small meat loaf than a small hamburger. The meat itself is not the only star of the show. Instead, the added ingredients (eggs, bread crumbs, spices) greatly contribute to the success of the finished product. An often overlooked meatball ingredient is the liquid. Using buttermilk insures a great tasting, tender meatball. The mild lactic acid in the buttermilk will enhance the flavor and texture of the final dish. *(Mama's Spaghetti and Meatballs, page 85)*

The "Whole" Truth Wheat kernels are much like eggs. The ''shell'' is the bran, the ''white'' is the endosperm and the ''yolk'' is the germ. All-purpose flour is made by removing the bran and germ and grinding the endosperm. Flour labeled as ''whole wheat'' is made from the entire wheat kernel. Although nutritious, the bran and germ can wreak havoc on your baked goods. Just like a shell, the bran is hard and sharp. When ground into flour it can ''cut'' into the structure of your bread or muffin, ruining the tender crumb and making it dense and soggy. If you want to use whole wheat flour in recipes that call for all-purpose flour, it's best to substitute no more than half whole wheat flour for all-purpose flour in baking. *(Whole Wheat Waffles with Maple-Apple Syrup, page 27)*

Helpful Nutrition and Cooking Information

Nutrition Guidelines

We provide nutrition information for each recipe that includes calories, fat, cholesterol, sodium, carbohydrate, fiber and protein. Individual food choices can be based on this information.

Recommended intake for a daily diet of 2,000 calories as set by the Food and Drug Administration

Total Fat	Less than 65g
Saturated Fat	Less than 20g
Cholesterol	Less than 300mg
Sodium	Less than 2,400mg
Total Carbohydrate	300g
Dietary Fiber	25g

Criteria Used for Calculating Nutrition Information

- The first ingredient was used wherever a choice is given (such as 1/3 cup sour cream or plain yogurt).

- The first ingredient amount was used wherever a range is given (such as 3- to 3 1/2-pound cut-up broiler-fryer chicken).

- The first serving number was used wherever a range is given (such as 4 to 6 servings).

- "If desired" ingredients and recipe variations were not included (such as sprinkle with brown sugar, if desired).

- Only the amount of a marinade or frying oil that is estimated to be absorbed by the food during preparation or cooking was calculated.

Ingredients Used in Recipe Testing and Nutrition Calculations

- Ingredients used for testing represent those that the majority of consumers use in their homes: large eggs, skim milk, 80%-lean ground beef, canned ready-to-use chicken broth and vegetable oil spread containing not less than 65 percent fat.

- Fat-free, low-fat or low-sodium products were not used, unless otherwise indicated.

- Solid vegetable shortening (not butter, margarine, nonstick cooking sprays or vegetable oil spread, as they can cause sticking problems) was used to grease pans, unless otherwise indicated.

Equipment Used in Recipe Testing

We use equipment for testing that the majority of consumers use in their homes. If a specific piece of equipment (such as a wire whisk) is necessary for recipe success, it is listed in the recipe.

- Cookware and bakeware without nonstick coatings were used, unless otherwise indicated.

- No dark-colored, black or insulated bakeware was used.

- When a pan is specified in a recipe, a metal pan was used; a baking dish or pie plate means ovenproof glass was used.

- An electric hand mixer was used for mixing only when mixer speeds are specified in the recipe directions. When a mixer speed is not given, a spoon or fork was used.

Cooking Terms Glossary

Beat: Mix ingredients vigorously with spoon, fork, wire whisk, hand beater or electric mixer until smooth and uniform.

Boil: Heat liquid until bubbles rise continuously and break on the surface and steam is given off. For rolling boil, the bubbles form rapidly.

Chop: Cut into coarse or fine irregular pieces with a knife, food chopper, blender or food processor.

Cube: Cut into squares 1/2 inch or larger.

Dice: Cut into squares smaller than 1/2 inch.

Grate: Cut into tiny particles using small rough holes of grater (citrus peel or chocolate).

Grease: Rub the inside surface of a pan with shortening, using pastry brush, piece of waxed paper or paper towel, to prevent food from sticking during baking (as for some casseroles).

Julienne: Cut into thin, matchlike strips, using knife or food processor (vegetables, fruits, meats).

Mix: Combine ingredients in any way that distributes them evenly.

Sauté: Cook foods in hot oil or margarine over medium-high heat with frequent tossing and turning motion.

Shred: Cut into long thin pieces by rubbing food across the holes of a shredder, as for cheese, or by using a knife to slice very thinly, as for cabbage.

Simmer: Cook in liquid just below the boiling point on top of the stove; usually after reducing heat from a boil. Bubbles will rise slowly and break just below the surface.

Stir: Mix ingredients until uniform consistency. Stir once in a while for stirring occasionally, often for stirring frequently and continuously for stirring constantly.

Toss: Tumble ingredients (such as green salad) lightly with a lifting motion, usually to coat evenly or mix with another food.

Metric Conversion Guide

Volume

U.S. Units	Canadian Metric	Australian Metric
1/4 teaspoon	1 mL	1 ml
1/2 teaspoon	2 mL	2 ml
1 teaspoon	5 mL	5 ml
1 tablespoon	15 mL	20 ml
1/4 cup	50 mL	60 ml
1/3 cup	75 mL	80 ml
1/2 cup	125 mL	125 ml
2/3 cup	150 mL	170 ml
3/4 cup	175 mL	190 ml
1 cup	250 mL	250 ml
1 quart	1 liter	1 liter
1 1/2 quarts	1.5 liters	1.5 liters
2 quarts	2 liters	2 liters
2 1/2 quarts	2.5 liters	2.5 liters
3 quarts	3 liters	3 liters
4 quarts	4 liters	4 liters

Measurements

Inches	Centimeters
1	2.5
2	5.0
3	7.5
4	10.0
5	12.5
6	15.0
7	17.5
8	20.5
9	23.0
10	25.5
11	28.0
12	30.5
13	33.0

Weight

U.S. Units	Canadian Metric	Australian Metric
1 ounce	30 grams	30 grams
2 ounces	55 grams	60 grams
3 ounces	85 grams	90 grams
4 ounces (1/4 pound)	115 grams	125 grams
8 ounces (1/2 pound)	225 grams	225 grams
16 ounces (1 pound)	455 grams	500 grams
1 pound	455 grams	1/2 kilogram

Temperatures

Fahrenheit	Celsius
32°	0°
212°	100°
250°	120°
275°	140°
300°	150°
325°	160°
350°	180°
375°	190°
400°	200°
425°	220°
450°	230°
475°	240°
500°	260°

Note: *The recipes in this cookbook have not been developed or tested using metric measures. When converting recipes to metric, some variations in quality may be noted.*

Index

Italicized page references indicate photographs or illustrations.

Complete your cookbook library
with these *BettyCrocker* titles

Betty Crocker Baking for Today
Betty Crocker Basics
Betty Crocker's Best Bread Machine Cookbook
Betty Crocker's Best Chicken Cookbook
Betty Crocker's Best Christmas Cookbook
Betty Crocker's Best of Baking
Betty Crocker's Best of Healthy and Hearty Cooking
Betty Crocker's Best-Loved Recipes
Betty Crocker's Bisquick® Cookbook
Betty Crocker Bisquick® II Cookbook
Betty Crocker Bisquick® Impossibly Easy Pies
Betty Crocker Celebrate!
Betty Crocker's Complete Thanksgiving Cookbook
Betty Crocker's Cook Book for Boys and Girls
Betty Crocker's Cook It Quick
Betty Crocker's Cookbook, 10th Edition—*The* **BIG RED** *Cookbook*®
Betty Crocker's Cookbook, Bridal Edition
Betty Crocker's Cookie Book
Betty Crocker's Cooking Basics
Betty Crocker's Cooking for Two
Betty Crocker's Cooky Book, Facsimile Edition
Betty Crocker Decorating Cakes and Cupcakes
Betty Crocker's Diabetes Cookbook
Betty Crocker Dinner Made Easy with Rotisserie Chicken
Betty Crocker Easy Family Dinners
Betty Crocker's Easy Slow Cooker Dinners
Betty Crocker's Eat and Lose Weight
Betty Crocker's Entertaining Basics
Betty Crocker Everyday Vegetarian
Betty Crocker's Flavors of Home
Betty Crocker 4-Ingredient Dinners
Betty Crocker Grilling Made Easy
Betty Crocker Healthy Heart Cookbook
Betty Crocker's Healthy New Choices
Betty Crocker's Indian Home Cooking
Betty Crocker's Italian Cooking
Betty Crocker's Kids Cook!
Betty Crocker's Kitchen Library
Betty Crocker's Living with Cancer Cookbook
Betty Crocker's Low-Carb Lifestyle Cookbook
Betty Crocker's Low-Fat, Low-Cholesterol Cooking Today
Betty Crocker's New Chinese Cookbook
Betty Crocker One-Dish Meals
Betty Crocker's A Passion for Pasta
Betty Crocker's Picture Cook Book, Facsimile Edition
Betty Crocker's Quick & Easy Cookbook
Betty Crocker's Slow Cooker Cookbook
Betty Crocker's Ultimate Cake Mix Cookbook
Betty Crocker Win at Weight Loss Cookbook
Cocina Betty Crocker